DIRECTORS IN PERSPECTIVE

General editor: Christopher Innes

# Edward Gordon Craig

What characterizes modern theater above all is continual stylistic innovation, in which theory and presentation have combined to create a wealth of new forms – naturalism, expressionism, epic theater, and so forth – in a way that has made directors the leading figures rather than dramatists. To a greater extent than is perhaps generally realized, it has been directors who have provided dramatic models for playwrights, though of course there are many different variations in this relationship. In some cases a dramatist's themes challenge a director to create new performance conditions (Stanislavski and Chekhov), or a dramatist turns director to formulate an appropriate style for his work (Brecht); alternatively a director writes plays to correspond with his theory (Artaud), or creates communal scripts out of exploratory work with actors (Chaikin, Grotowski). Some directors are identified with a single theory (Craig), others gave definitive shape to a range of styles (Reinhardt); the work of some has an ideological basis (Stein), while others work more pragmatically (Bergman).

Generally speaking, those directors who have contributed to what is distinctly "modern" in today's theater stand in much the same relationship to the dramatic texts they work with, as composers do to librettists in opera. However, since theatrical performance is the most ephemeral of the arts and the only easily reproducible element is the text, critical attention has tended to focus on the playwright. This series is designed to redress the balance by providing an overview of selected directors' stage work: those who helped to formulate modern theories of drama. Their key productions have been reconstructed from promptbooks, reviews, scene-designs, photographs, diaries, correspondence and – where these productions are contemporary – documented by first hand description, interviews with the director, and so forth. Apart from its intrinsic interest, this record allows a critical perspective, testing ideas against practical problems and achievements. In each case, too, the director's work is set in context by indicating the source of his ideas and their influence, the organization of his acting company, and his relationship to the theatrical or political establishment, so as to bring out wider issues: the way theater both reflects and influences assumptions about the nature of man and his social role.

*Christopher Innes*

Gordon Craig at work: a marionette, Florence 1914 and (*facing page*) a model stage, Moscow 1910.

# Edward Gordon Craig

CHRISTOPHER INNES
*York University, Toronto*

**CAMBRIDGE UNIVERSITY PRESS**
CAMBRIDGE
LONDON   NEW YORK   NEW ROCHELLE
MELBOURNE   SYDNEY

Published by the Press Syndicate of the University of Cambridge
The Pitt Building, Trumpington Street, Cambridge CB2 1RP
32 East 57th Street, New York, NY 10022, USA
296 Beaconsfield Parade, Middle Park, Melbourne 3206, Australia

First published 1983

Printed in the United States of America

*Library of Congress Cataloging in Publication Data*
Innes, Christopher
Edward Gordon Craig.
(Directors in perspective)
Bibliography: p.
Includes index.
1. Craig, Edward Gordon, 1872–1966. I. Title.
II. Series.
PN2598.C85I56   1983   792'.0233'0924   83–1829
ISBN 0 521 25371 3 hard covers
ISBN 0 521 27383 8 paperback

# Contents

# Illustrations

# Acknowledgments

This study could not have been completed without the cooperation and active assistance of many institutions and individuals. In particular, I should like to thank Edward Craig, who offered encouragement, advice, and criticism, opened his personal archives to me, and was always prepared to answer questions that arose during the writing of the book. He provided many of the photographs as well, and very kindly gave permission to reproduce some of his own reconstructions of his father's work. I am also extremely grateful both to Peter Fozzard, for giving me the considerable benefit of his experience in organizing a centennial exhibition of Craig's work, and to Dr. Arnold Rood, for his hospitality in allowing me to work with his Craig collection as well as for his generosity in sharing his wide knowledge of Gordon Craig.

Without the assistance of the Social Sciences and Humanities Research Council of Canada, as well as the additional support provided by the Deans of Arts and Research at York University, it would have been impossible to gather the necessary material, which has been widely dispersed and is now held in many different centers. At the Bibliothèque Nationale my job was made much easier by the kindness of Professor André Veinstein and Mlle. Cecile Giteau, as well as by the helpfulness of Mme. Lalais and Mlle. Coron. I am also very grateful for the friendliness and cooperation of both Ellen Dunlap and the staff of the Humanities Research Center in Texas, and of Dr. Brooke Whiting and his staff at the University of California at Los Angeles.

I am grateful to Edward Craig and Arnold Rood, who both provided illustrative material. I should also like to thank the following for permission to reproduce work from their collections as illustrations in this book: the Bibliothèque Nationale, the Humanities Research Center, the British Library, the University of California at Los Angeles, the Novosti Press Agency, the Lincoln Center for the Performing Arts, and Helen Craig. I am also deeply grateful to H. E. Robert Craig for his generous permission to use copyrighted material in the Edward Gordon Craig, C. H. Estate.

xiii

In addition, my special thanks go to Ronald Bryden for his constructive suggestions and editorial comments, and to my wife, Eva, who helped me in gathering material and clarifying my ideas.

Christopher Innes

# 1    Prologue: The argument

In 1890, at the age of eighteen, Gordon Craig was hailed as the most promising young actor in England. Ten years later he had turned his back on the conventional stage and devoted himself to a vision of theater so radical that it seemed to have no place for the actor at all. His work as a director established techniques that have become axioms of modern stagecraft, but his theories were so extreme that they had little chance of being accepted or even understood. He was an enigma from the first, and for the last seventy-five years has been one of the most fought-over names in world theater. He was one of the innovators who shaped the development of modern theater, yet the exact extent of his influence is almost impossible to measure. His early productions introduced revolutionary techniques of lighting and new principles of grouping and scene design that are now accepted without question. Yet these productions had little direct impact. Practically no other theatrical reformer saw them and the information to reconstruct them has only recently become available. Craig was a leader without clearly identifiable followers, yet a magnet for almost all who reacted against realistic staging; a director with only seven mature productions he could call his own, who denied that even these were true examples of his theatrical concept. He was a founder-member of the new movement that included Copeau and Jouvet, Appia and Reinhardt, Tairov and Vaktangov, Poel and Granville-Barker – but unlike those others, who have won general recognition, Craig has never commanded any critical consensus. From the first, his work either attracted exaggerated praise or was rejected out of hand.

On the one side, artists such as Yeats hailed him as a theatrical messiah. Indeed, by 1931 his early collaborator, Martin Shaw, could fairly claim that Craig was "acknowledged by most people on the continent . . . to be the most significant force in the theatre today." On the other, standard source books on twentieth-century staging tend to dismiss his work (together with Appia's) as representative of a "synthetic movement." Because it "produced no new plays and no new actors," it is taken to be merely a superficial "scenic reform in which suggestive simplicity covered with 'a veil of light or darkness' the clumsy literalism of the naturalists' 'tasteless parlour' . . ."[1]

1

This tendency to see Craig solely as a scene designer, and therefore to dismiss his vision as an attempt to substitute visual spectacle for drama, is an all-too-common error. Even Isadora Duncan, whose dancing inspired Craig and confirmed his belief that the essential element of his art had to be movement, referred to his work only as "the perfect setting" – which led Craig to exclaim that "even after 20 years . . . she thought I was thinking of scenery!"[2] The unfortunate fact is that, having no steady income from productions, Craig lived mainly by exhibiting and publishing his designs. Because designs can be easily reproduced, this is the sole aspect of his work that became generally known, apart from one collection of essays. So it has been all too easy to assume that his theatrical reform was limited to stage settings, whatever Craig himself claimed. This is also partly because his drawings have such artistic merit, partly because he misleadingly labeled one of the prototypes for his new theater as "Scene," and partly because innovations are easier to carry out in scene design than in any other element of staging. Indeed this mistaken emphasis has made it possible to ignore the real implications of Craig's theories, because (as the commercial theater repeatedly demonstrates) a style of setting or lighting can be used completely independently of any aesthetic values it was created to express. But Craig always insisted that he was a director, a *metteur-en-scène*, vehemently rejected the view that he was primarily a designer of scenes, and denied that scenery was anything more than one of many elements in his concept of theater. For him, the essential qualification for a director was acting experience, and he defined a "designer" as anyone with a specifically theatrical vision.

As evidence about the other aspects of his theatrical work has emerged, the critical pendulum has swung more in Craig's favor. However, by now so much time has passed since Craig's major involvement with the stage that his ideas are usually treated as historical curiosities, rather than as the inspiration to the present that he intended them to be. This is reinforced by the way he presented his work – stressing the continuity with tradition as well as the decisive break with it – and by the number of elements in his productions that in fact harked back to the nineteenth-century theater, which they were designed to replace. The paradox was summed up in one of Craig's obituaries, which labeled him "the last Victorian of the English stage and the first prophet of a new order in the theatre, an order still in the making, and, some would add, incapable of being made."[3] As such, however, his vision not only helps to illuminate a past turning point in stage history, out of which our modern theater evolved, but also offers a continuing challenge.

The case against Craig was perhaps put most trenchantly by Lee Simonson in 1931, and the terms of his attack deserve note if only because they have been picked up unthinkingly and repeated frequently. But his criticisms also bring out unintentionally the real issues that shaped the unusual course of Craig's career: How much can be achieved by working within an established tradition, when the aim is to change it so radically that in effect it will become a new art form – and how can the true qualities of this new art be understood, when the terms that might be used to describe it can only be drawn from the form it is meant to supersede? Simonson's argument was that it is absurd to extol someone (as Craig's converts did) "as the source of every important innovation in designing stage settings" over the past twenty-five years when that person had not staged any work he could call solely his own during that whole period. Craig's withdrawal from practical theater is explained as "a flight from reality" following the shock of "defeat" in his early productions, which led him to make extravagant demands – a specially constructed stage and sole artistic control – in order to avoid any test of his theories. This "fear of failure" is then taken as support for the contention that Craig's designs are – and perhaps at least subconsciously were even intended to be – unrealizable on the stage, and his essays are dismissed as "a maze of suggestions . . . a mass of evasions and contradictions." The fact that Craig never managed to put his ideas into practice, even though this was at a time when a wide range of experimental art theaters was able to find support, is offered as proof that those ideas are incoherent and impracticable. The only way his apparent importance can then be explained is by characterizing him as "a demagogue . . . an exalted mountebank."[4]

Ironically, the passion of this denunciation itself indicates how dominant Craig's influence is felt to be. But, leaving that aside, from a different perspective the qualities singled out as flaws are precisely what gives Craig's work much of its value. His retreat from the stage was a refusal to compromise with existing conditions that would have destroyed the integrity of his ideas. So was his demand for autonomy and complete control of anything he produced. This assertion of the right to be in sole charge of every element in a production – orchestrating light, music, movement, the setting, and the actors, so that a performance became the work of a single artist – was hardly new. Dramatists such as Goethe and actor-managers such as Macready had called for it up to a century before as the only means of achieving artistic unity. The need for integrating the diverse elements of an increasingly spectacular and technically complex theater was the reason for the rise of the director, and it was largely Craig's claims that legitimized the modern director's position. A generation before, the Duke of Saxe-Meiningen, able to exercise autocratic control because of his social position, had demonstrated what was possible. But it was Craig who provided the theoretical justification for the preeminence of the director as the only way to implement synaesthetic ideals of theatrical performance in which all the different art forms are integrated to create a single emotional harmony. On this level at least he could be said to have shaped one of the determining factors of twentieth-century theater. At the same time, in his own case this claim ruled out what might otherwise have been potentially valuable collaborations with better-established directors such as Reinhardt, even when they shared many of the same principles.

Because Craig saw his work as the antithesis of all accepted theatrical standards, even critical acclaim became suspect, because it meant that his productions fulfilled those conventional expectations he rejected. So it was hardly surprising that, at the very time he was writing his first major theoretical statement, "On the Art of the Theatre," he remarked, "The nearer I come to success the more form and beauty I see in what's called failure."[5] His series of early operatic productions between 1900 and 1902 in fact did correspond to the type of experimental "art theater" Simonson claims he avoided because of the impracticability of his theories. But Craig moved beyond that possibility as his ideas developed. He came to see that such a framework could only promote partial reforms, reforms that represented innovations in technique and presentation rather than a completely new art form.

If so many of Craig's ideas seem negative, it is because his concept of what theater might become could not be realized (as Isadora Duncan noted in the margin of "On the Art of the Theatre") until "the great incubus of the present theatre is destroyed . . . leaving CLEAR SPACE." If his essays seem impressionistic and imprecise, exaggerated and enthusiastic, that is because they were intended as a fundamental challenge to all preconceptions. It is true that there is a strong vein of mysticism in Craig's vision, yet on a practical level any coherent manifesto would have been too limiting. The value of Craig's theories, like those of Antonin Artaud a generation later, is precisely that they free the imagination instead of providing a specific program. Indeed this can be seen as one reason why Craig deliberately turned from producing tangible examples of his new art of the theater – although he continued to experiment privately on model stages – and instead turned to writing.

In a critical commentary on one of the early books dealing with his work, which described him as one of "the three giants who led the charge" against realism (the others being Appia and Reinhardt), Craig made the distinction between visionaries such as himself, who acted as catalysts for change, and "organizers" like Reinhardt or Stanislavski, who put new artistic ideas into practice at the expense of popularizing them. At the same time Craig was alive to the contradictions inherent in the attempt to revolutionize the most physical of all art forms, which in a sense only exists in performance, by moving into abstractions. Finding himself labeled as "fundamentally a theorist," he insisted that practical experience was the basis of all his work: "I acted and produced long before I dreamt of enunciating any theory." Even while formulating his theories he had noted that though knowledge of stage history, paradoxically, was a prerequisite for meaningful change, "the more an artist studies the theatre the further he finds himself from the theatre."[6] So in one sense the critics who labeled Craig's work impractical were correct. Even the towering monoliths and shifting architectural shapes, the stairs and skies leading to infinity in his scene drawings, were not designed for the conventional stage, but were attempts "to record what is seen in the mind's eye." Yet his theater of the imagination was always conceived in concrete terms and precise dimensions that generally corresponded to those of a regular proscenium – apart from the single exception of a festival theater he envisaged with a stage opening 170 feet high. He demonstrated the "infinite sky" effect in his early productions, and frequently created scale models to show how designs would be translated into stage terms. Commenting on seventeenth- and eighteenth-century costume designs, he picked out technical drawings that showed the construction rather than the effect for spectators – "Is not one such plate of more true value to us than a hundred fantastic whirling designs by some studio painter?"[7] – and many of his own costume designs include detail on cut, texture, or fastenings. This combination of practical concern (taking all the conditions of the stage into account) and fantasy that breaks out of conventional limitations is characteristic of Craig's work as a whole.

When he came to write his autobiography, *Index to the Story of My Days*, Craig originally planned to focus on his stage work. The first section would "describe the conditions of 1899 . . . so you may see what it is I thought I would change and how I would change it . . . Secondly my first seven productions . . . Then must come a break in the story and we must see what others are doing."[8] The final section was to be a description of the forms he had evolved to embody his vision of a new theater: the abstract choreography of moving geometrical shapes that he called Scene, and the production plans for festival performances of *The St. Matthew Passion*. He admonished himself to "write only of the *mise-en-scène*." But, despite all this, his autobiography turned out to be a chronological diary concentrating on personal relationships, beginning on January 16th, 1872, the day of his birth, and breaking off in 1907 before he started publishing *The Mask*, the journal that became the major vehicle for his ideas, and before he developed his theories in such essays as "The Actor and the Uebermarionette" and "The Artists of the Theatre of the Future."

Craig – passionate, improvident, mercurial, a self-taught genius who mastered almost everything except self-discipline and who scattered his energy among multitudinous projects; dogmatic yet secretly self-doubting, whimsical as well as visionary – comes across in his *Index to the Story of My Days*. His personality is also described by Edward Craig in his biography of his father, where all the details of his life can be found. So this study concentrates solely on his theater: his theories, his productions, and his plans. The primary aim is to reconstruct and document his stage work, and to analyze how it relates to his developing vision of a new art. It is therefore appropriate to adopt the broad framework that Craig himself never carried out, and to begin with an overview of the late Victorian stage – in particular, Irving's Lyceum Theater, where Craig received his training and against which he reacted.

Craig believed correctly that his first seven productions represented his most significant work in the live theater, although he always undervalued the contribution of his eighth production, the 1912 *Hamlet* at the Moscow Art Theater, and overestimated his first independent venture as a director, the 1893 staging of *No Trifling with Love*. He liked to see *No Trifling* as the start of his theatrical revolution, despite the fact that it contained few hints of what was to come, whereas he tended to dismiss the *Hamlet* – a landmark production by anyone else's standards – because he had not had complete artistic control and believed Stanislavski had compromised his conception. Later work, like *The Pretenders* in 1926, mainly recapitulated his turn-of-the-century stage achievements. The approach was essentially the same, the ideas he had been exploring over the preceding two decades were not incorporated, and the technical problems remained, even if they were to some extent more successfully disguised.⁹ So *The Pretenders* and the New York *Macbeth* are dealt with only briefly.

The next sections analyze the burst of creative energy between *Dido and Aeneas* and *Much Ado About Nothing*. Craig's eighth production, the Moscow *Hamlet*, is discussed separately, because it embodies the new stage concepts that Craig developed following his stage experiments between 1900 and 1904. As the only real test of his new vision of theater, these must form the main focus of this study. In one sense, of course, they were no more than the initial steps in a lifelong campaign to revolutionize the stage, and still contain many of the conventional concepts from which Craig gradually freed himself. But it was in these early productions that he worked out the principles of what was later to become his "Art of the Theatre." As he always emphasized, "I was practising [as a] *metteur-en-scène* long before I wrote about *l'Art du Théâtre* – and I *did* then what I wrote of later – the theory came after the practice."¹⁰

## 2 Scene changes: Victorian theater, an acting career, and points of departure

The theoretical nature of Craig's published writings and the tendency to abstraction in his designs, many of which are unrelated to any specific play, give the misleading impression that he was a reformer working from outside. In fact, he always asserted that his aim was to revolutionize the theater from within. One characteristic that could almost be said to define contemporary drama is its continual process of rejection. Directors jettison whatever stage conventions have been established by the previous generation or movement as "culinary" (Brecht) or "deadly" (Brook) in order to create new forms through a *via negativa* (Grotowski). Craig was no exception. But he, far more than other revolutionaries of the stage, was a part of the theatrical tradition he came to reject. With Ellen Terry as his mother, and the most famous actor-manager of the late Victorian period, Henry Irving, as his mentor, he could be said literally to have grown up in the nineteenth-century theater. Indeed, in some ways he never completely freed himself from it, which occasionally gives his work the disturbing flavor of old wine in new bottles.

Craig was very much a man of his time, and although he lived until 1966, his time was the turn of the century. He was twenty-seven when he started the production of *Dido and Aeneas*, a work that marked his emergence as a director in 1900, and it was at the same time that he first began sketching ideas for *The St. Matthew Passion*, which was to be his final, unstaged work. He continued to write and design until after the Second World War, but his career could be said effectively to have ended with his production of *The Crown Pretenders* in 1926. He always referred to his new Art of the Theater, which he began to define between 1902 and 1905, as an integral part of the wider European movement that he associated with Appia, Diaghilev, Meyerhold, Reinhardt, and Stanislavski. But he also claimed that in attempting "to revitalize our European theatre from within" he was directly following Irving, who epitomized so much of the nineteenth-century theater that his movement opposed.[1]

Henry Irving established the Lyceum as the foremost London theater, and himself as the leading English actor, with a single production in 1871. This was *The Bells* by Leopold Lewis, still in the

8

Lyceum repertoire thirty years later and performed so many times that the scenery literally disintegrated. Adapted from a French original with a plot that recurred in several other plays (including *Paul Zegars, or The Dream of Retribution*, which failed in London just two weeks before *The Bells* opened), this was a psychological melodrama based on the idea of poetic justice: A guilty conscience alone is enough to betray secret crime behind the front of respectability and to destroy the criminal. The dialogue is full of clichés and the dramatic situations are remarkable only for the openness with which the villain – always the active agent, but usually presented as a stock figure, motivated by a simple desire to do evil – is recognized as the true focus of Victorian melodrama. Indeed, all the other characters are little more than symbols of his desires, representing the family happiness and social acceptance that Matthias committed murder to secure, or projections of his fears in the forms of an imagined mesmerist who could hypnotize him into admitting his guilty secret and judges who would condemn him. It was Irving's acting alone, therefore, that was responsible for the success of the play, and Craig's description of his performance vividly evokes some of the key elements in what became known as the Lyceum style. At the same time, his retrospective enthusiasm for the effects Irving achieved reveals something of the qualities he was searching for in his own art.

The only function of the other actors was to support Irving in the main role: to prepare his entrances, to take up groupings that would focus the audience's attention on his figure. Indeed, according to Craig the necessary qualities for a Lyceum actor were those of "the leg of a table," so that "to obtrude would have been out of the question"[2] – and in this overstatement we can see Craig defending his own concept of acting. But this was very different from our modern conception of ensemble performance, and the way Irving organized a production around himself is amusingly illustrated by an anecdote about the rehearsals for another standard Lyceum piece, *The Corsican Brothers*. Running through the duel scene, the actor fighting with Irving broke off and asked, "Don't you think, Guv'nor, a few rays of the moon might fall on me – it shines equally on the just and the unjust." In this case Irving agreed to share the limelight a little. But behind this personal dominance was an ideal of artistic unity, as his remarks about the costuming of *Faust* show: "I have studiously kept as yet all the colour to that grey-green. When my dress of flaming scarlet appears amongst it – and remember that the colour will be intensified by that very light – it will bring the whole picture together in a way you cannot dream of."[3]

Clearly the effect attempted was one of balance as well as contrast, and the subordination of all the other figures to the leading role was one way of achieving harmony. In contrast to Charles Kean, the other great nineteenth-century actor-manager, whose productions set the earlier theatrical fashion and stressed visual variety as well as historical accuracy, Irving required an atmospheric unity in scene and costume design that carried through the whole play. In 1881 the Meiningen company had appeared in London. The way it integrated acting with the setting through a discipline directed at building a single and consistent impression, even in mob scenes, was a revelation. The Duke of Saxe-Meiningen's complete control of the smallest details of costuming, lighting, and gesture gave every element interpretative value. It made the human figure in movement the primary pictorial unit. Irving immediately took up the challenge, and the Meiningen influence was already clear in the 1882 Lyceum production of *Much Ado*. Unlike the Meiningen ensemble, in which every actor took his turn as a supernumerary, Lyceum actors remained fixed in subordinate positions around their star, but Irving's rehearsals became meticulous in their attention to precise timing and positioning. Groupings, moves, and gestures were rhythmic, planned, and measured. As Craig commented, Irving "was forever counting – one, two, three – pause – one, two – a step, another, a half, a faintest turn, another step, a word."[4] This detailed precision was the most obvious sign of the change in Irving's methods after the Meiningen visit. However, in the Meiningen performances the aim was primarily realistic, whereas Irving emphasized the aesthetic quality of their techniques. In his hands their approach created a symphonic totality. For the audience it produced an emotional unity of vision and atmospheric effect, although it was almost solely concerned with the external aspects of performance, such as intonation and attitude, rather than the psychological interpretation of character, and was therefore highly artificial.

In their own terms, however, the results achieved were strikingly powerful. For instance, during the low-key opening of *The Bells* suspense was slowly built up to such effect, leading up to Irving's first entrance, that the audience always burst into spontaneous applause when he appeared. This allowed him to demonstrate his control by breaking character and intensified the energy of his performance by showing a sharp distinction between the actor and his role. "The shout of applause going up, he lowers his arm, he lowers his head, he relaxes his force all over, seems to turn it off to an almost dead calm . . . and then as the applause dies away . . . the actor clips it off by a sudden gesture of awakening from his long and patiently endured ordeal – flings cap and whip to right and left." In his lectures entitled "The Art of Acting," Irving defined the actor's approach to a role as "a double consciousness," wherein the actor gives his emotions free rein while simultaneously remaining aware of all the expressive techniques by which these emotional states can be communicated. In doing so, he provided a solution to the debate over identification versus objectivity. Diderot's paradox – that an actor can portray emotions effectively only if he does not experience them, but instead analyzes his role intellectually – had been restated by Coquelin, the leading French comedian, in the 1880s. In reply, Irving synthesized the two poles of the argument in a way that anticipated Stanislavski's theories, although his style of performance was very different. For him, the primary aim of the actor was "the representation of passion."[5] This stress on extreme emotional states was essentially Romantic in that it equated greatness with depth of feeling, and it led in fact to a highly idiosyncratic, exaggerated, and even grotesque form of acting.

The intensity with which Irving expressed emotion often seemed to give a spiritual dimension to his performance, and his interpretations of characters frequently contained striking insights. Hamlet became an introvert whose habitual self-contemplation had the effect of fostering and aggravating his own emotions to hysteria. Shylock became a Jew with a genuine cultural background whose depth of psychological suffering compensated for his crimes and whose forlorn dignity made all the Christian society that baits him seem contemptible by comparison. At the same time this magnification of every trait into passion reduced everything, even *Macbeth* and *Othello*, to melodrama (a simplified view of Shakespeare's tragedies that Craig himself was never able to break free from completely), and neither the intention nor the effect could be called naturalistic.

As Craig pointed out, in his characterization of Matthias "Irving set out to wring our hearts, not to give us a clever exhibition of antics such as a murderer would be likely to go through." So terror was always abject, anguish never less than infinite, hatred or love all-consuming. Drama, for Irving, meant the opposite of the society problem play with its restrained drawing-room conventions of acting. Craig, who heartily agreed, neatly characterized this genre as a form of pseudorealism in which "the villain of the play comes onto the stage smiling: he is quite alone; and although he remains alone for five minutes, he does not dare to tell us that he is 'the villain' – has not dared to let any tell-tale look escape him." By contrast,

Irving never sacrificed any potentially dramatic moment to verisimilitude. As a result, his acting was overtly artificial and highly
mannered. His hands became talons, his face was transformed into
a mask by muscular tension, his movements were either extremely
dynamic or tended toward cataleptic stasis at points of extreme intensity – all comparable in some ways to the "schemata" of classical
Greek tragedy. In many ways Irving's approach was a prototype for
the ecstatic style of expressionist acting. They had similar aims: to
communicate emotions directly and in a pure state to the audience.
So Bernard Shaw's unsympathetic description of "the condition in
which he works" as "a somnambulist one: he hypnotizes himself
into a sort of dreamy energy, and is intoxicated by humming of
words in his nose" parallels Strindberg's claim that the actor should
function like a spiritualist medium in a trance, or the typical expressionist statement that "the actor who knows his inner strength goes
onto the stage as someone sleepwalking."[6]

Craig's description of Irving's performance as Matthias is a sensitive illustration of these qualities and their effectiveness, though he
shows his characteristic disregard for plot detail or dialogue in con-
flating two separate points in the scene. Take the commonplace business of Matthias unlacing his boots while (according to Craig) the talk
turns to the storm during which the Jewish traveler disappeared:

The way Irving did it had never been thought of till he did it, and has never
been done since.

It was, in every gesture, every half move, in the play of his shoulders,
legs, head and arms, mesmeric in the highest degree . . . We suddenly saw
these fingers stop their work; the crown of the head suddenly seems to
glitter and become frozen – and then, at the pace of the slowest and most
terrified snail, the two hands, still motionless and dead, were seen to be
coming up the side of the leg . . . the whole torso of the man, also seeming
frozen, was gradually seen to be drawing up and back . . .

Once in that position – motionless – eyes fixed ahead of him and fixed on
us all – there he sat for the space of ten to twelve seconds, which, I can
assure you, seemed to us all like a lifetime, and then said – and said in a
voice deep and overwhelmingly beautiful: "Oh, you were talking of that –
were you?" . . . Time seemed out of joint, and moved as it moves to us who
suffer, when we wish it would move on and it does not stir.

And the next step of his dance began . . . He glides up to a standing
position: never has anyone seen another rising figure which slid slowly up
like that: with one arm slightly raised, with sensitive hand speaking of
far-off apprehended sounds, he asks, in the voice of some woman who is
frightened, yet does not wish to frighten those with her: "Don't you . . .
don't you hear the sound of sledgebells on the road?"[7]

In the actual performance, Matthias spoke of the mesmerist while changing his footwear, and his consternation was caused by the word "conscience." The comment about "the Polish Jew's Winter" occurs later, when he is about to drink some wine. Treating both moments as a single emotional unit may simply be a slip of Craig's memory, but the change is still significant. It reflects the way Craig himself treated dramatic material, simplifying action to create clear emotional progressions and substituting physical movement for speeches. Equally significantly, his description evokes a simultaneous impression of calculated preparation and psychological automatism. The meticulous timing and rehearsed precision, which made Irving's acting an art in Craig's terms, allowed him to draw directly on emotions from a subconscious level. Perhaps because of this, Craig associated stylization with intensity, and his description is dramatized to bring this out.

Irving treated dialogue in much the same way, and his delivery was as mannered as his movement. Words were distorted for musical or emotional effect – "Cut thrut dug" for "cut throat dog" (Shylock), "Tack the rup frum mey nek" for "Take the rope from my neck" or "Ritz" for "Rich" (Matthias) – or elided for ejaculative force, like Matthias's opening speech, "It is I," which Irving transformed into an exclamation: " 't's I!" Critics who supported Ibsen and the new naturalism, such as William Archer, found it easy to be amusing at Irving's expense. "Not a vowel but has undergone a change into something new and strange, not a consonant but is jerked out with a convulsion of the throat or a spasm of the under jaw, while every dental at the end of a word is prolonged into an unmistakable sneeze . . . Trained elocutionists have assured me that, considering Mr. Irving's ignorance of the art, the effects he produces are marvellous." But what some critics condemned as the screeching and staggering style, Craig admired. In his eyes the harsh flattening of vowels gave a graphic register of the character's emotional tension. The stress on sibilants gave the thrilling impression of a hissing serpent. "In short, his tendency was to enrich the sounds of the words – to make them expressive."[8]

Craig served a long apprenticeship at the Lyceum, with Irving's example continually before his eyes. He made his first public appearance on stage at the age of six, started learning his craft (as he put it) at the age of twelve with a walk-on part in *Charles I* and a small speaking role in *Eugene Aram* during Irving's 1885 American tour, and joined the Lyceum company in 1889. From then until 1897 he acted the "juvenile lead" roles in a repertoire of Shakespeare, melodrama, historical romance, restoration comedy, and farce: Cromwell in *Henry VIII*, Richmond in *Richard III*, Arviragus in *Cymbeline*; Henry Ashton in *Ravenswood* (an adaptation of *The Bride of Lammermoor*), Cavaradossi in *La Tosca*; Arthur St. Valéry in *The Dead Heart* (a story of the French Revolution), Caleb Deecie in *Two Roses*, Moses in *Olivia* (based on *The Vicar of Wakefield*); Charles Surface in *School for Scandal*, and Abel Quick in *A Regular Fix*. As early as 1890 he won recognition as one of the most promising young actors – a newspaper cartoon of all the great stars included Craig, representing "the stage of the future" – and he began touring the provinces between Lyceum engagements. This was the traditional training for an actor, and Irving, who himself had started his career in a provincial stock company playing 429 different parts in two-and-a-half years (or a new part every two days), personally selected the roles the young Craig was to play.

At the Lyceum the old established ways of producing a play were disguised by technical sophistication and spectacular realism. In these touring companies Craig experienced them in a pure form, and his reaction against this particular type of traditionalism can be seen motivating much of his later work. When he joined the W. S. Hardy Shakespeare Company in 1894 at Hereford, for instance, he found that almost the whole stage area was taken up by a huge tank filled with water:

This was because Miss Ida Millais – probably related to the great painter – was performing in some melodrama called, I imagine, *Ida's Escape or the Last Leap*; for in the last act she, the heroine, had to jump from a big rock into this tank of water, which splashed up, of course. And then the villain jumped in after her and the hero jumped in after the villain, and finally she came up drenched and the body of the villain floated down to the green room. I think we were all fairly brave, looking at this damnable tank and realizing that we only had a yard or a yard and a half of stage in front of it in which to go through all the hither and thither of the five acts of *Hamlet* and the five acts of *Romeo and Juliet*.[9]

Quite apart from the sacrifice of all but the simplest possibilities of blocking and movement in the whole repertoire to a single spectacular climax, the Hardy company's approach to a text had severe interpretative limitations. It was traditional practice for the leading actor to control the tone and set the pace of a production, and when they began rehearsing *Hamlet* Mrs. Hardy, who was playing Gertrude, asked Craig to "tell us exactly what you want, and we will fit in." In addition, as was usual at the time, no member of the cast had the complete text. Each was given only a copy of his or her own words and cues. This was traditional practice as early as the Renaissance. Indeed, cue scripts were still widely used in provincial repertory theater as late as the 1950s, having clearly practical advantages for any actors performing a continually changing repertoire of short-run plays. But, with the large Victorian casts, this had become an almost universal phenomenon, and it had far-reaching effects for nine-teenth-century dramaturgy. According to Craig, it was not until much later that he himself came to realize that a play was written as a whole, instead of as the series of fragmented parts that he was accustomed to acting from: "I forget exactly when this illumination came, but it surprised me exceedingly." What this meant was that the emphasis was solely on portraying individual character, with little concept of central ideas or through-lines in a play, and that – just as in the Lyceum under Irving – everything would inevitably be arranged to make the leading figure the focus of a production. Such an approach also meant that remarkably little time and expense were required for rehearsing, as most of the moves and business were bound to be traditional. And indeed the W. S. Hardy Shake-speare Company completed what rehearsals were thought necessary for *Hamlet* in three days, and for *Romeo and Juliet* in two. As Craig later remarked, such productions merely rearranged old bits: "The actors between 1800 and 1900 never made new bits – it was ever the same old show done differently." What the audience saw was "the same Hamlet sitting in the same chair, with no marked sign of difference from any Hamlet seen before."[10]

When Craig founded his own touring company in 1894, however, its repertoire was exactly the same as any other stock company of the time.

## Mr. GORDON CRAIG'S COMPANY.

### Repertoire:

"HAMLET." — "A BLOT IN THE 'SCUTCHEON." — "FANTASIO."
"TAMING OF THE SHREW."  (From the French.)
"LADY OF LYONS." — "SHE STOOPS TO CONQUER." — "RAISING THE WIND."

*The Costumes for all the Plays have been kindly lent*
BY
MR. HENRY IRVING.

And when he first brought his own production of *Hamlet*

to London in 1896 it was basically conventional. His death scene was accompanied by melodramatic music, and his costume was the one used by Irving himself when he first played Hamlet at the Lyceum twenty-two years earlier. Reviewers certainly saw Craig's own performance as an example of "the new school of acting," on which opinions were sharply divided. One praised his "endeavor to be natural and unstagey . . . as opposed to the stilted, ranting delivery and often mechanical methods of the old." Another found him "altogether too 'modern' in style" and advised him "to work within the limits of convention . . . There is danger in being too original."[11] But the reviewers had also described Irving as an exponent of the "modern" school because his style was equally different from the stock rhetorical gestures of the traditional theater. The psychological focus of his characterizations of Shylock and Richard III had also been taken, however incongruously, as "naturalistic."

Craig was greatly influenced by Irving both as an actor and in his later ideal of a theatrical form that would be an "Art" rather than an imitation of life. The stress on patterned and precise movement and the use of color harmonies to create atmospheric effects were primary elements in his early operatic productions. He compared Irving's acting to the "noble artifice" of Nō drama because it transposed diction into "song," movement into "dance." He believed its overt artificiality was a way of portraying essences instead of appearances – and demanded a similar style for his Moscow production of *Hamlet* with Stanislavski. The harmonic integration of all the elements of a performance into a unified vision under the sole control of a single artist became the fundamental principle in his new theory of theater, though everything was to be subordinated to the central idea of a play and not (as with Irving) to the personality of the central figure. Above all, his much-misunderstood image of an ideal actor came from Irving. What he singled out was the way Irving's elimination of chance or apparent spontaneity in movement and diction made "each moment significant" because "all was sharp cut at beginning and end, and all joined by an immensely subtle rhythm," thus creating a true synthesis of passion with controlled expression. "Indeed," he remarked, "Irving was the nearest thing ever known to what I have called the Uebermarionette."[12]

It is this close connection between Craig's principles and the Lyceum conventions that helps to explain the curiously anachronistic quality of some of his work. By the time of the last Lyceum production, Sardou's *Dante* in 1903, Irving's acting seemed very dated. As Craig himself realized at the time, Irving's style had become set at the very beginning of his career and his most effective roles were

Craig the actor, as Hamlet at the Olympic Theater, 1897.

those he had created thirty years earlier. In addition, Irving's repertoire conditioned Craig's dramatic taste. Craig's earliest attempts to prepare scripts for production followed Irving's practice in cutting dialogue to enhance the more striking plot situations or in transposing and rewriting whole passages to achieve more spectacular effects – and toward the end of his career Craig was still announcing that "it is only the more melodramatic plays and operas which appeal to me as a producer."[13]

Two other elements of Irving's staging also deserve mention: his use of lighting and the type of setting employed at the Lyceum. The Lyceum was the first London theater to keep the houselights dimmed throughout a performance. This was purely for reasons of atmosphere – to create a sense of magic and to draw the audience emotionally into the production – rather than to shift emphasis toward the "fourth-wall" naturalism of Antoine or Stanislavski. It was the importance of this quality that led Irving to insist on gas lighting – and to take his own lighting equipment even on his American tours – long after electricity had become standard in the theater. This gas lighting, with its individual limelight spots used to reinforce the emotional tone of each moment in a play by subtle changes in color, was highly impressionistic. It provided all the suggestiveness of semiobscurity, and Ellen Terry summed up Irving's reasons for retaining it when she commented that "the thick softness of gaslight, with the lovely specks and motes in it, so like *natural* light, gave illusion to many a scene which is now revealed in all its naked trashiness by electricity."[14] At the same time he was prepared to use electricity for elaborate stage tricks, as in *Faust*, where live plates were set in the stage floor and wires ran from the actors' shoes to their gloves for the duel scene, so that blue flashes sparked from sword to sword as the electrical circuits shorted at each contact.

A similar stress on visual spectacle was characteristic of Irving's scenery. This was two-dimensional and painted, rather than architectural, but the pictorial realism was historically accurate and meticulously detailed. To prepare *Faust*, for example, Irving took his scene painters, costume designers, and property master to Nuremberg to collect materials and make drawings. Elaborate scenes could be changed quickly (with the help of no fewer than ninety stagehands, thirty gas men to handle the flexible hoses and the lights, and fifteen property men). They were painted on a combination of front cloths, back cloths, and "cut" cloths, which unrolled from the flies, and flats, which could be pushed on from each wing, or split horizontally, one half of the set ascending as the other dropped through narrow openings in the stage floor. Thus, in *The Corsican*

This abrupt mounting Staircase was my good - by Banquo's son when they go to bed -

This is an exceptionally poor interpretation of what was really the best scene in the play - The tower & seemed thicker than here & the figures much smaller in proportion -

a front scene - a drop-scene -

Where I have drawn a line there was a line - the wooden roller of the drop-scene -

So that all this is humbug & duoh Partridge -

*Brothers,* an exact mirror image of the Lyceum auditorium could be dismantled behind a cutcloth during a short banquet scene. This in turn was changed in under forty seconds behind a front cloth that rose to reveal a forest with free-standing (though two-dimensional) trees, among and behind which the actors could pass, and thick snow (salt) covering the whole stage floor. It was only occasionally that the settings were three-dimensional. Then the effects tended to be even more elaborate: The scenic auditorium in *The Corsican Brothers* had practicable boxes seating a whole stage audience in perspective, with children representing adults at the rear. But sometimes a simpler architectural quality was achieved, as in Macbeth's castle – a scene that directly influenced many of Craig's designs, with its steps winding round a broad column, and its steeply mounting staircase, up which the characters climbed to their beds.

As an actor, Craig found the two-dimensional Lyceum sets fake and incongruous, although for the audience the illusion would have been complete, with the softness of the gas lighting blurring joints and hard edges and giving depth to the trompe l'oeil highlights and shadows painted on the flats. Yet the continual and almost instantaneous transformations of scene that such sets allowed remained central to Craig's later ideas and formed the basis of both his screens and Scene, though in very different terms. Similarly, although he turned to the new medium of electric lighting, his principles for illuminating the stage remained much the same as Irving's – the atmospheric or symbolic use of "natural" light. He later commented that "few actors have acted in darker scenes than Irving . . . It was from Irving that I learnt to plunge my scenes in a good deal too much gloom."[15] Where Craig differed radically from Irving, however, turning all the elements he adopted from the old Lyceum upside down and transfiguring them, was in his complete rejection of spectacular realism. But this came later.

His very first attempt at production was indeed almost a straight copy of the Lyceum style. This was a gothic historical romance, Alfred de Musset's *No Trifling with Love,* which he staged at Uxbridge in 1893. He was still a member of the Lyceum company, and most of the costumes came straight from its wardrobe, with additional headdresses and decoration copied as usual from Viollet le Duc. The scenery (kept simple only because of Craig's slender finances) – damask curtains for interior settings, a painted backdrop, a front scene – was representational and in period. The program announced, "We intend giving as *thorough* a performance as possible." The interpretation was equally conventional. The text was "adapted

by Mr. Gordon Craig," which meant that he had reorganized the
scenes to strengthen melodramatic effects and had cut the dialogue
by about one-third. (Looking back on it fifty years later, Craig acknowledged that for "adapted" one should "say 'mutilated,' but I
adopted one of the many theatrical conceits of those days.") The
plot was reduced to its basic situations. Perdican's father arranges
for him to marry his cousin Camille. Each has long loved the other
in secret, but Perdican mistakes her modesty for coldness and Camille interprets his bashfulness as rejection. They quarrel, and at a
peasant festival to celebrate their engagement, which Craig transformed into an elaborate dance, Perdican sees Rosette – in this version the stock figure of a "simple yet lovely village maiden." He
pursues her to spite Camille, who overhears him proposing to her.
Camille discovers that Rosette's innocent, trusting nature would be
heartbroken if she were to be abandoned. So when she meets Perdican, who is now suffering from a crisis of conscience, she decides to
resolve his dilemma for him by disguising her true feelings and
withdrawing into a convent – though in Craig's overheated interpretation, "Camille gets frightened at his words and at his face and hot
breath as he whispers his soul out." She goes to pray – in "despair
absolute" reads Craig's direction – and faints on the altar steps,
where Perdican finds her. Believing she is dead, he acknowledges
his true passion, and the shock of finding he has never loved her
kills Rosette, who had followed him secretly to the oratory. This
climax Craig heightened with every means at his disposal, replacing
lengthy poetic sentiments with exclamations and sound effects.

> PERDICAN: Mine, mine!
> (*He kisses Camille. A great cry is heard from behind the altar. A rush of
> wind extinguishes the candles – wind continues to sigh to end of scene
> [blowing the curtains behind which Rosette lies] . . . Thunder. A big
> drum. Lightning.*)
> She is dead![16]

Craig's acting was appropriately Irvingesque. As the only review
commented: "With frenzied passion he invokes the deity to restore
[Camille] to him . . . in fervent tones tells of his *passion tendre*." Yet
within this conventional treatment there are certain elements that
point forward to Craig's later work. Perhaps not altogether surprisingly, the plot of his adaptation was found "somewhat weak," but it
was recognized that sacrificing the story gave "opportunity for
many graceful tableaux." The action was restructured to gain a lyrical progression, beginning with the hopefulness of early morning
and the ripening warmth of a summer day, and following through a

symbolic natural sequence in which sophisticated lighting effects were used to shape the audience's emotional response. "Evening stars and sinking sun – the sun sinks deeper and as it sinks it darkens and gets deeper red. *Always changing.*" This was intended to have spiritual significance, and Craig's notes refer to "the setting sun as a suggestion or sign of the promised land." Then came full night, and for the final scene the ghostly light of a rising moon. In addition, the weight Craig later gave to movement as the key element of theater can already be glimpsed in the emphasis placed on the dance, which the reviewer singled out as "certainly bizarre, and what with the delicately hued costumes, altered in tone from time to time by the changing limelight and backed by the deepest shades of foliage, [it] presented the prettiest scene in the play."[17]

When he became aware that his ideas were leading him to a radically new form of theater, Craig labeled his work "the revolution that started in Uxbridge." But looking back over his career as a whole, he dismissed the production as "really . . . of little significance" because it did not reflect any of the other influences to which he had already been exposed, influences that were to act as catalysts for his theatrical vision.

Until 1897, when he left the acting profession altogether, Craig hardly seemed to be on the verge of any revolutionary breakthrough. The productions he planned were as conventional as those he staged. When he prepared the play-within-a-play scenes of *A Midsummer Night's Dream,* his sketches show a naturalistic setting for both the carpenter's shop, with a rear wall parallel to the proscenium and a beamed roof, and for the wood, with a hawthorne brake for Snug to fall backward into when the "translated" Bottom appears. There were to be several additional nonspeaking actors simply "to convey *bustle* and excitement," and much of the "business" was to be left up to the actors, indicating that the production was traditional. The only unusual touch was that in acting the Pyramus and Thisby piece the mechanicals would each wear "a real Greek tragedy mask."[18] Similarly, the last play he actually mounted with himself in the lead role was a melodrama from his stock repertoire, with all the usual wind effects and "hurry" music, and a villain (François Villon, played of course by Craig) turned from his evil path by the kindly treatment of a priest. This was part of an impromptu evening's entertainment, arranged practically on the spot to raise money for a stranded theatrical troupe. The other half of the program, a sentimental recitation, contained one element that was to recur in Craig's later work, the simple white costume and bold black pom-pom buttons of a Pierrot. Yet, despite the freedom offered by the improvisational nature of this performance, it held nothing that suggested anything new.

But beneath the surface, fresh ideas were clearly taking shape. Craig had already come across what he later listed as his three major sources of inspiration. And although his decision to give up acting may have been precipitated by the breakup of his marriage, behind it was a growing realization that the theater in which he had served his apprenticeship was on the wrong track.

The first of these influences came in the shape of magazine articles. These articles, which reflected the growing interest in theater history at the time, made Craig aware that radically different and nonnaturalistic stage conventions had not only existed once, but could still be viable. One in particular that impressed him was an imaginative reconstruction of "A Christmas Mystery in the Fifteenth Century." It emphasized the sacred nature of medieval drama, its links with the liturgy, and its status as a communal "ceremony of public worship." It drew a picture of a sumptuous and symbolic performance: Even those playing beggars were dressed magnificently, and "solemn" aesthetic qualities took the place of realistic illusion – to the extent, it was claimed, that actors chosen solely for their beauty mimed the parts while "the real players and singers were hidden behind the scenes." In short, mystery plays were described as a visionary representation of spiritual existence, the opposite of any naturalistic copy of life: "The stage was . . . the materialization of all those medieval frescoes and bas-reliefs where we see represented in different planes of the same expanse the different phases in the life of man . . . The upper floor was open to the sky and in the middle was a golden throne surrounded by golden rays, in which God sat, an attentive and permanent spectator of the play."[19]

Another article, which gave a different example of much the same elements and which Craig claimed had "more positive influence on my scenic work than any other," described the performance of *Oedipus* and *Antigone* by the Comédie Française in 1894 in the ruins of the Roman theater at Orange. This description stressed the effectiveness of visual simplicity and the absence of any representational scenery in contrast to the elaborately carpentered settings for the mystery plays. It portrayed this simplicity as "a direct reversal of the ordinary effect in the ordinary theatre," where a proscenium, stage lighting, and the machinery of illusion "compels us to perceive that the palace is but painted canvas. The palace at Orange – towering up as if it would touch the very heavens and obviously of veritable

stone—was a most peremptory reality." The stateliness of this facade was described as reducing light comedy or social problem plays
to insignificance, while amplifying the noble passions of high tragedy or grand opera "in keeping with the devotional solemnity of the
early theatre . . . when the play itself was a religious rite."[20]

It was only after seeing the illustrations of the permanent scene (330
feet wide by 120 feet high) in the Roman theater at Orange, Craig later
said, that he "realized the possibilities which are opened by height,
space and background to the stage."[21] But the other qualities praised
by these articles were also to be reflected directly in his work. His idea
of a "rich theatre" with costumes created out of "exquisite and precious" materials can be traced back to the description of mystery
plays. So can his plans to separate mimed action from vocal accompaniment in *The St. Matthew Passion,* and his ideal of performance as a
public ceremony. His concept of architectural settings, with light
playing on scenery like the gradually changing light of the sun, the
visual simplicity of his later designs, and his clear preference for
tragedy and opera paralleled the elements of the Roman theater. In
particular, the stress on the religious and spiritual nature of both
medieval and classical drama struck a chord in him. But two other
influences were of even more immediate importance to Craig's development. One was the experiments of Hubert von Herkomer; the
other the stage work of his father, Edward William Godwin.

Perhaps it was precisely because Craig never knew his father, who
had separated from Ellen Terry and their two illegitimate children
when Craig was only three, and knew relatively little about his
work, that Godwin became a focus for his dreams, an ideal to emu-
late, and an imaginary rival. By profession, Godwin was a successful
architect of the Victorian gothic school, but began to write occasional
drama criticism in Bristol in 1857, and after meeting Ellen Terry was
gradually drawn into theater production. In his early reviews, Godwin criticized Charles Kean's productions for their lack of historical
accuracy, and by the 1870s he was writing articles on how the background to Shakespeare's plays should be presented. He was opposed to the popular drama of the time, dismissing melodramas
such as *The Wandering Heir* (even with Ellen Terry in the cast) as
"stagey" productions with "altogether complicated and uninteresting" plots. He proposed instead that unity and realism be the guiding principles of the theater, that the scenery should be an "exact
representation" of the location of the action, and that the actors
should discard conventional histrionics.[22]

When Bancroft produced *The Merchant of Venice* in 1875, the program acknowledged Godwin's "invaluable aid in archeological re-

search." The reviews singled out the "attention to minute details" in the elaborately carved arches of the Doge's palace, with a panorama of canals and medieval buildings beyond, which put Venice "on the stage with a completeness and picturesque beauty of scenery, costumes and other accessories rarely equalled." Whatever the historical justification, this was pure spectacle, and even the critics who praised it recognized that "extravagance of decoration has a natural tendency to subordinate the action," particularly when a cast "underact . . . in the approved drawing room style." Productions like *The Cup* by Tennyson, on which Godwin advised Irving in 1881, or *Claudian*, which he designed in 1883, were perhaps more suited to his principles. Roman architecture called for severe lines, which threw into relief not only the proportions but also the figures of the actors by the absence of distracting decoration, and Godwin was thereby able to gain a type of visual unity that reinforced the emotional tone of the action. In *The Cup* it was noted that the harmony among the actor's poses, their costumes, and the scenery achieved the effect of elevated solemnity, with Ellen Terry's "snake like draperies" falling "into the exact folds of the garments of an ancient Greek statue or a Pompeian fresco."[23] In *Claudian* Craig himself was vividly impressed by the destruction of a temple in an earthquake that brought columns and cornices crashing down around the protagonist.

When Godwin turned to directing, it was this emotional unity – an integration of all the visual elements of a production in order to bring out the essential quality of the action in such a way as to envelop the audience in the dramatic experience – that became his primary objective. Accuracy of historical detail, though of scholarly importance, was now theatrically significant only insofar as it contributed to this unity. But to achieve such an ideal, Godwin had to move out of the conventional theater. The plays in three of his four productions – *As You Like It*, *The Faithful Shepherdess*, and Tennyson's *Fair Rosamund* – called for natural settings. These were mounted in woodland glades at Coombe or Wimbledon, where there was no "scenery" or "stage illusion" as such. The audience shared the environment with the actors, who passed in and out of the trees, a historically neutral background that could be given any "period" by details of costume.

There were, of course, many different kinds of outdoor theater at the time, from popular entertainment to high culture. At the seaside pierrots played on platforms rather like the traditional booth stages. Festivals were held in special auditoriums, like the Roman amphitheater at Orange. But this totally natural type of open-air performance was an innovation in the 1880s. It was not, of course, new in itself, as Jacobean masques like *Comus* had been specifically written for exactly the same kind of performance. However, Godwin's experiment soon became almost standard practice in England. After the turn of the century there was Ben Greet, of whom it was once remarked: "Just as Mr. Wemmick said in effect, 'Holloa! Here's a church! Let's have a wedding!' So Greet would say, 'Here's a lawn! Let's do the *Dream!*' ";[24] and such open-air productions reached their apogee with Reinhardt's 1933 *Midsummer Night's Dream* outside Oxford.

Godwin's only other production applied the same principles in a very different way, though again outside the limits of the conventional stage. This was *Helena in Troas*, John Todhunter's highly lyrical compression of the Homeric legends about the Trojan war into a single day's action and nineteen pages of dialogue carefully structured into the classical strophe/antistrophe/epode pattern. To bring this highly stylized drama to life, and to involve the audience in such an unfamiliar theatrical form, Godwin accentuated its ritualistic qualities. He staged it in 1886 in a large arena, Hengler's Circus, which he altered to create an archeologically correct "Greek arrangement of Pro-scenium, Orchestra and Thymele." (Not perhaps altogether coincidentally, the production was "performed for the Benefit of the British School of Archeology at Athens.") In the center a large circular space, enclosed by a low wall and covered by a floor cloth that was painted to represent a tessellated marble pavement, separated the audience, seated in semicircular tiers modeled on the well-known amphitheater below the Acropolis, from a long, narrow upper stage. The panels covering the front of this structure were reproductions of friezes at the Temple of Phigalia. The arrangement of columns that formed the permanent set of Priam's palace, through which a backdrop of clear blue sky appeared on either side, was copied from the Temple of Empedocles. Incense burned in the altar to Dionysus that took up the center of the orchestra. This aspect of the production was imaginatively effective, particularly when the whole was bathed in "a dim religious light." It was described as "elevating, imposing and very beautiful, full of exquisite grace and refinement." Its impact on the audience was compared to that of a performance of *Oedipus* in another reproduction of a Greek theater at Harvard five years before, when the spectators "dispersed afterwards as if they were leaving a religious ceremony" rather than a theatrical entertainment. This response was attributed "in great part to the fact that the tragedy appeared in its own dignified surroundings and as far removed as possible from the flimsy and artificial accessories with which the modern playgoer is too easily satisfied."[25]

Indeed the visual spectacle must have been exceptionally powerful to achieve anything like this effect, as so many other elements in the production were working against it. According to Beerbohm Tree, who played Paris, there were only two rehearsals of the principal scenes. The amateur chorus moved clumsily and had to be restricted to aesthetically decorative but undramatic groupings, which did little to offset the static nature of the play. The script itself transformed passion into rhetorical clichés:

> PARIS(*to Helen*): Immaculate womanhood . . . O river of bliss
> Where deeper plunged than vexèd Tantalus
> I stand, and gape with my deluded lips
> To assuage the thirst that fills me at thy sight!

It also reduced the fall of Troy to a purely personal level, with little of the ethical questioning or religious significance of the Greek tragedy it was copying. As one reviewer commented, "For a noble scene we must have a noble art, but to strive after it is at least something."[26]

In his emphasis on historical accuracy, and also in this archeologi-

E. W. Godwin's production of *Helena in Troas*, Hengler's Circus, 1886. Production marked by archeological accuracy and aesthetic grouping.

cal attempt to reproduce a theater of the past, Godwin stood for much of what Craig rejected. But Craig's psychological need for a father figure led him to adopt Godwin, as he had adopted Irving, as an artistic progenitor, translating Godwin's approach into his own terms, stressing any parallels with him, and ignoring the very real differences. Thus, even after he had established his own antinatural-istic style and had left England for Berlin, Craig believed that he "could create great interest [there] in my father's work for the stage . . . it bears on mine, and the [two] things together would make for strength." It was specifically his own principles of visual unity, the creation of an emotional harmony out of all the elements of a performance, the bridging of the stage/auditorium division to involve spectators more immediately in the dramatic action, that Craig saw reflected in his father's work. The notion that directing as such was an activity comparable to architecture, as well as the con-sistently architectural quality of his designs, relates to Godwin; and even Godwin's realism carries over into Craig's work, though in an anti-illusionistic form, in his rejection of scenic artificiality. Above all Craig saw his aims as a continuation of his father's, for one of Godwin's obituaries had described him as motivated in all his stage work by "the absolute necessity for a reform in the usually accepted notions of theatre design."[27]

Irving had acted as Craig's artistic godfather. In Godwin, his bio-logical father, Craig believed he had found a forerunner whose par-entage might also legitimize his revolutionary theatrical concepts. He was to pay homage to both of these father figures, writing the book on Irving that has, perhaps more effectively than anything else, preserved interest in his acting achievements, and rescuing Godwin's ideas from oblivion by reprinting his articles on staging Shakespeare in *The Mask*. Yet on a practical level the influence of Hubert von Herkomer, which Craig never directly acknowledged, was even more decisive.

Born in Bavaria in 1846, Herkomer became part of the English artis-tic establishment. He exhibited at the Royal Academy, lectured at Oxford as the Slade Professor, and founded an art school at Bushey, then a village just outside London, in 1883. The work produced by the students was in the Pre-Raphaelite and Victorian gothic tradition, but they were taught that "dramatic expression – any outward, visible sign of any possible emotion – is proper pictorial matter; and move-ment is such in a special degree." For Herkomer, therefore, the theater was a logical extension of the easel, and he constructed a small stage for his students to experiment with lighting effects, per-spective, figure grouping, and the creation of emotional mood through story situations, "unfettered by tradition, or by the demands of a paying public."[28] Only two productions were finally mounted there: *The Sorceress* in 1889 and *An Idyll* in 1890. But these attracted a great deal of interest because of the novel scenic concepts they displayed. A select audience of leading theater artists was invited to each performance, and in 1892 Herkomer gave a public lecture entitled "Scenic Art" at the Avenue Theater in London.

At first glance these productions seem unlikely material for the seeds of Craig's ideas. They were lyrical rather than dramatic, and reflected the careful balance and sentimental detail of the popular genre painting of the period. The subjects were medieval, and the treatment was realistic to the highest degree. But Craig, who attended all three events, found Herkomer's stage techniques fascinating. He described the performances as "most moving," and commented on the potential value of the ideas put forward in the lecture, regretting that "the Profession" showed no signs of adopting them.[29]

Herkomer always denied that his aim was to reform the theater. Instead he presented his ideas as *improvements* on standard practice. But because neither he nor his students knew anything about traditional stagecraft, they started with a tabula rasa, and although the effects they wanted were basically conventional, the means they invented to achieve them led Herkomer to reject all established practices. In particular he criticized the flatness of two-dimensional scenery, the unnatural shadows thrown on an actor's face by footlights, and the perfunctory nature of stage illusion:

It is quite safe at present to let your moon rise perpendicularly up the sky, very quickly, until your mechanism is exhausted, and then let it stop. Further, that the moment this red, rising moon appears over the horizon, it shall send rays of blue light from the opposite direction from which it rose. It is safe to let down a "wobbly" sheet of canvas, close to the footlights, with a scene painted thereon representing [static] breakers dashing over the cliffs, and perhaps a sinking ship in the distance, to which the actor may have to refer in his speech. It is safe to have layers of canvas hanging from the "sky," like so much washing hung on a line; and certainly nobody has ever questioned the prerogative of the "firmament" to come together at right angles in the corners.[30]

By contrast, in his school's productions all the scenery was built-up, footlights were replaced by lights set back on either side of the auditorium, level with the actor's faces and boxed in so that the audience was unaware of them, and the "sky" was an unbroken, seemingly limitless expanse. In addition, a simple mechanism allowed the moon to rise naturally.

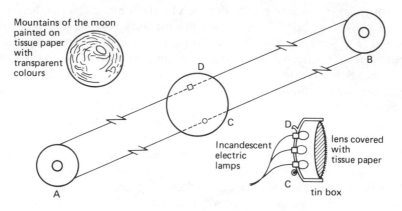

Two wires stretched between wheels attached to the rear wall of the stage at A and B carry the "moon-box," fixed at either D or C, which is moved by a stagehand slowly pulling on the wire. The mountains of the moon are painted on the tissue-paper cover, illuminated by three "incandescent lamps" with a transformer to reduce or increase the electric current.

Herkomer's lighting was so effective that many in his audience were convinced he had opened out the rear wall of his theater so that what they were seeing was the real sky. The only way to dispel this mistaken but flattering belief was to take a group (which included the young Craig) behind the scenes at the end of the performance and physically demonstrate how the impression of distance had been achieved. Across the back of the stage was a canvas painted in graduated shades of blue. In front of this a sheet of gauze was stretched, angled so that the gap between was two feet at the bottom and twelve feet at the top. Lights were set behind as well as in front of it, so that the surface could be made opaque or transparent, and projections were used to throw moving clouds onto it. As Herkomer described the effect:

With but little hastening of nature's time – the forty minutes of the act would be long enough to represent the last rays of the sun, casting its long shadows from the different objects on the distant slopes – time enough for the land to darken into that bewitching colour which is to be seen between the setting of the sun and the rising of the moon. Then for the moon to increase in strength as it rises (correctly) into the sky, showing a halo of ever-increasing brilliancy [through the reflection of the lights in the "moon-box" on the gauze in front] as the whole scene darkens almost into night.[31]

When, eight years later, Craig came to mount *Dido and Aeneas*, the first production in which he broke away from the conventional theater, he copied exactly this method of creating an "atmospheric" sky, together with the technique of positioning lights on either wall of the auditorium. In fact it was Herkomer's techniques that made the greatest impact in that performance, and Craig's obvious debt in stage lighting has been recognized for some time.[32] What does not seem to have been realized is how pervasive Herkomer's influence was on Craig's artistic principles in general, and how specifically it shaped many of the other elements in *Dido* and the group of productions that followed.

Herkomer realized that this sort of "stereoscopic" illusion could be created only if all the spectators viewed the stage from the same perspective. The theater he constructed was modeled on a scaled-down version of Wagner's theater in Bayreuth and was limited to an audience of 150 people, all of whom were seated on one level. This was an ideal that Craig also called for and carried out in his early productions, though Herkomer was aware – as Craig apparently was not – that "a non-subsidized theatre constructed in this way would not pay its way." He also outlined plans for an adjustable proscenium, so that the "frame" could contract to accommodate interior scenes or, when a single actor was on stage, to make "the human figure . . . duly prominent." In addition, he emphasized that design and proportion in the relationship of figures to a group or to objects in the setting could transform the scale, apparently magnifying an actor's stature or making him recede into the distance – ideas that Craig later picked up and expanded. He believed that scenic illusion could be created only if the stage floor were made as three-dimensional as the setting, and in *An Idyll* it was built up into an uneven surface of cobbles (for a village street) and curving slopes. As he noted, this had the additional advantage of preventing "my young performers from attempting the so-called stage-walk." In his production of *The Vikings* Craig used the same device for precisely the same practical purpose. But he accentuated the slopes, partly because instead of dealing with amateurs he was attempting to break down the long-established acting habits of professionals, and in place of Herkomer's subtle details he substituted steep cliffs in the bold lines that were characteristic of his art. Later, divorced from Herkomer's realistic context, this was to become one of Craig's most challenging concepts – transforming the stage floor into an active dramatic element. Even the darkness of the scenes in *The Vikings*, which followed Irving's practice, could equally be traced to one of Herkomer's suggestions: "Pictorial brilliancy is obtained by the very *economy of light* . . . leaving some parts of the stage-picture suggestive and indistinct."[33]

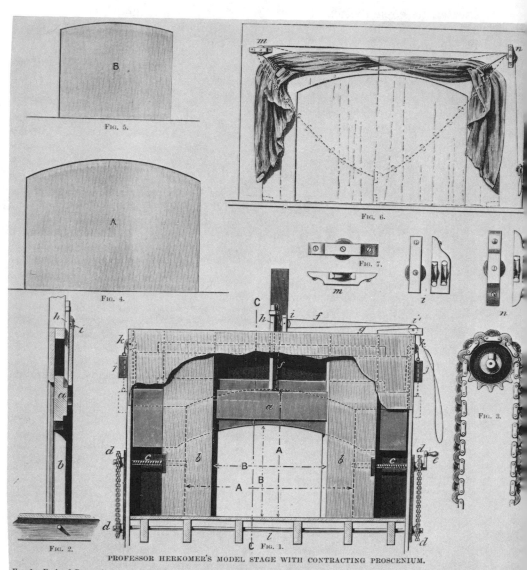

FIG. 5.

FIG. 6.

FIG. 4.

FIG. 7.

FIG. 3.

FIG. 2.

FIG. 1.

PROFESSOR HERKOMER'S MODEL STAGE WITH CONTRACTING PROSCENIUM.

FIG. 1.—Back of Proscenium, partly in section: A, A, Opening, normal size; B, B, Opening, reduced; *a*, Sky Piece; *b, b*, Sliding Wings; *c, c,* Right and Left-handed Screws, respectively; *d, d, d, d,* Toothed Pulleys; *e,* Handle; *f, f,* Rope for raising Sky Piece; *g,* Rope for lowering same; *h,* Guide; *i, i,* Pulleys; *j, j,* Counterbalance Weights, working over Pulleys *k, k; l,* Shaft connecting Pulleys *d, d.* FIG. 2.—Section on line C, C: *a,* Sliding Sky Piece; *b,* Sliding Wing; *h,* Guide; *i,* Pulley. FIG. 3.—Front View of Toothed Pulley *d,* and Connecting Chain. FIG. 4.—Greatest Size of Opening. FIG. 5.—Least Size of Opening. FIG. 6.—Method of Raising and Lowering the Curtain; the dotted lines represent the Curtain lowered; *m, n,* Pulleys. FIG. 7.—Elevation and Side View of Pulleys *m, n,* and *i* respectively.

Herkomer's plans for an adjustable proscenium, illustrating the "screw" mechanism (*The Magazine of Art,* 1892).

Herkomer corresponded to Craig's ideal of the theater artist. He not only acted the leading role in his own productions, directed, and rehearsed the cast, but also designed the scenery, wrote the dialogue, and composed all the music, and even drew the plans for his own theater as well. Like Craig, he emphasized that even "if a thousand people are needed to carry out an art scheme, it must be planned and directed by the *one man* who stamps it as his work." Craig later pointed to what he considered an essential distinction between Herkomer's intentions and his own, not mentioning him by name, but referring specifically to the natural moonlight effect that had become a symbol of Herkomer's improvements in scenic art: "The reproduction of nature's lights is *not* what my stage-manager ever attempts," and the aim should be "not to *reproduce* nature, but to *suggest*." Yet, beneath Herkomer's surface of extreme and detailed realism, the principles on which his work was based were remarkably similar to Craig's. He stressed that "natural phenomena must always be expressed through art," which by definition was subjective, and that "the very foundation of scenic art is *artificiality*." Like Craig, he believed that movement, not dialogue, should communicate meaning (though he was referring to representational mime rather than abstract dance), and that the function of every element in a performance was to contribute to "the 'mood' or, as the Germans say, 'stimmung' of the scene." In *The Sorceress* he had experimented with contrasting the moods of juxtaposed scenes in a way that was very similar to some of the effects Craig was to gain in *Dido*. "Heathen worship . . . song and dance . . . [and] incantations of the queen sorceress" during the night were set against the calm "peacefulness" of daybreak and shepherds. Perhaps most significantly, his definition of a "pictorial music-play" – the term he gave to his scenarios, in which the plots were little more than visual situations developed out of some of his own paintings, and in which for every speech or song there were ten pages of musical score accompanying and illustrating the actions of the characters – could be applied almost without change to the dramatic "visions" that Craig created for his Scene. "The first word denotes the plastic picture; the second, the musical sounds that are to attune one to the picture; and finally, the word play, to give sufficient motive for the display of the two arts – painting and music."[34]

However, Craig emphasized the qualities of overt artifice and impressionistic suggestion to an extent that made his debt to Herkomer almost unrecognizable. Whereas Herkomer's plasticity tended to stasis, Craig made movement the key element in his theatrical theories.

In addition, his representationalism was highly stylized from the first and quickly moved toward abstraction. His demand that every facet of the stage be transformed, from the architecture of the auditorium and proscenium, to the scenery, lighting, stage floor, and even the actor, may have been a response to Herkomer's call – more all-embracing than Godwin's – for reforms. Yet his vision of an Art of the Theatre was qualitatively different from Herkomer's Scenic Art, not just an extension of it.

Nonetheless, even in its urgency to find new theatrical forms for a new age, Craig's work has to be seen as a direct development of the theater at the end of the nineteenth century, retaining some of its most traditional aspects as well as building on those new techniques of staging that were already available. His aim of totally renewing the theater was to some extent characteristic of the time, and his first productions after he parted ways with Irving and left the Lyceum were at least partly a logical continuation of well-established trends, with Herkomer's experiments as their starting point.

# 3    A rising action: Design and movement

In 1900 Craig proposed for himself a characteristically far-reaching scheme of work: designing "Scenes, Costumes, Props, Movements and the rest" for seven of Shakespeare's plays (including *Hamlet*, *Macbeth*, and *The Merchant of Venice*), for romantic poetic dramas such as *Peer Gynt* and *Faust*, for "pantomimes and masques," and for musical productions ranging from "Symphonies by Mozart and Beethoven" and Bach's *Passion* to three Wagner operas and Purcell's *Fairy Queen*.[1] This "list of things to be prepared and done" ends with the note, "Prepare slowly my book on the Theatre and its Art," and the fact that this is the final item is significant. Productions precede theory. In a sense the main outlines of all his works for the conventional theater are contained in these early notes. He was later to design *The Merchant of Venice* for Ellen Terry, *Macbeth* for Beerbohm Tree in 1909 and then for Tyler in 1928, and *Hamlet* for Stanislavski. One of Ibsen's romantic plays was the first straight drama he directed, and another closed his stage career; and he worked on masques and *The St. Matthew Passion* off and on over the next thirty years. The fact that, right at the outset of his career as a director, so much of his future program was already articulated in outline gives unexpected consistency and coherence to his development, which otherwise seems so full of fresh starts and new directions. What the list also indicates, however, is a simultaneous preoccupation with such a wide diversity of projects that the odds were against any single production ever being completed – and this scattering of energy is indeed one of the reasons why Craig achieved relatively little on the stage.

But at this point he had someone who helped him focus his ideas: Martin Shaw, whose interest in early opera led him to found the Purcell Society. So Purcell became Craig's starting point. As he later said, "I rang up the curtain on my work in *Dido and Aeneas*" (a more modest and therefore more practicable choice than *The Fairy Queen*), although "without Martin Shaw I should never have thought to do this or done so."[2]

Martin Shaw, unlike Craig's later collaborators, was not another director, but a composer. So his approach complemented Craig's ideas, rather than competed with them; and over the next three years

35

they mounted six productions in which Craig worked out the principles of his theatrical art. *Dido and Aeneas* was repeated in 1901, together with *The Masque of Love* (built around the ballet and incidental music composed by Purcell for Betterton's adaptation of Beaumont and Fletcher's *The Prophetess, or The History of Dioclesian*). *The Masque* was performed again with Handel's *Acis and Galatea* in 1902, followed by Laurence Housman's nativity play, *Bethlehem*. Then in 1903 came Ibsen's *The Vikings at Helgeland* and *Much Ado about Nothing*. For various reasons – the use of amateur performers, the choice of a theater too far off the beaten track, censorship that restricted *Bethlehem* to "private performance," or the general public's lack of comprehension about something so different from their theatrical preconceptions – none ran for more than a few performances. Yet, perhaps because this was the era of new movements, Craig's work was immediately recognized as "the first step of a new movement which is destined to revolutionize the poetic drama." So *Dido* was hailed as "the way for which we have looked so long – the way in which we may see Shakespeare and Maeterlinck in all their poetry . . . the middle way between ugly pedantry [Poel's Elizabethan Stage Society] and superfluous detail [Irving and the Lyceum]."[3]

For this first production, Craig was literally forced to design his own stage, as the only available space the Purcell Society could afford was the Hampstead Conservatoire. This concert hall – forty-four feet wide, and with a fixed series of steplike platforms built across one end to seat an orchestra – was at first sight an unpromising theater. But the compromises forced on Craig by this shape and structure became characteristic features of his work. The ceiling height was the same throughout the hall, and to use Herkomer's techniques of overhead lighting and sky effects, he had to construct an exceptionally low proscenium to hide not only the frames for back cloths and gauzes, but also a bridge above the stage for a lighting man and his equipment. At the same time, to fit a cast and chorus that together numbered forty-two (swelling to seventy-five for the second production) onto an exceedingly shallow stage area, he had to use almost the entire width of the hall. The effect was strikingly panoramic, and he reused it not only for *Bethlehem*, which was presented in a similar though larger hall, but also in the Coronet and Great Queen Street theaters, where he lowered existing prosceniums by as much as twelve feet to create an impression of width. He also found (as Jessner was later to do in Germany) that stepped platforms made three-dimensional groupings and movement possible, and promoted as well a symbolic ranking of characters. So he designed a series of six steplike platforms for *Acis* (though in the actual production this was reduced to a single low rostrum across the rear, broken in the middle) and planned steps leading down to the orchestra for *The Masque of Love*. Similarly, in *The Vikings*, "instead of the stage level" he created "a slope of broken ground . . . to assist proper grouping" and to prevent all the actors from gathering downstage center and facing the audience – as they had become accustomed to doing with the footlights that he was responsible for abolishing.[4]

Two further factors imposed by the concert-hall structure also had a decisive influence on Craig. With four different scenes to mount, six changes, and no space for wings or flies, there could be no conventional settings. So the only physical scenery consisted of three or four poles hung with ropes to represent Aeneas's ships in act 3, and Dido's throne, arched over with a dome supported on four slender columns and flanked by six-foot trellis fences covered with dark green vine leaves and purple clusters of grapes. All of these could be easily moved and stacked flat against the side walls. This simplicity of scene, remarked on by almost all the reviews as responsible for much of the beauty of the production, became one of Craig's main principles. As he later noted:

Remember generally to seize one property . . . and round that conceive and build your scene – accompanying it always with its like a cross [*sic:* i.e., giving it the status of a symbol such as the cross, in order to make the scene] a place for PRAYER, an *emblem*. When you do this, you are able to help the theatre – [and it will be] full of spectators.[5]

The second factor was the unified, single-level seating in the hall. There were no side boxes, parterres, or galleries. This allowed all the spectators to see the play from the same perspective. Craig found it so effective that while working on *Venice Preserved* for Otto Brahm he even tried to persuade him to remodel the Lessing Theater along the lines of the Bayreuth auditorium, and accompanied one of his designs with the declaration, "I would not propose such a scene for any theatre except one of a special form – that is to say, with all the seats on an inclined floor."[6]

These qualities of simplicity and unified effect, together with exceptional possibilities for movement, were already present in Purcell's score. Originally commissioned by a dancing master for his Boarding School for Girls in Chelsea, the libretto calls for no less than seventeen dances and was modeled on the plan of Lully's operas, with choral scenes of spectacle linked by ballet dances and a

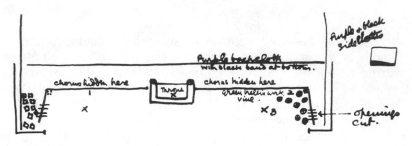

**PURPLE** ~~object~~ · vermilion dot.

From red ~~dot to red~~ dot stands a ~~green~~ hedge of green · Purple flowers a ~~thing~~ trellis upholds the green · it is semi transparent the ~~chorus~~ are behind · it dressing ready for the witches scene · _____ , ( more ⑤)

At the end of this scene on page 23 on removal of the Hedges 1 + 2 everyone behind must come down close to curtain at the word "Dance of ...". This will be done noiselessly, + in order.

———

Properties on stage · Throne · Canopy · Step · 8 cushions Rof 5 red side up 3 black.

Offstage (L) (1) Wreath of purple + green ·

" (2) Crown on silver cushion + robe ·

(R) (3) 2 Cornucopiae · 8 Spears + SPQR's 8 Shields · Shield + Spear for Aeneas.

Lights · 4 Blue + Purple from top on backcloth 3 Amber ~~from stage~~ top onto stage xxx 2 ambers from front on people only.

● Girls in green + purple ·

:: Two little black boys sit in corners - green + black ·

□ men with Aeneas · Purple + black

Craig's stage plan and lighting notes for the opening of *Dido and Aeneas* from the promptbook, showing the shallowness of the stage and the tight grouping of the chorus.

minimum of narrative. As a result, Virgil's original story is reduced
to five basic situations. Dido recognizes that she has fallen in love
with Aeneas, who woos and wins her with only token resistance.
All join in a "Triumphing Dance." The Sorceress and her witches
plot to destroy Dido by sending an evil spirit in the shape of Mercury to command Aeneas to leave Carthage. Then comes an "Echo
Dance of Furies." Dido and her maidens, resting by a fountain during a hunting party, are forced to take shelter from a storm, during
which the false Mercury appears to Aeneas. He promises to obey
the demands of fate, and the witches dance at their success. Aeneas
prepares to sail, while the witches delight in the coming destruction
of Carthage. A second "Witches' Dance" follows. Aeneas offers to
disobey the gods and stay, but Dido rejects him for being capable of
intending to abandon her, and throws herself on a funeral pyre
when he leaves.

This schematic story was simplified still further by a subtle shift in
the opening situation. In the libretto Dido's "torment not to be con-
fest" refers to the passion she is refusing to acknowledge, although
Aeneas's pleas make her "eyes confess the flame her tongue de-
nies." In Craig's version Dido was assumed to have acknowledged
her love before the opening of the opera. Her inner conflict became
"a Presentiment that her love for Aeneas will end in Disaster," and
Aeneas's declaration of love a reassurance that "revives her." This
gave an even greater emotional unity to the opera and increased its
powerful concentration still further. In addition, Craig's synopsis
makes quite clear that the emphasis is not on plot. After a bare
outline of the Sorceress's plan of deception, the whole action of the
last two acts is given a single sentence: "This has the desired effect;
the Witches exult, and Dido is left alone to mourn her Loss." The
subtitles given to the scenes stress specific moods and indicate that
Craig changed the settings to produce a structure of emotional
tones, even at the expense of verisimilitude. Instead of a palace we
are given "The Arbor," with its connotations of a lover's meeting
place and cultivated garden. Instead of a cave, the Witches were set
under water in a "long, low waste of dunes to which had drifted all
the wreckage of the world."[7] The hunt took place in "Moonshine,"
and the scenes of act 3, with the witches divided from the sailors by
a set change, were labeled "Departure," "Under the Ground," and
"Death." The effect is both of chiaroscuro and emotional progression. A cultivated garden as "the Morning breaks" is contrasted
with a dark wasteland of dashed hopes. The sylvan innocence and
tranquillity of a moonlit grove – brought out by Craig's opening

stage direction: "A laugh. R two fawns leap out startled and race off to L" – are set against the violence of a storm and Aeneas's anguish.[8]

The reviewers found the unity of the whole amazing as "a new and distinct art." They praised in particular what they (mistakenly) called "decorative scene painting" and pointed out that the settings were "as inseparable from the movements as from the robes of the players and from the falling of the light," all of which "mingle with the tones of the voices and with the sentiments of the play without overwhelming them under any alien interest."[9] This was clearly not a single-tone unity, however, but a higher type, the synthesis of opposites. Even the colors of the first scene were deliberately strong, jarring, and discordant to contemporary taste: vivid green, deep purple, black, and light scarlet cushions on Dido's throne, against

The use of gauze and cut cloth to create ghostly effects in the Witches' scene.

purple and black side cloths and a background modulating from sky blue to lilac during the scene. The same colors were carried over into the costumes: a red wig, and a green robe with a yoke of purple for Dido, green drapery with purple gauze veils for her maidens, and purple and black for Aeneas.

There were equivalent contrasts between the color schemes of each scene. The vibrant brightness of the arbor switched to blacks and whites in the Witches' scene, and the color of the stage floor changed too, with a green floor cloth replaced by a gray one. Even the textures of the scenes were set against one another. The clarity of shape and color and the impression of immense depths – Craig used Herkomer's combination of light thrown onto a plain back cloth from both behind and in front of a gauze for scene 1 – were followed by muted indistinctness. With cloth draped over the platforms so that all contours were lost and camouflaged in gray rags against the floor, the Witches seemed to rise out of nothing. Behind a gauze over the proscenium, surrounded by a cut cloth representing driftwood and wreckage, the figures seemed distanced and ghostly, and Craig's lighting notes underline that this was the effect he intended:

> Black snow is falling as curtain rises. One lime moon. One lime on Sorceress. Rest black. Keep light away from side cloths at edge and bottom edge. During this scene huge shadows sweep across the floor and people on the floor (not on the side or back cloth though).
> SORCERESS: Appear! Appear! Appear! Appear!
> Everyone else flat on ground, heads covered. Their dresses and floor cloth same tone: mixed green and grey.[10]

Two further types of contrast also deserve mention because they challenged the audience's imagination in a way that was to become characteristic of Craig's work. On one hand the production was openly theatrical, with obviously imitation vine leaves and grapes on the trellis of the arbor, a crude papier-mâché boar's head on the end of a spear in the hunting scene, and oversize bright pink paper rose petals for the death scene. On the other hand, as critics noted enthusiastically, the deliberate avoidance of conventional realistic detail and the "simple effects of colour . . . leave the imagination free" – achieving a suggestiveness that Craig underlined in the program for the second production by announcing that he had "taken particular care to be entirely *incorrect* in all matters of detail." This reminded one reviewer of the more delicate friezes of Pompeii, or, as Yeats wrote, "created an ideal country where everything was possible, even speaking in verse or in music, or the expression of the whole of life in a dance" (a phrase Craig was later to repeat).[11]

Similarly, the heroic was set against the grotesque. Craig's costume list emphasizes the "grand plumes" of Aeneas's helmet and the "large spears" of his men, and his prompt notes for the hunting scene deliberately echo seventeenth-century paintings of classical picnics: little black boys with turbans carrying trays laden with fruit and cakes, one holding up a cluster of grapes while a half-reclining maiden stretches up after the fruit, a loving cup ceremonially handed round. At the other extreme the witches were half-animal, half-vegetable, or half-human: deformed shapes with extravagantly fantastic accoutrements. One male witch

> . . . wears a fool's headdress and seaweed, green grey and black (velvet). The one black note.
> Strong handles to be attached to [the 1st and 2nd female] witches as if their hair.
> The rest have twigs with green leaves which seem to sprout from their fingers about 8 inches . . .
> Two have a skull between them (extra large. White).
> A model of a child. A bleeding head.
> The 5 men who cross after dance — owls' heads (Rosetti?)[12]

Like the Jacobean "antimasque," the effect of juxtaposing two such contrasting scenes heightened the essential quality of each. At the same time the introduction of overtly theatrical elements, as well as the unhistorical approach and a high degree of artifice in the patterning of movement, increased the audience involvement. They raised the imaginative stakes, challenging any too-easy suspension of disbelief by requiring the audience to assimilate discordant and unrealistic elements, and to create a synthesis for themselves in their own minds. (Equally, of course, this stylization ran the danger of making the whole seem absurd if spectators were not capable of taking the imaginative leap. In the second production at the Coronet Theater, which attracted numbers of the regular and less artistically inclined patrons of Notting Hill Gate because of the presence of Ellen Terry in a crowd-drawing curtain raiser, there was raucous laughter from the gallery and heckling at some points.)[13]

However, the general consensus of the reviews was that Craig's mise-en-scène harmonized with the dramatic emotion of the opera, creating a remarkable unity of figures, scene, music, and mood through "simplicity both in colour and form." "For the first time perhaps, those present saw operatic singers using gestures of real dramatic significance." In addition, the main idea was never lost sight of, no detail was allowed to detach itself from the picture, and every touch was of importance in the gradual development of the tragedy."[14] It was the lighting and the movement – the two elements that were to become central to Craig's concept of "a new theatre" – that contributed more than even the colors and costumes, to this unified effect.

Craig never prepared a full *mise-en-scène*, but by collating his notes for both productions a fairly complete picture emerges, as the second reproduced the first with only relatively minor variations. For instance, a special backdrop of hills and woods arched by a rainbow was painted for the hunting scene and Craig noted that it was "to become more mysterious. More moonlight." Similarly, for the opening scene he noted that "Dido *must* stay near or under the canopy. In 1900 she moved too much."[15]

By removing the footlights and replacing them with lights concealed in boxes at the sides of the auditorium and above the stage, not only could the figures be lit naturally, but also a wide range of shadow effects could be created. By using a single-color back cloth with a gauze stretched at an angle in front of it onto which light of another color was projected, "an astoundingly three-dimensional effect was achieved" which, to Yeats, seemed "like the edge of eternity."[16] The lighting was coordinated with the music, as at the opening, when "drums, lights swell and fall. Lights fall as drums fall." It was also largely responsible for giving an overall unity to the contrasting scenes. For the Witches' chorus "in our deep vaulted cell," Craig intended "a lime light under stage to come through 6 or 10 holes in the floor and steam which ascends as cigarette smoke in heavy atmosphere" (at least for the second production; such an effect was not possible in the Hampstead Conservatoire). This would have provided a parallel to the death scene, where rose petals fluttered gently down onto Dido's body in a vertical shaft of sharply focused white light against the gradually darkening purple sky as the chorus sang, "Scatter roses on her tomb." Perhaps more obviously, the rising dawn of the opening – darkness, with purple, then blue light thrown on a pale indigo back cloth from the top, gradually strengthening amber light on the stage and the green and purple figures – was balanced against the close. There Dido, robed in black on black cushions, and her surrounding maidens, now entirely covered in their purple gauze veils, were bathed in green light, while blue light was thrown from the top onto the indigo back cloth, yellow onto the gauze. The yellow gradually dimmed, then the blue, leaving the sky deep purple, which darkened until the chorus was lost against it and only their waving arms could be seen.

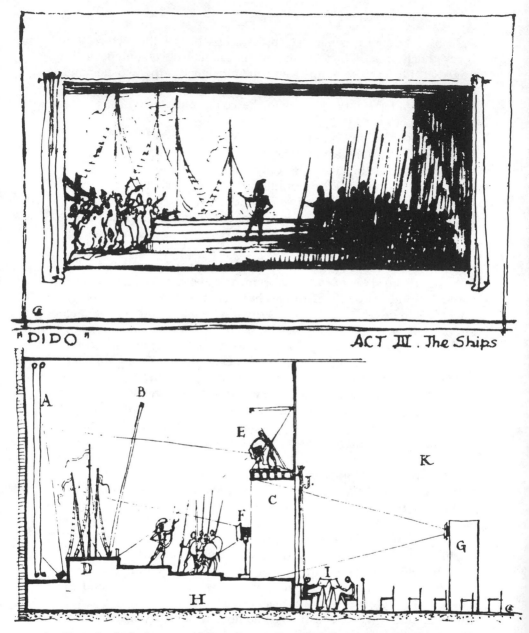

**"DIDO"**　　　　　　　　　　　　　**ACT III. The Ships**

A. Two backcloths—one blue, one grey.　　B. Grey gauze on a stretcher.
C. Temporary Proscenium-cum-spotting rail, faced with grey canvas.
D. Slender scaffold poles and thin rope to suggest ship's masts.　E. Battery
of 5 electric lamps with coloured filters.　　F. Floor lamps on either side of
Proscenium.　　G. Auditorium lights concealed in boxes.　　H. Permanent
platform of concert hall.　　I. Orchestra.　　J. Grey curtains.　　K. Auditorium.

Edward Craig's reconstruction of the lighting system and the pictorial effect
with massed choruses and minimal scenery.

Patterns of mood and movement: the Mourners' dance of white arms.

Craig's first reaction once *Dido and Aeneas* was suggested had been to visualize not the scenery, but patterns of movement and grouping to bring out the mood of the music. This final effect was one of his earliest concepts: "One dance I'll make a dance of arms – white, *white* arms – The rest of the scene dark – and out of it the voices – with arm accompaniment."[17] While Shaw rehearsed the members of the cast musically, Craig insisted that from the first they should be required to move around as they sang so that eventually they would be able to follow his direction to "walk with or counter to music. Continuous movement." As he later noted, "It is the large and sweeping impression produced by means of . . . the movement of figures which is undoubtedly the most valuable means" for trans-

mitting the essential meaning of a drama. So his production notes
dictate a highly formalized style of groupings and gesture, which
one critic found too "rigidly . . . decorative."[18] For instance, on the
last line of Aeneas's recitative on entering in the first scene – "Let
Dido smile, and I'll defy/The feeble stroke of destiny" – the elaborate
procession of his attendants with cornucopias, trophies, gold and
ivory trays laden with gifts, and spears and shields, makes "a descending movement. All spears slope on the syllable 'destiny.' "
With the next line, "Cupid only throws the dart," the chorus of girls
"go[es] off slowly, fingers to lips then slowly extend [arms]. Four
men move into a group [downstage R]. Stand still. Heads up. Two
slaves carry fruits, presents in golden baskets and lay them each
side of Dido. The 4 [men] sink." At the final line of the chorus,
"boys [put] fingers on lips. On last 3 notes the 2 slaves move arms
and swirl cloaks around (sticks in cloaks)." Frequently the movement directly illustrated Craig's principle of building a scene round a
single emblematic property, as at the end of the Triumphing dance,
when the girls, grouped in pairs, pick up the flowers that Aeneas's
attendants have scattered across the floor,

filling their hands and scarves with them.
   One girl finds the shield left by Aeneas. Trying to lift it. It falls on her.
She puts up one arm – the others, 3 or 4, run to help. They get under it
slowly and with difficulty raise it – a slow movement – everyone throws their
flowers into it and exeunt.
   All the girls who raise it must be same height from head to wrist.

This way of indirectly building up Aeneas's heroic stature risked
ridicule, as the shield was barely large enough for six girls to stand
shoulder to shoulder beneath its rim. But an accompanying sketch
emphasizes the graceful draping of the group holding the shield,
piled with blossoms, at full stretch above their heads, and the movement is carefully broken down into beats.

1.2.3.lift/hold shield with left hands.
1.2.3.wait/throw up with right.
1.throw high. Shield is heavy.
[Others] run off.

   By far the most complex patterning of movement comes in the
witches' scene. There are effective arrangements at other points,
particularly at the thunderstorm of act 2, when the chorus gathers
round Dido in a swirling group, the maidens taking shelter under
the soldiers' upheld shields at the extreme left,

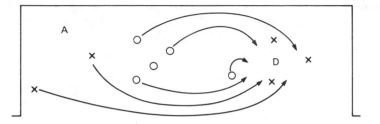

then dashing diagonally across the whole width of the stage in a linear movement to exit with the words, "Haste, haste to town."

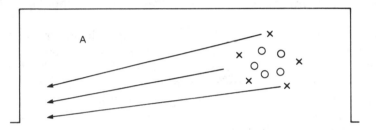

But the orchestration of the large numbers of witches shows Craig's choreography at its best. As the witches appeared, writhing in the shadows sweeping across the floor, structural patterns of sound were created. First "ah," which was picked up person by person across the stage from left to right. Then one wail at the right and a sigh traveling around from the left, then "whine (one)–2 gutteral noises and wail. Whine." The line rose silently up, starting at one side, "arms slowly out and up." Singing "Harm's our delight," they advanced one pace and sank a little at each line, to gather in a half circle with the tallest in the center, until "on the end of the last note the hands sweep round from R to L near floor."

Chanting "Ho! Ho! Ho!," the half-circle then advanced inward "swaying, clawing and singing," while from the center the figure of the fool, flanked by the two most grotesque witches with "handle-hair," marched straight toward the audience. With a shriek on the last "Ho!" all sank waving toward the sides of the stage. But the effect was not so much one of careful patterning as of threatening confusion, with the orchestrated gestures embedded in passages of "general movement, commotion, no one to be still for an instant." This reached a choreographed climax in the Echo Dance of Furies. The chorus accompanied the music with sung chords, with the girls echoing the men one bar later, and with sharp laughs, with the men echoing the girls. The dancers were divided into two groups of five to create "echo in movement also," and at the end of the sequence the performers in the first group "throw themselves back R and men go off 3 strides at [bar 3]," while those in the second group

at echo go up 3 strides, leap and turn sharp on [bar 5]. They start making circle, 2 one way 2 the other. They get into the right arm and leg position. Move round. [bar 15]. As the dancers begin to go off [re]enter first group. Mysterious steps. Owls' heads.
Noise . . . echo noise . . . laugh . . . echo laugh.
The lights die out. Circle. Enter others hold[ing] long sticks with rags and heads on them . . . all raised at end in centre.[19]

Throughout, the (male) Sorceress towered almost motionless at the rear.

As the number of notes relating to choreography and gesture indicates, movement was already one of Craig's primary concerns in the first of his mature productions. Another touch that foreshadows one of his central concepts was the use of masks. For the Sorceress and the two leaders of the chorus Craig noted: "Masks for witches – see Japan play." This was his earliest reference to the Nō drama, which was to become one of the models for his new theater. But the influence was limited to a type of stylized distortion. The features remain Western rather than become copies of specific symbols from a foreign tradition, and it was the impression of masking – not the masks in themselves – that was significant. As Craig noted in one copy of the program opposite the woodcut of a mask, "Wig and beard in one. Rest *can* be painted on face . . . nosepiece needed." At first sight his designs seem merely ideal conceptions. But he was dealing with broad effects, which made their realization easier, and was always concerned with the practical details of how his vision could be represented on stage. Opposite the drawing of a skeleton, for example, there are detailed directions for constructing the costume: "This figure wears a cloak of net over garment, bones painted on the under dress." Alternatively, the dress was to have a cage of wire beneath representing the ribs, while the upper part of the skull was to be "painted on old bowler hat" and "the lower jaw to be worn under the chin (the chin to be blackened)" to form the gaping mouth of the drawing.[20]

Craig always selected the most economical means of creating visual effects, and some of these masks were almost as simple as the modern burglar's nylon stocking: "Costume of witches. Net – black. Masks cut to mouth or gauze [stretched] over the upper part of the face. Very scarlet mouths. The gauze passing behind neck and swathing body. Tightly fixed at girdle." Even so, not all of his tech-

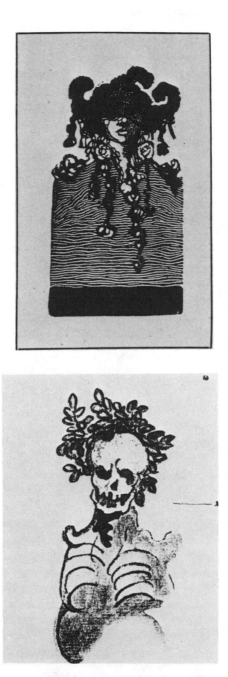

Rich imaginative effects gained by economical means: costume designs for a witch and a skeleton for the "wreckage" scene of *Dido and Aeneas*.

nical innovations were fully controlled. On the first night, as Martin Shaw recalled, "The limelight men supplied us with two moons; one of them was obviously excessive, but as neither of them would give way, both remained to the end of the scene." Indeed, some of Craig's ideas for this production were clearly beyond the resources of even the professional theater of the period, let alone the Hampstead Conservatoire. There are suggestions for making illusion more complete by involving the audience's sense of smell, as well as their eyes and ears, by filling the hall with the odor of sulphur during the witches' scene, and with "rare perfume" as the rose petals fall on Dido's corpse. And one note suggests something that Craig was later to experiment with in his search for a totally flexible theater form: "Proscenium to alter in size."[21]

With *Dido and Aeneas* recognized as the first step toward a significantly new kind of theater, Craig's next productions can be seen as extending and refining the principles he had established in that work. *Dido* had appealed to him because of "its directness and unconventionality of expression."[22] His subsequent vehicles were even less conventional, and allowed Craig even more latitude for interpretation. Although *Acis and Galatea* had been rewritten in the nineteenth century to conform with the theatrical taste of the period – Galatea being provided with a sister as mate for Damon and a father en route to the Trojan war, which allowed for the introduction of Ulysses and a scene adapted from Shelley's *Prometheus Unbound* – Craig returned to the original version, with its undramatic title "A Serenata." According to Handel's 1732 advertisement, "There will be no action on the stage, but the scene will represent, in a Picturesque Manner, a rural prospect, with rocks, groves, fountains and grottos, amongst which will be disposed a chorus of Nymphs and Shepherds, the habits and every other decoration suited to the subject." As for *The Masque of Love*, removed from the context of *The Prophetess* it had neither story nor situation to limit Craig's imagination, only a series of choral songs, music for a "Furies Dance," a "Chair Dance," and a "Butterfly Dance," and the emblematic characters of an Arcadian Shepherd and Shepherdess, Cupid, Bacchus, and Bacchanals. Perhaps because of the freedom these librettos allowed, Craig later rated both far higher than either *Dido* or *The Vikings*, and called *The Masque of Love* "the best thing I ever did on a stage."[23]

Needless to say, Craig ignored Handel's picturesque prospect in *Acis and Galatea*. For one scene, "The Shadow," he used the three-dimensional effect of limitless sky – blue darkening through deep purple to black at the base – as a backdrop for the lovers, who were seated in a vertical circle of pink light on a small mound of cushions and roses in the center of the stage. Behind them stood "a long dim line of cloaked figures melting into the gloom, yet seen; a row of faces peering from out the black, now a white arm uplifted, now the mass swayed and bent like human reeds." But this was the only scenic effect repeated from *Dido*, and even here he added a new technique. When the chorus bade the "wretched lovers" to "behold the monster Polypheme," a wire frame behind the gauze was illuminated and the impression of "a towering castle emerged in golden outlines."[24] A similar, but even more spectacular piece of theatricality closed the opera, when the dead Acis was transformed into a "Water God." A figure formed out of sparkling drops of water, which appeared to rise and fall like a fountain, appeared against a sheer blue sky. The effect was so magical that one reviewer believed he was seeing an entirely new technique of projected light. But, as Edward Craig has pointed out, this was an old pantomime trick used by Charles Kean: The light from lamps with large perforated discs revolving in front of them shines from behind through holes pierced in the back cloth.[25]

Apart from such spectacular effects, which show the links between Craig's new art and the artifice of traditional theater, the major scenic development in both this production and *The Masque of Love* was toward suggestiveness, simplicity, and austerity. One aspect of this movement, as in the earlier representation of Witches, was Craig's use of indistinct forms and semidarkness to allow each spectator to fill out a picture of horror with his own imagined fears. But in *Acis* this became pure suggestion, without grotesque accoutrements. When Polyphemus was first introduced, it was only as an enormous shadow projected on the back cloth to tower threateningly over the lovers, a tableau that gave Craig his title for the scene. When Polyphemus appeared in the next scene, "The Giant," at first only "one single fold of a vast purple mantle, sweeping down from the darkness" could be seen. Then, as the light grew, all that stood revealed was "a huge, brooding form upon a throne of heaped shadows, a haunting shape, barely seen, yet difficult to forget," and it was precisely this allusive bareness that led Max Beerbohm to call Polyphemus "the only real and impressive giant ever seen on any stage."[26]

Even more significantly, the first scene, "The White Tent," showed that Craig could move beyond the easy suggestiveness of semidarkness. Instead of displaying the romantic Arcadian land-

BYAM·SHAW·DEL·1902

ACIS·AND
GALATEA

MARCH
1902

An artist's impression of the "Wretched Lovers" duet in *Acis and Galatea:* In
the original the lovers appear light purple against the wall of black figures
behind, harmonizing with the deep blue sky. Craig's design for the moment immediately following the lovers' duet: chorus and castle fade away,
to be replaced by a gigantic shadow projected onto the back cloth.

Stage plan for *Acis and Galatea*. R and L stand for the two trelliswork columns; the inner frame represents the webbing of the "tent" and the outer frame the back cloth. The large circle shows the position of the "mound" for the lovers. For the opening scene brightly colored cushions are spread on the platforms at the rear, and the only props listed are two "long sticks with Honesty," a bunch of bells, and balloons.

scape of Sicily, Craig hung a bar right across the stage toward the rear, over which he draped a complete row of long two-and-a-half-inch-wide strips of upholsterers' webbing. At the front these were attached just above the sight lines behind the proscenium to form a gently curving roof, through which light filtered from above. At the back they hung down like a curtain, striped with the narrow gap between each one. This gave an effect of transparency, with the strips swaying and opening as the actors moved past and through them, and the rough material appeared so delicate that one reviewer believed the tent to be made of silk. Behind was a back cloth with circular clouds at the base of a sky that went from white through pink to indigo at the top. (Craig had actually designed this three years earlier in 1899 – the first example of the way he created generalized scenes that could then be incorporated into any production to establish mood rather than representing a specific place, as in more conventional settings.) On either side of the stage two slim columns of trelliswork entwined by vines appeared to be supporting the roof and emphasized the tentlike form. As in *Dido*, the colors of the costumes echoed the background – white, pink, and silver here; brown and black in the later tragic scenes – and in addition gave the effect of shimmering movement. Made of inch-wide tapes, cream outside and colored on the reverse, they looked like drapery when the figures were motionless, swirling ribands of red or blue when they moved. These techniques were intended to convey the floating evanescence of a dream and, as Craig noted, "the strings" of the scene were "to wave now and then as if in the mind." Out of these simple materials and light, a completely original world of poetic fancy was created.

"O the Pleasure of the Plains!" sang the chorus, and the fierce mid-day light beat down, tempered softly by the draperies of the white tent under which they lay. Of scenery, in the ordinary sense, there was none; all was suggestion, but such skillful suggestion that into the cool, white shadow came the very heat and glare of midsummer's meadows under a burning sun.[27]

The action Craig created to accompany this effect was equally simple and fanciful. Among the drowsy nymphs and shepherds, white-frocked children danced beneath pink and white penny balloons that were tied to a hoop above their heads. These they handed out, one to each dreamer as a symbol of their desires, until the whole scene was filled with dancing figures and floating balls.

The setting for *The Masque of Love* was even simpler: plainness carried to austerity. Instead of using suggestion, Craig reduced the scenery to a neutral ground for the imagination – three monotone gray canvas walls, a gray floor cloth patterned in squares, and a double gauze front curtain, one ribbed with a grille of dark gray bars, the other hatched with white squares, for "The Prison of Love." Craig found this sort of grille (derived from Inigo Jones) so effective that it reappeared when he designed *For Sword or Song*, in which it was used as a semitransparent "front scene" with dark ragged figures outside toward the audience, and warm candlelight and song behind. He used it as well in the *Caesar and Cleopatra* designs he did for Max Reinhardt. In both productions it was clearly

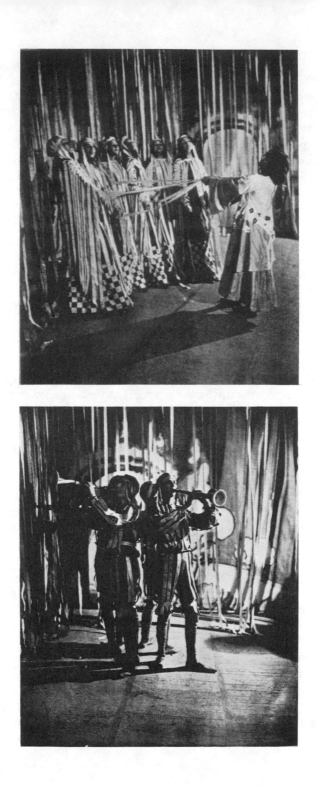

Stylized movement, the transparent "tent," and the effect of tapes in the costumes of the chorus (white outside, showing red reverse when swirled apart) in the opening scene of *Acis and Galatea*.

a distancing device, a way of creating the separation between art and "the pushing world" that a symbolist poet like Yeats believed essential if an imaginary vision were to keep its integrity. But in *The Masque* there was also an element of optical illusion directly anticipating the "op art" of later painters such as Vasarelli. The spacing between the bars grew narrower toward top, bottom, and sides, and curved into the corners, so that the grille appeared to bulge out toward the audience, giving a dreamlike effect. Initially Craig had contemplated using elaborate stage properties, and one of his drawings shows Cupid seated on a towering throne, arched with a dome very reminiscent of Dido's arbor. A flight of steps lead down to an elaborate two-tier altar, flanked by ten massive candles, and Craig's notes alongside suggest the full deployment of such pantomime techniques as the "Water God":

A golden rain descends as the curtain rises.
Inside dome is a white light – hidden.
Altars . . . incense bowls from which smoke ascends in a quite straight line, silver rain descending on same.

In the actual production, the only parts of this used were the candelabra, a pair of which was set on each side of the stage. (The bowls of incense were transferred to *Acis*.) Instead there was an almost toylike simplicity. Cupid's throne was transformed into a small wooden play cart, drawn around the stage by small children, in which a real infant was set as Cupid (with the soprano singing the role offstage – the first use of a technique that was to be developed in Craig's later, unstaged work). Even the costumes were plain and muted. A chorus of Pierrots was clad in loose white smocks with black chiffon scarves hanging from simple headdresses, Harlequins wore surcoats of dark gauze over the traditional pattern of lozenges on their tight-fitting costumes, and a group of Kings and Queens was robed in long sweeping cloaks painted with large patterns in faint gold. But these neutral tones set off the bright yellow of crowns and candelabra, the floral wreaths carried by the Harlequins, and "touches of red, the more brilliant for their rarity," while the "white figures and greys and greens" took on different hues as they moved through the pools of colored light that covered each area of the stage – blue and green and red and yellow.[28] At the same time this plainness also set off the occasional grotesque touches (like the masks worn by Comus and Silenus and the elaborately beribboned loops and furbelows of the gray-and-black dress of the

Shepherdess), and Craig's costume notes bring out the diversity within this overall unity. Kings were

to look as dignified and gorgeous as the costume can manage. Crown gold and crystal with turban – underdress reaching to ground to be cross and dot pattern, yellow and dark grey – overmantle: long train, with pattern round shoulders and bottom edge in dark grey – overmantle to be of heavy stuff. Lining of mantle, yellow and white.

Bacchanals, in contrast, wore skintight "green costume, with leaves down seams of legs and sleeves, at wrists and in ruff at throat. Headdress of leaves and red berries, carrying branch with leaves and berries."[29]

This was all in such stark contrast to the conventional theater's tinsel-and-pretty-lace treatment of imaginary visions (the best example being the usual nineteenth-century gossamer fairyland of *Midsummer Night's Dream*) that at least one reviewer "found a dream that had come true."[30] In a sense it could be called minimal art, gaining richness from a simplicity that made each detail full of significance; and the austere straight lines of the box set, the neutral tones brought alive by complex lighting effects, form a basic prototype for later developments like Craig's use of screens.

Yet this apparent artlessness was achieved only through considerable technical complexity which, like anything complicated, was prone to accidents – and the slightest of mishaps was enough to endanger such a delicate emotional tone. There was laughter from the gallery, for instance, when a dancer brushed against one of the high candles, making it wobble, and on the first night of *The Masque*, according to Martin Shaw, "the children upset the infant in his car and while the unlucky babe (where was the L.C.C.?) hung perilously downward, howling, his attendants shrilly disputed the question who was to blame for his ungodlike position." Similarly, although *The Masque* had only a single set, changing even the apparently almost nonexistent scenery for *Acis and Galatea* caused all-too-obvious problems. After the opening night, one of Craig's friends and supporters, the critic Haldane Macfall, commented:

Between the acts you lose your public whom you have captured . . . is there no bridging over this gap? . . . of course, I quite allow that your bawling behind the curtains was wholly delightful; but while vibrant with suppressed emotional intensity it was not in the picture. You very nearly got an encore once, all the same. It was when you told the carpenter he was ruddier than the cherry.[31]

Contrasting costumes: Pierrot and Harlequin.

This was the more potentially damaging because the key factor was not scenic effect, but movement: movement not only within each act in the form of dances, choreographed gestures, and groupings, but also movement between one act and another through developing parallels and contrasts on all levels, gradations of light and shade or color scheme, and variations of human mood and movement.

Preparing for *Acis*, Craig noted: "The stage movement to be far more elaborated, and simpler than 'Dido and Æ.' Conventionalize the actions and retain the general one – movements of the crowd."[32]

Working on this principle, Handel's single tableau had been transformed into a series of orchestrated groupings, stylized moves, and symbolic positions. This was even more the case in *The Masque*, in which Craig had effectively created a wholly new work around the bare indications of action contained in the lyrics. Here the movement was so central that he later tried to create a vocabulary of notations based on the choreography. A single downward stroke indicated the posture of the body, a triangle the head (tilted for various positions: to one side �triangle, back ⬆, down ▽, or with a line through it for closed eyes ⬆), and an inverted "t" for whichever leg was "pointed" or not bearing weight ( ⬆ ). A horizontal line represented three arm positions (raised to the shoulder ⬆, to the ears ⬅, over the head ⬇). A circle stood for a complete turn, with segments of the circle for one-quarter, one-half, and three-quarter turns. Lines and dots showed the direction and number of steps, as well the type of pace (walking on flat foot ----, on toes ||||, running on flat foot --. --. --., on toes . . . .). A square stood for an unmoving figure, and ⊠ indicated a figure holding a fixed posture. These symbols may seem crude. After all, Craig was to some extent pioneering a new field, and a satisfactory system of dance notation still has yet to be developed. But the fact that the range of things that can be recorded by these signs is limited is not accidental. It corresponds to the type of movement in his productions. Obviously this had very little to do with conventional ballet, and that there are no symbols for leaps and pirouettes is significant. Craig's system of symbols is based on ordinary gestures and ways of moving, which are restricted and standardized – three clearly differentiated arm positions, four basic steps – and which can be built up into easily perceived visual patterns. This simplification would be more effective for group movement than for a solo dance, and the tendency is toward geometric abstraction.

Even if the program defined the masque form as "a link between the medieval pageant and the play proper," Craig clearly thought of *The Masque of Love* as "a ballet."[33] Indeed, any outline of its contents is a description of dances and symbolically choreographed movements rather than of dramatic actions.

In the vague and mysterious depths of a hall, very empty and very spacious . . . is trod the first measure of the Masque of Love. We see, but only darkly as yet, through the bars of an immense window, that Love for all his great power is a very little god. The children surrounding Love are behind these prison bars, not as captives of the invincible captor, but as his fellow-jailers. They, impersonal little beings, are as gods, and do the god's bidding unvexed by whip or chain. These are the orders which Cupid gives them:

Cupid. Call the Nymphs and the Fauns from the wood.
Children . . . The Nymphs and the Fauns from the wood.
Cupid. Call the Naiads and Gods of the Floods.
Children . . . The Naiads and Gods of the Floods.
Cupid. Call Flora and Comus . . .
   Silenus and Momus . . .
   Call Bacchus and his merry fellows . . .
   Silvanus, Ceres, and Tellus . . .
   All leave for awhile their abodes.
Children . . . Leave for awhile their abodes.

The children run out swiftly, and return as swiftly, dragging a car full of masks and disguises. In pageantry it is the habit which makes the god or goddess, and Cupid's will is done when the messengers have assumed the guise of the gods whom they were sent to find. As they put on their divine cloaks they sing exultantly:–
   "Come, come away;
   No delay, no delay.
   All bow to his will,
   And all show their skill,
   To grace Love's triumphing day."

The hour has struck for the coming of Love's captives. Darkness falls, and a solemn prelude ushers in the procession. Between sleeping and waking heralds of its advance tread a grotesque measure. Here now are the prisoners of Love. They enter in three groups, from the east, from the west, from the north, and the names of these groups are Rank, Riches, and Poverty. They enter at no visible doors, . . .

Splendid victims . . . their wrists are bound, their step is slow. They are here, but chained to a rod of captivity; they are here, but dragged by one only less powerful than Death. As these shapes pass, they sing:–
   "Behold, O mightiest of gods,
   At thy command we come–
   The gay, the sad,
   The grave, the glad,
   The youthful and the old all meet,
   As at the day of doom."

Hardly have they finished their stately declaration of allegiance to Love, than their master, with sweet duplicity, will have them think that their slavery is perfect freedom. Love's little fellow-jailers enter, and strike the fetters from the wrists of the captives. A sprightly "Paspe" (passe-pied) strikes up.

The barred window fades and vanishes. The rod to which the "splendid victims' " wrists were tied by long lengths of cord becomes "a maypole of merriment," and "deliverance is symbolised by a dance," after which "a solemn movement" gives visual expression to the simple descants of "Hear, mighty Love!" that end the second section.

Craig's notes for movement at "Behold, oh mightiest of gods" in the promptbook of *The Masque of Love*. The strings are attached to a long stick held by one of the Harlequins above his head.

At the conclusion of this high invocation, a mysterious rustling and a trampling of feet are heard outside. The worshippers of Love are filled with mingled consternation and curiosity, which give place to open fear. They flee like startled fawns when a company of Bacchanals rush in with uproarious merriment.

The joy of living, as symbolised by Bacchus and his train, at first astounds and shocks the devotees of Love, but step by step they draw nearer, fascinated by the gay green god and his wild followers. . . . Very soon the two parties mingle. Bacchus and his men sing a rollicking chorus of the vine, which is followed by a chorus and [an interweaving] dance even more full of joy and movement, and delight in living. This prepares us for the coming of Mirtillo and Corinna, the only names in this crowd of nameless wooers and wooed. The man woos, the woman hesitates; he entreats her reason – Tell me why? – she has none. It was ever thus, even in dreamland. She yields at last, and her winning is the signal for all the maskers to move in a courtship dance. This gives place to another dance, and yet another, this time the "contre-danse." All the dancers except the children are blindfold. Could these blind ones see, their chorus in praise of Love might be a shade less triumphant.

"Triumph, victorious Love,
Triumph o'er the universe."
During this exalted song the maskers resume their chains; but now through
the magic of the masque we dream a marvellous dream. It is their persecu-
tors, not they, who wear the fetters. Triumphantly free, they lead captivity
captive – and are gone.[34]

Beneath his copy of this summary Craig wrote the words "well
described," and what the description brings out is the symbolic nature of the performance. The characters are not simply mythical or
metaphoric – even the two figures individualized by names are those
traditional fictions, of the Arcadian shepherd and shepherdess. They
are also imaginary and overtly theatrical, created by donning masks
and costumes in full view of the audience, and similar in many ways
to the Commedia dell'Arte (even though at this point Craig knew
nothing about this Italian theatrical tradition). Relationships and
emotional reactions are communicated by groupings and postures, so
that the stage presentation was almost equivalent in its abstraction to
the music. Many of the audience found all but the most obvious
references obscure, and as one reviewer admitted,

I could not quite follow all the inner meanings of the show – some were a
trifle cryptic. But the triumph of Love was clear enough, and it even caught
up a timid nun hovering round the edge of forbidden joys. In the end she
too secured one of the strings which hung from the maypoles and followed
in the train.[35]

However, the general moods were clear enough, communicated by
blending the choreography of the players, the patterns of color and
light, and the musical orchestration into a single, unified form of
expression – the basis for Craig's new art of the theater.

In *The Masque of Love*, even more clearly than in the two operas,
the dominant element was the movement. In *Acis* the dances visually reinforced the scenic effects, as with the transformation at the
end, when the flow of the fountain was "echoed in the bending,
swaying forms, floating scarves and waving arms of the chorus" so
that "music and singers alike seemed to melt together and ripple in
a silver flood round the feet of the new-born Water God." But the
essence of *The Masque* was in the "ballet," and in an advertisement
of 1904 Craig offered to perform "his unique entertainment . . . at
Town or Country Houses, either in the open air or in a large hall."
So little in fact did he consider it dependent on the technical appara-
tus of the theater, or on the conventional relationship between audience and actors, that he even suggested performing it on railway-
station platforms as a traveling show.[36]

In both these productions reviewers noted a "large display of symbolic suggestion in posture and grouping" and an "unconventional conventionality." At the same time, in the dance steps, as with the masks in *Dido*, Craig deliberately used indigenous forms for their familiarity, rather than copy foreign traditions, and he replaced Purcell's original pavanes and minuets with English country dances. The choruses were divided into groups of three and four so that movements could be counterpointed, or a balance created in stylized groupings. Other positions and gestures were deliberately copied from seventeenth-century paintings. For instance, the dance illustrating "the sweet delights of love" in *The Masque* was modeled on a reproduction of Fra Angelico's *Dance of the Angels* that Craig pasted into his promptbook. The gestures for the chorus in the death scene of *Acis* were described as "hands above head, fingers open and bent back – grief: Rubens." Other patterns of grouping were designed to create a geometry of movement – sometimes in three dimensions, as when children with bells climbed up into the trellis columns of *Acis* – each move in a pattern being carefully coordinated with the words and music. This was emphasized in *The Masque*, in which the different groups were all instructed to take "a step on the first beat in each bar" and to move forward and sink "on the word 'Down' . . .", and the geometrical effects were particularly striking.[37] Repeated parallels were set up. A circle of children moved around Cupid, a circle of dancers around the maypole; first the Poor from the left, then the Kings from the right, each led in on their knees by a Harlequin who held the ends of the ribbons tied around their wrists high over his head. Symmetrical patterns were duplicated on each side of the stage, with groups dancing from the center diagonally down to the right and left, or curving out down from a line along the back to return up the center in a double circle. At one point eight Bacchanals flanking three Harlequins in a long line across the stage pranced forward through a second line of eleven Pierrots in a series of three strongly marked moves. Diagonal movements were executed by triangularly shaped groups. Marchers formed rectangles. The impression of rigid structuring was so strong that Arthur Symons described Craig as working

in squares and straight lines, hardly ever in curves. He drapes the stage into a square with cloths; he divides those cloths by vertical lines, carrying the eye straight up to an immense height . . . he sets squares of pattern and structure on the stage; he forms his groups into irregular squares and sets them moving in straight lines which double on themselves like the two arms of a compass . . . He prefers gestures that have no curves in them: the arms held straight up or straight forwards or straight sideways. He likes the act of kneeling in which the body is bent at a sharp angle; he likes a sudden spring to the feet, with the arms held straight up. He links his groups by an arrangement of poles and ribbons . . . each figure is held to the centre by a tightly stretched line like the spokes of a wheel. Even when, as in this case, the pattern forms into a circle, the circle is segmented by straight lines.[38]

A description like this brings out the essential unity of Craig's theatrical vision over his whole career. It could be applied, almost without change, to the final stage of his development that is represented by his notion of Scene. At the same time, although the effect from the eye level of the stalls may have been linear, this was an illusion. In the ground plans that Craig drew, curving and circular move-

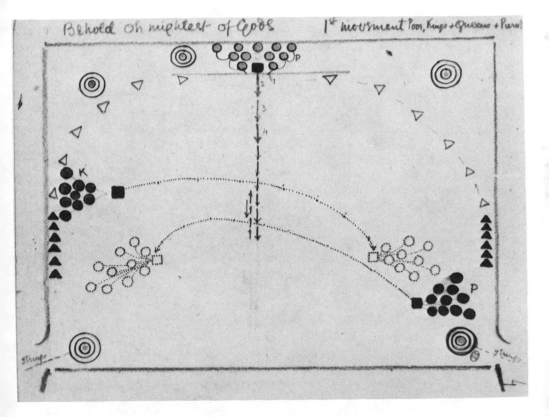

Craig's blocking for "Behold, oh mightiest of gods." The large concentric circles represent the positions of the candlesticks. The triangles show the starting points and movements for the "Torches," and the groupings of dots those for the Kings and Queens (st. R), the poor (st. L), and the Pierrots (upstage); the squares stand for the Harlequins.

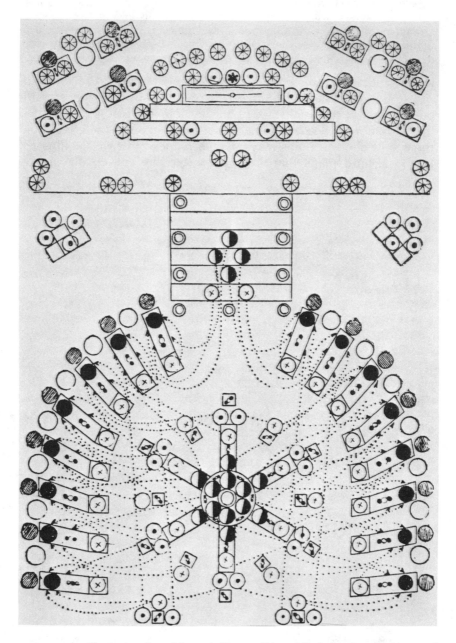

An illustration from Moynet's *Trucs et Décors* (1890) showing the system of ballet notation used by Craig for *The Masque of Love*.

ments predominate. These diagrams are tangible indications of the link between *The Masque of Love* and Craig's later work. Completed more than two years after the production itself, the patterns still follow the sketches for movement in his promptbook in their general outline. However, they are even more schematic than the actual dances performed, as they were exercises modeled on a system of ballet notation Craig had discovered in Moynet's *Trucs et Décors*, exercises through which he was working out the principles of a more abstract, completely formalized theatrical art.

For Craig – again looking forward to Scene – this geometry contained symbolic, almost mystical meanings, and as he noted in 1907, "movement can be divided into two distinct parts, the movement of two and four which is the square, the movement of one and three which is the circle. There is ever that which is masculine in the square and ever that which is feminine in the circle." In this metaphysical perspective "perfect movement" came from combining these masculine and feminine elements, which would (supposedly) unite a stage performance with the universal rhythms of nature. The choreography of *The Masque of Love* is clearly an attempt in that direction. When Symons commented that "Mr. Craig aims at taking us beyond reality; he replaces the pattern of the thing itself by the pattern which the thing evokes in the mind, the symbol of the thing," Craig noted in the margin, "Right, right so!"[39]

# 4    Problem drama: Texts and performers

In his early operatic productions Craig achieved a remarkable unity of acting, music, scene, and costume that became his standard for subsequent work. To some extent the circumstances that allowed this were not repeatable. Arguably, it was his success under such special conditions that made him dissatisfied with his next productions. It may explain to some extent his insistence on founding a school instead of on giving practical examples of his theories on the stage, and perhaps even contributed to his eventual abandonment of the theater. The prime characteristic of Craig's style was neither the often-referred-to purple or blue of his apparently infinite skies, nor the reform of stage lighting that followed his removal of the footlights. Nor was it the imaginative use of masks, the color harmonies, or the move away from realistic settings toward a simplification that liberated the audience's imagination – though Craig, considered solely as a scene designer, may be credited with the invention of scenic impressionism. The vital quality was Craig's symbolic choreography of patterned movement and stylized gesture. As any careful examination of his notes and directions for *Dido*, *Acis*, and *The Masque of Love* show, it was this that preoccupied him and gave his work its characteristic style as well as much of its powerful imaginative effect.

Three of the factors that created these special conditions for his early operatic productions were inherent in the material. For Purcell, "as poetry is the harmony of words, so music is that of notes," and the continuous musical accompaniment, the frequent reprises and refrains, gave a clear structure around which Craig could orchestrate sweeping or repeated movements. At the same time the simplicity of the librettos and the absence of any stage directions (or even, in Handel's case, of any intention that the music should be accompanied by illustrative action) allowed Craig almost complete imaginative freedom. He could create ideal forms to express pure emotional states, corresponding to and reinforced by the music, with minimal constraints of story and characterization. (Indeed, the absence of characterization was one of the criticisms voiced against his first production, in which Aeneas had seemed so much an echo of Dido's visual environment that it was hardly credible he should ever contemplate abandoning her.) In addition, subliminal forms of communication – visual patterns, expressive gesture, sound rather than verbal sense – could legitimately be emphasized at the expense of the more intellectual qualities of dialogue. Quite apart from their share of belcanto arias or reprises that add little to the meaning, as Martin Shaw pointed out, "the libretto of both these pieces is such sorry stuff that it is amazing that Purcell could have written such inspired music to much of it. In *Dido & Aeneas* particularly one meets with such absurd phrases as 'Let Dido die!' and 'Thus, on the fateful banks of Nile/ Weeps the deceitful crocodile.' "[1] In short, the operatic form not only gave Craig the scope to move toward a new concept of theatrical art, transforming the mimetic nature of conventional stage representation into something nearer to the abstract qualities of music and architecture, but also encouraged this development and provided a framework for it.

Equally significant was a fourth factor: his use of amateur actors. Because they had no previous stage experience at all, they had no preconceptions, no conventional techniques of characterization, and no established mannerisms and ways of moving that might conflict with Craig's vision. On one level, their lack of expertise (together, of course, with the fact that all had other commitments) meant an inordinate – and commercially impossible – length of time had to be devoted to rehearsing them, starting at the most basic level. As Craig later commented, "These ladies and gentlemen not being dancers (never having had a day's training) were made to walk – to run (now and again a few steps)" and were "given discreet exercises to execute." Preparing *Dido and Aeneas* took six months, all for only three performances. Four months went to rehearsing *The Masque of Love*, whereas it took barely two weeks to mount Craig's production of *Much Ado* with a professional cast. At the same time, if Craig were to create model productions for an entirely new kind of theatrical experience, it was essential for him to return to first principles, which this work with amateurs forced him to do. As he said, they became "excellent in their stepping out – and far better than ballet dancers would have been – for they and I together expressed something and what we said was no echo of what the theatres were at that time repeating over and over like parrots."

In addition, this lack of previous training meant that, however complex Craig's choreography, its components – the actual gestures, groupings, and dance steps – had to be *simple every way* (as Craig reminded himself on the opening page of his promptbook for *The Masque*). It also meant that the actors had to be willing to submit themselves totally to his directions, so that every movement and position corresponded to his vision. The same applied to the cast as singers. As Martin Shaw remarked, "There was hardly a trained voice among them," so they accepted being required "to sing their choruses crawling, leaping, swaying, running – any way that Craig fancied."[2] Most professionals would have considered that such demands would cramp their singing and would have refused to do such things. Even with the large numbers in his chorus, the long rehearsal times allowed him to elaborate separate roles for each individual within the overall structure, and the absence of any "stars" accustomed to center stage made it possible for him to go a long way toward his ideal of a unity in which scene, music, and actors harmonized. At the same time, because most of his original cast for *Dido* also acted in *Acis*, *The Masque of Love*, and *Bethlehem*, by the second or third production he possessed a chorus fairly expert in his requirements. They were capable of reaching a high performance standard – even if filling the major roles satisfactorily continued to be a problem – and it seems probable that working with the particular limitations of this group both contributed to making simplicity

Suggestive simplicity and chiaroscuro in the opening scene of *Bethlehem*.

one of his guiding principles, and led him later to his ideal of the actor as "Uebermarionette," totally under the control of the artist–director.

In many ways *Bethlehem* can be seen as an extension of the earlier productions. Again there was a strong musical element. Laurence Housman had commissioned Joseph Moorat to compose arrangements for the lyrics – a score to which Craig and Shaw, who looked on Moorat as "an amateur composer . . . nothing but a stumbling block" added passages of Palestrina, Bach, Mozart, and others.[3] A proscenium was constructed in the same shape as for *Dido*, and there were similar orchestral platforms on the stage to aid in creating effective groupings. There were the same indigo skies and simple but striking visual effects, such as twinkling stars (reportedly achieved by lights behind a pierced back cloth – as in the "Water God" – but in fact created by hanging chandelier crystals on black thread). These struck the only reviewer as inspiringly apt: appealing "to the imagination as the boundless sky of God" and "night as it had never been made before – night, simple as the Shepherds, sublime as the angel host and vast as the message delivered."[4] There was a similar use of suggestion instead of visual statement in the impression of the Shepherds' flocks conjured up out of sacks filled with wood shavings and tied off at the corners for ears. The cast was even larger – seventy-five performers are listed in the program – but its movements and groupings were equally tightly orchestrated. At the opening the Shepherds were all seated in two basic positions, bent forward, "hat over eyes. Chin in necktie. Both hands on knees. Heels drawn back," or stretched out against a hurdle, "hat back of head. Arms crossed. Legs right out." Then, as Gabriel enters stage left,

> *all move to end in fright.*
> WATCHER: Ay – oh! . . .
> *Out come heads. Silver bells. Music. From all the shepherds crescendo growl like dogs roused . . .*
> ANGELS: Glory be to God – *chorus*
>    In the highest – *semi chorus* . . .
> *The Angels disappear. Shepherds stretch their hands to heaven – 3 steps forwards. Pause. Hands up slowly. Swing down, dazzled.* "Redeems man's fall": *Shepherds stretch out arms after them as if wanting them back. Advance after them – 3 steps, one step.*[5]

The Masque of Love had concluded with a ceremonial procession. Here, the entire second scene, "The Coming of the Kings," was transformed into a procession. A King in black headed a retinue in

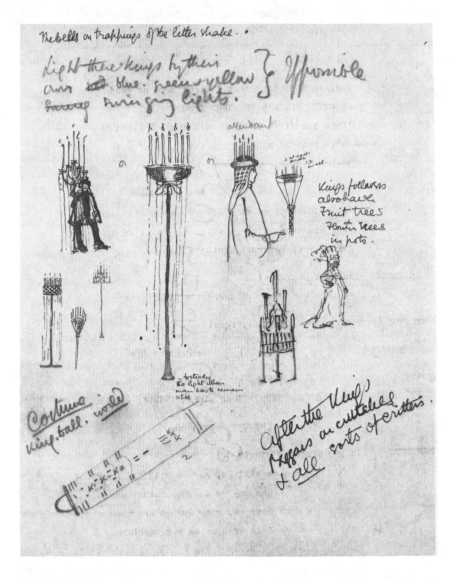

black and purple, a gray-clad King had followers in purple and green, a white King led a train in ragged gray. These last provided a grotesque contrast with the pomp of the other groups and represented "the grave, the sad, the poor, the bad" as "lepers, idiots, a murderer with red head and beard who never kneels, a travelling marionette showman, a musician, beggars . . . , " who moved onto

DEVILS

ENTER the ANGEL of the STAR. He crosses
the stage and departs,

ENTER the KINGS.

1st KING.      Hear me, oh King of Kings,
               And give me my desire!

2nd KING       Have me beneath thy wings,
               And guide my feet with fire

3rd KING       Unto that Holy Mount
               Where forth from Thee goes Light,

ALL            Whence springs a Living Fount
               To wash the whole world white.

GABRIEL        Peace be with you, and hail!
               Where go ye this fair night,
               Travellers, and what seek ye?

1st KING       We seek from the hill the vale,
               And from the vale the hill.

2nd KING       From the ends of the morning, rest;
               And from the East, the West.

3rd KING       In the darkness we seek fire;
               And out of dreams the heart's desire!

Craig's notes from the promptbook for *Bethlehem*, showing alternatives for lighting the procession and the positions on the side stage, the vocal orchestration, and the replacement of dialogue by visual effects. (The last four speeches on the page were cut.)

the stage to form a half circle around Gabriel on a central mound.[6] These costumes and props were far more elaborate than any Craig (helped by his sister, Edy) had designed before: richly embroidered, fur-edged, and vividly colored robes of medieval cut; ornate cruci-fixes and shrines, fantastical lanthorns and offerings; extravagantly different crowns for each of the Kings. The richness of detail here, to be extended in Craig's next production, *The Vikings*, anticipates his later demand for a "rich theater," which he associated with the earliest form of Christian drama, the celebration of the Mass: "In place of vulgar materials such as canvas and wood, papier masche [sic] and paint, I want more *precious* material made use of for a durable theatre: ebony and ivory–silver and gold–copper and brass–silk and the rarest dyes–marble and alabaster–and fine brains."[7] Indeed, all the props for *The Vikings* were made by crafts-men in real wood and metal. But although this richness was to become one of Craig's less realistic ideals, it was in no sense whimsi-cal or arbitrary here. It sprang naturally from the play's thematic connection with church ceremonial, which Craig emphasized in his direction – so much so that there were complaints from Roman Cath-olic members of the cast who felt that the representation was verg-ing on blasphemy, and Housman had to intervene. "The Madonna seems to them to take too priestly an attitude in the words of the blessing, especially if the symbols of bread and wine are to be intro-duced," he contended.

The procession of Kings and their colorful retinues had originally been conceived as "The Pageant of Our Lady, which precedes the nativity play," and was therefore to some extent extraneous. In other respects the costumes repeated effects from previous produc-tions. Housman had wanted Craig to make the Angels "as invisible and like blue night air as possible," and his "first notion was to dress them in sky colour and have only silver faces and silver hair showing out."[8] Craig rejected this as too conventionally pretty and reused the swirling white strips from *Acis*, which appeared even more ethereal in contrast to the Shepherds. These wore cloaks and slouch hats of rough hessian which, with the sacks representing sheep, created a textural unity surpassing the color echoes of scene and costume in *Dido*, while the neutral tones had the same sugges-tive effect that freed the imagination in *The Masque*.

This production also introduced technical innovations that show the way Craig's ideas were developing. At one point Craig intended to use a double proscenium, with an upper stage behind a row of arched windows above the ordinary acting area. However this, like

his plan for reflooring the whole hall to bring the audience's eyes to
the right level, could not be carried out because it was too expen-
sive. Housman had envisaged a tangible Christ child, a baby whom
Mary would raise from the cradle and hold out to the adoring multi-
tudes, making the sign of the cross with him over their heads –
though he was obviously aware of the danger of humanizing what
his text had built into a transcendent symbol, and warned Craig that
"it is God himself she carries in . . . all dazed and wondering – so no
playing with his toes I beg of you!" In a brilliant stroke of imaginatively suggestive simplification Craig cut all physical representation
of the Christ child. Instead he placed a powerful light in the cradle
and reduced all other lighting to a minimum. When Mary raised the
cloth covering the cradle, it was the radiance from within that illuminated the surrounding faces, and their gestures and expressions
alone made the presence of divinity felt.

Still more significant as an advance were attempts to integrate the
audience into the performance. Housman's epilogue (which Craig
wanted to cut) tried to bring the meaning of the play home to the
audience in a rather overly obvious way:

> Oh Maid and Holy Child, where have ye gone? . . .
> Gentles, O ye that here have watched our play,
> Tell me, I pray you, did He pass *your* way?
> Say, have ye Him safe, each one, in his breast.

Instead, Craig, anticipating the ideas of Artaud and the work of
such directors as Barrault and Schechner, brought the action and
environment of the play out into the auditorium to gain relevance
on a more subliminal level. To some extent this effect was accidental. It was because the acoustics of the hall at the Imperial Institute
were so poor that Craig initially thought of hanging cloth on the
walls. But to solve this practical problem, he created the impression
of a simple tent, in which the blue of the cloth draped around the
auditorium merged with the skies in the stage picture, while the
cloth's coarse weave echoed the texture of the Shepherds' costumes.

At one point too, he contemplated spreading "lots of sacks to sit
and lie on" instead of ordinary seating for the public. This would
have placed the audience in the same physical posture as the Shepherds they were watching. However, in order for them to see the
stage from a prone position, it would have been necessary to raise
the floor level. Housman, who was personally financing the production, refused to consider "reflooring the hall from end to end" out of
his own pocket. So this particular part of the experiment in environ-

mental staging, which the LCC (London City Council) would never have sanctioned in any case, had to be abandoned. Instead Craig constructed a platform with steps that ran the whole length of one side of the auditorium and up onto the stage, so that the processions – first Angels, then Kings – entered from behind the audience and made their stately way through them. This manner of breaking down the separation of audience and action was felt by Craig to be so important that he insisted on retaining it, even though it drastically reduced the number of places in London where the performance could take place and led to continual complaints from Housman: "You don't seem prepared to cut down one plank of your platform to meet the exigencies of plan or space. No wonder then the Hall takes so long to find."

Yet Craig was careful to keep this sense of involvement on an imaginative rather than a purely physical level. The platform was lined with a gauze on its outer side to preserve an aura of mystery around the figures that passed in such close proximity to the spectators. To strengthen this further, Craig emphasized that the "orchestra must be hidden. Not a single one of the *works* must show . . . The whole thing must be free from effort and machines." To complete the illusion he equipped one group of Angels and one group in the Kings' procession with their own musical instruments: lutes, cymbals, and bells. He also had Housman write a short extra scene "outside Bethlehem," with lines spoken by a Pilgrim. There was a front curtain with a narrow opening in the center to represent the gates of the town, and just behind – borrowing directly from the medieval staging of passion plays – a miniature two-dimensional cutout of domes and roofs backed by a second curtain of black with "spangles here and there." As one of the actors noted, "The purpose of the scene is an introduction . . . the 'Chorus' invites the audience to follow him . . . to enter by the lower gate and pass through to the cradle."[9] In addition, to preserve the unity of mood and to remove the performance further from the conventions of traditional theater, the program specifically requested the audience not to applaud but "to keep silent throughout and after the performance" – an injunction that later directors were to repeat for similar reasons, as Piscator did in staging Weiss's *The Investigation*.[10]

In some ways, working with straight dialogue – for the first time since *No Trifling with Love* – and with a story that was part of his audience's immediate cultural background made Craig's style of representation more effective. Patternings of movement and grouping were given instantly recognizable symbolic resonance by their con-

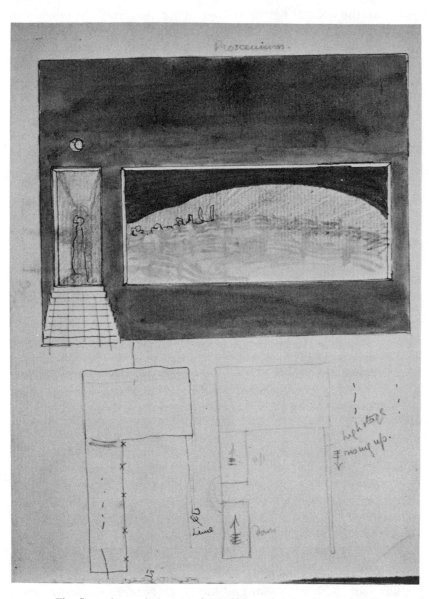

The floor plan and elevation for *Bethlehem*, showing the step construction of the side stage (with the gauze indicated along the inner edge) and the position of the light on one side wall.

texts. As the central figure in Housman's play was the Madonna, one aspect of "the eternal feminine," circles dominated. The semicircular formation of the kings around Gabriel, stepping forward crown in hand, prefigured the emotional climax in Bethlehem. There was no scenic representation of the manger. The figures that were massed in concentric lines on curving platforms, rising up around Mary and the cradle, themselves formed a living scenery. A floor cloth continued the circles of the steps round in front, and the movements emphasized the pattern. The Shepherds entered

> to the music, form in a semi-circle on top step and descend all to gather [round Mary]. End on knees . . .
>
> Shepherds give gifts – bread, milk, cheese, nuts, wine, a lamb and a song [a reprise of the opening Shepherd's song]. A circle and close so as to hide V. M. then let V. M. speak (when not seen) . . .
>
> "Angelus." All are kneeling up straight – then heads go down – they sink backwards, hands before clasped chest-high – sink to ground – fingers touching ground . . . Joseph stands several tiers up – and apart always from the mother and child.
>
> JOSEPH: Stand near in faith, behold . . .
>   Here shepherds, is your fold.
> Mary raises the veil from the cradle, keeping it covered for audience but open for shepherds. All the shepherds make signs to cries of wonder [which substituted for several whole pages of speeches cut by Craig]: Some are dazzled by the light from the cradle. The light grows.

The production received little critical attention because it had to be given as a "private performance" – the Lord Chamberlain refused to license the representation of the Holy Family on a stage. Its only review stated that it was a striking "example of the symbolic element in Mr. Craig's staging" because the circles directly represented "the divine, the perfect figure."[11]

In other ways, however, working with a dramatic text was alien to the style Craig had developed. Craig later commented that he hadn't done Housman's play full justice because "after Purcell and Handel the words of his piece (good as I find them now) then did not move me." His autocratic handling of the material provoked continual conflict with both its author and the composer. His earliest notes to Martin Shaw had emphasized that this production "must in no way be an OPERA," and initially he even thought of separating the singing from the dramatic action by keeping all the singers offstage (extending into a general practice what he had been forced to do by having an infant Cupid for *The Masque of Love*).[12] Yet he clearly felt the lack of continuous musical accompaniment. In his previous work music had inspired and controlled every movement. Here his inability to find a satisfactory equivalent in Housman's rather static poetry was indicated by the amount of music eventually added. This superimposed a kind of formal organization on the play that was qualitatively different from the structure of the text. The first scene, for instance, became an allegretto, followed by two solos (a Shepherd and Gabriel) and two choruses (Angels, then Shepherds); the final scene was transformed into a counterpoint of chorus and solo, framed by offstage choruses at the beginning and the end. Not surprisingly, Housman complained that Craig's "exquisite Allegros" were "swamping my Penserosos."

Certainly the thrust of Craig's production brought out some of Housman's intentions: for instance, "by symbolic action to quicken the imagination of the beholder so as to make the beauty of holiness more evident" or, instead of simply representing the events of Christmas, "to realize their appeal to the hearts of all to whom they convey a living truth." But Housman's almost daily letters during the rehearsal period are a record of desperate, and almost always vain, attempts to preserve the integrity of his text. Craig cut away at many of the speeches, which he found too long, and omitted several entirely. Housman, in turn, suggested that he see Poel's production of *Everyman* for an example of how "devoutly" an audience could be brought to accept even longer speeches.[13] Craig criticized "the pompous note" in the dialogue, which he set to music to disguise; Housman protested that what he was obliterating was the note of "restraint and wonder and adoration . . . quiet and natural." Craig called Housman's Madonna "a prig," omitted several of her speeches, and gave others to Joseph; Housman complained that "the rollicking note of 'Tis Christmas Morn' comes too close and abruptly on the offerings of the Kings and the music of the Adoremus . . . [because of Craig's] overcutting and bringing things, which were schemed to be separated, too closely together."

In fact, almost the only element that Housman managed to reinstate was the epilogue. Craig himself epitomized his approach when he referred to the play as "a recipe." Housman's–or any playwright's–position was summed up in his plaintive question, 'You do see, don't you, that there is this inner unwritten text to be thought about which is the author's own? And the recognition of it leads to unity, not diversity of effect."[14]

Laurence Housman's graphic expression of his feelings about working with Craig.

In a play of just over 600 lines (before cuts), yet with a performance time of almost two hours, the musical and visual elements of the production clearly overwhelmed the poetry. Hardly surprisingly, Housman regarded this as "a beautiful perversion" of his work, though according to one member of the audience his attitude in fact was one of "resigned complacency – he was sorry so much had to go, but – *que faire* – another effect and a beautiful one had been attained." In this case Craig's autocratic disregard for the text was due to a basic lack of sympathy for its theme. As he commented, "I am nearly suffocated by the halos and holiness of this play. The unbelievers and the no church people *ARE* the only true believers, and the sincere religionists there are only eye and voice lifters."[15] But Craig's treatment here of a dramatist's theme and words, subordinating all elements to a sometimes idiosyncratic vision, was to become characteristic of his approach. At his request Housman had cut all stage directions from the text of *Bethlehem* to leave Craig more freedom for visual invention. Three years later Craig was dispensing with the dialogue too – even that of such a verbal playwright as Bernard Shaw, who liked to say that the basis of his work was "the argument" rather than the plot or action – in order to bring out the symbolic essence of a drama.

In fact his description of the way he arrived at his designs for *Caesar and Cleopatra*, which Reinhardt commissioned from him in 1905, provides an excellent example of both his creative method and his belief that the stage could communicate most powerfully on the subliminal level of mood and metaphoric suggestion. First he cut

the author's stage directions . . . And as I read the words, I wanted to omit these too . . . When I had got the words out of my head I looked to see what was left of the First Scene and I found this First Scene to be like a great rat trap in which figures were hurrying and scurrying to and fro like so many squeaking animals, one real figure standing out in a comic tragic mask – Ftatateeta.[16]

When working on *The Vikings at Helgeland*, too, he asked Ellen Terry to cut out all the stage directions before sending him the text. But on this occasion there was no author in the wings and the public had little knowledge of Ibsen's early plays. So Craig was almost as free to interpret the text here as in his earlier operatic productions, though at least one critic complained that his grouping of the actors seemed solely for aesthetic effect and bore little relation to the dramatic action, which therefore became meaningless. Instead he came into conflict with the acting profession. Working with amateurs had presented only one difficulty: lack of expertise. This was one of the reasons why he reduced the importance of the focal figure in *Bethlehem*, cutting her speeches or transferring them to others because "I see Madonnas every day and none knows how to speak . . . Have now tried 5 Marys, but none can do it."[17] Here his problem was very different. For the first time each member of his cast was a trained performer. Most of his principals were established theater figures. His protagonist, Ellen Terry, was a traditionalist, the leading lady of Irving's Lyceum melodramas, and she was used to playing on the

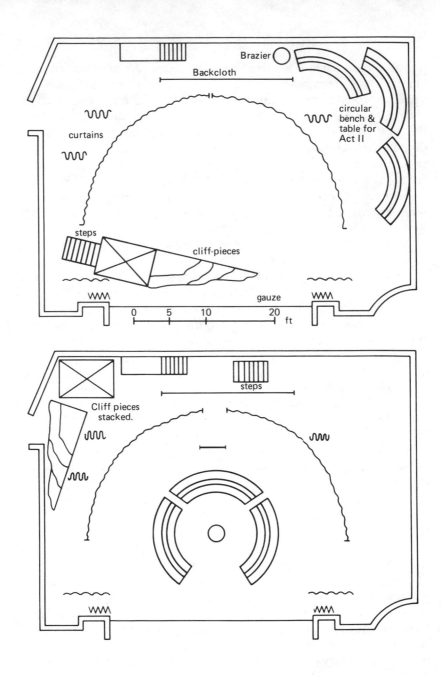

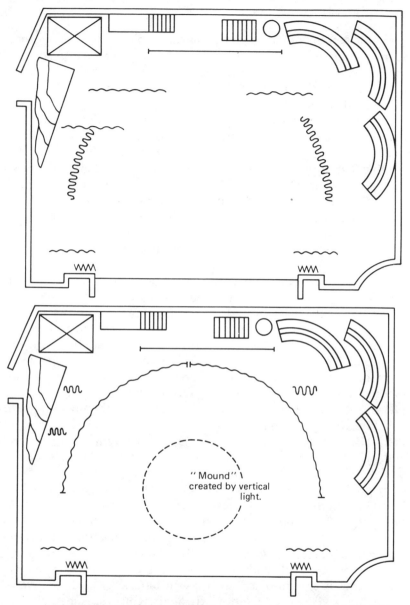

A reconstruction of the stage layout for the four scenes of *The Vikings,* showing the way the built-up pieces might be stacked for the "bare stage" of the last scene, even in the confined space of the Imperial Theater. *Top left,* act 1. The cliff construct. (The curtains, unlit, would be invisible.) *Bottom left,* act 2. The banquet tables. *Top,* act 3. Curtains forming the interior walls of a hall, with the brightly illuminated back cloth visible through the opening. *Bottom,* act 4. The cleared stage and the optical illusion of a mound. (Created by lighting effects alone.)

romantic sentiments of her enthusiastic public, who expected her to be the dominant focus of each scene. All of the cast's experience ran directly counter to Craig's concepts, in particular to the visual unity and ensemble acting he demanded and to the ritualistic style of movement he had developed.

To some extent he was able to impose these concepts through the inanimate elements of the production – lighting, setting, costume – that were completely subject to his control. He thus reversed the relative significance of the actor and the visual background in a way that looks forward to his later, more theoretical development. In *Towards A New Theatre* Craig contrasts two scene designs: one that any actor could dominate, even if with difficulty, and another (with the actor dwarfed by towering geometric masses) that would need "a Hero" to dominate. The *Vikings* production was somewhere between the two.

In the first scene a gauze was stretched across the proscenium opening, blurring outlines so that shadowed parts of the figures shaded into the background, and distancing the actors from the audience. As one reviewer described the effect, 'Behind the thin gauze curtain they flashed out and faded away like the strange and gorgeous fish of some aquarium." The costumes were all tonal variations of a single neutral colour, gray, with each of the principals merged into a particular group – Ornulf and his six sons in gray picked out with white, Sigurd and his ten men in gray and green – and Ellen Terry's dresses echoed the emotional tone of each scene. Her robe of blue was covered in the first act by a surcoat of green and gray strips and a white bearskin that hung from her shoulders, in the third act (where Hjordis weaves a magic bowstring from her own golden hair) by an ash-colored cloak bordered with dull yellows, and in the final act of death and transfiguration by a surcoat of black strips patterned with a network of silver. These costume designs alone were enough to create a unified visual effect, but they also harmonized the figures with their backgrounds. In the first act this was misty black with a sinister purple light playing over dull gray rocks. In the third act, ash-gray curtains suggesting the walls of a hall flanked a huge window through which streamed the cold, pale yellow daylight of the far north. In the final act, the blackness of night surrounded a central snow-covered mound under which Ornulf has buried the dead bodies of his seven sons and on which Hjordis stands to shoot Sigurd.

As Craig later remarked,

Obviously . . . it is a sensible thing to place a white costume against a dark background and a dark costume against a light background. It makes the figure stand out; but what should you do when you want the figure to be merged in the scene, if not lost in the scene? Macbeth roaming around his castle at night-time seems to be part of his habitation; and I remember that when Irving played the part he was dressed in a costume almost the same colour as the walls.[18]

But this appeal to tradition in the form of Irving is misleading. At the Lyceum this sort of effect was rare, and when it occurred the scene became an extension of a central figure's consciousness. Here, actors and setting together reflected an abstract mood symbolizing the underlying tone of that point on the emotional scale of the drama as a whole. Even in the banquet scene of the second act, where the assembled characters wore bright cloaks of multicolored squares and stripes, the same unity was achieved by setting them against a curtain striped in the same colors. This formed a huge half circle, dark gray at the edges and the center, with a spectrum of vermilion, purple, blue, green, yellow, and crimson on each quadrant. The curtain was made of gauze, and through it the flames of torchbearers could be seen dimly as they moved behind. This linked the actors still more fully with their background, as Craig also used torches in the hands of the servants around the tables to transfer the focus from one speaker to another. In fact the flickering light of the torches held over one or another actor's head drew the eye so effectively that several reviewers believed they illuminated the actors' faces, while those of the rest were shadowed by the general overhead lighting for the scene. (In reality, these torches – long rods with small metal cups at the top holding cotton wads soaked in methylated spirits – could never have acted as a light source.)

The actors were also grouped into a single unit, with no one dominating position, by the shape of the banquet tables around which they sat. These formed a raised circle with a downstage opening, which echoed the shape of the curtains behind and of a massive circular candelabrum suspended above. This concentric amphitheater form clearly repeated the configuration of the manger scene of *Bethlehem*, but there it had been designed to focus all attention on Mary and the crib. Here the central position was empty – and to ensure that no actor take it, Craig placed a fire there in a circular brazier.

Even those props and details of costume that distinguished one character from another were designed to cloak the actor's individual-

A torchbearer in the banquet scene.

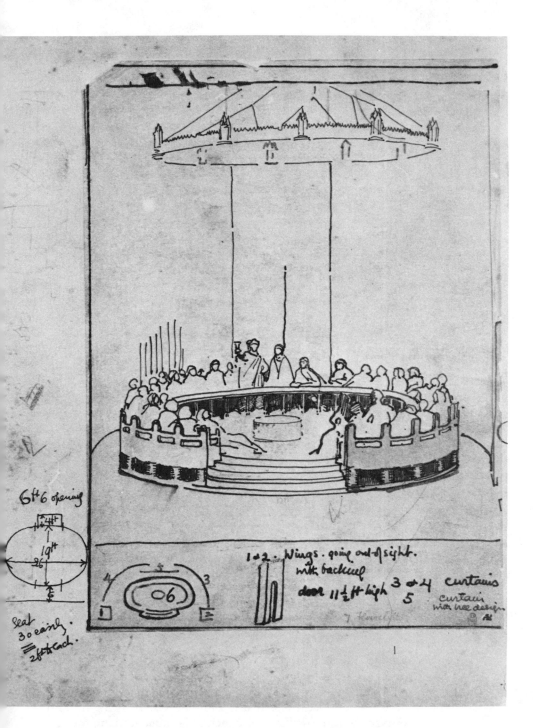

Craig's design for the circular banquet table and candelabra.

ity. The shields (as in *Dido*) were large and, with their sharply etched Celtic designs, tended to attract attention away from the persons who carried them. So did the torches, five feet high with the lower one-and-a-half feet weighted ribbons, and the necklace worn by Käre's wife, which was a prehistoric fantasy of teeth, beads, and wild birds' skulls. Similarly, each of the protagonists, including Hjordis as a warrior–maiden, wore a sharply different helmet crested with horns, seabirds' wings, or porcupine quills. With the top lighting, these threw deep shadows on the actors' faces, making it almost impossible to see any emotion that might have been expressed by their features. According to Edward Craig, this was an undesired consequence of the attempt to recreate the lighting effects of *Dido* in a procenium three times as high with the primitive equipment of the time, which could not project an intensive enough light so far. There is some truth in this, but in fact the height of the proscenium opening at the Imperial Theater was not much more than half again as high as the one Craig had constructed in Hampstead (twenty-seven feet as opposed to sixteen), and Craig himself claimed that the darkness was deliberate – to correspond to "a gloomy subject."[19] A further reason for thinking it intentional is that Craig's initial designs for the helmets had shown them coming down over the actors' faces and in two cases almost completely covering them. Protests from those who wore them forced Craig to alter these, but the male protagonists were given thick beards instead, which served much the same purpose. The major complaint against the production was that in all acts except the third (titled "Light" by Craig in the program) the stage was too dark to discern the faces. Yet, as Max Beerbohm pointed out, this was a way of transforming individuals into symbols of passions or elemental forces: "In the case of a play demanding subtle interpretation this complaint would be justified. But *The Vikings* is a play in which nothing would be lost if all the characters wore masks. Indeed, it would be all the better, if the masks were sufficiently grotesque."[20]

As for the ritualistic movement, the steeply angled platforms constructed to represent the rocky cliffs of act 1, with uneven ledges sloping at an angle of thirty to forty degrees, were designed as obstacles to the actors' acquired habits of movement on the traditional flat stage. These platforms also made it impossible for the cast to take their customary turn-of-the-century positions in a line downstage along the footlights Craig had removed. Edward Craig recounts how, when Oscar Asche and Holman Clark, as Sigurd and Ornulf, refused to fight on this rocky incline because it made the fast footwork, slashing, and parrying of the standard Shakespearean duel impossible, Craig first explained that their combat should be like the slow swinging movements of the ancient samurai with their great curved swords, then discomfited them by demonstrating how effective this unorthodox manner of stage fighting could look. But Craig was not content with having them imitate what he could demonstrate. Once an actor himself, he was well aware that in performance it is all too easy to revert to old acting habits, whatever the director may have imposed in rehearsal. He provided them with five-foot doubleheaded axes, swords with "heavy weights" built into them, and spears "eight foot high and extra thick." With this massive armament, any clash was necessarily ponderous, all slashes sweeping, all movement stylized – and the same principles were carried over into other scenes. Where one of Ibsen's stage directions reads, "All rise; violent excitement," Craig substituted, "Up very slow. Move as one."[21]

This archetypal, even alien quality was reinforced by other elements of the production. As several reviewers remarked, the lighting, apart from obscuring the players' faces, was more natural (in illuminating the stage from above – by now the connection with Herkomer had been made). It also created the sense of "an age almost immeasurably remote from our own . . . unlike anything associated with ordinary life." The stage had been stripped of the conventional borders and "ceiling" battens or "flies," so that the eye reached out into the darkness of shadows or the apparent depths of sky in Craig's back cloth and gauze, instead of meeting any tangible enclosure, or was drawn upward by the vertical lines of curtain and falling light, which seemed to continue above the proscenium. This effect of limitless space gave the impression that the characters were "sunk in a gigantic shaft," and "utterly precludes any notion of realism" in the normal sense.

The result combined all the powers of suggestion achieved in the earlier Purcell Society productions so successfully that spectators literally filled in the blanks for themselves. For example, in the first act the darkness surrounding the sloping platform (the only actual scenery on stage) was described as "the sea, an inky pool, mist-hemmed, washing at its base." Paradoxically, this combination of natural and unnatural effects gave the impression of "a real unreality."[22] The light fell as in the everyday world – a contrast to the conventional stage illumination still as striking in 1903 as it had been in 1900 – yet its color was purely emotive: A sinister purple tone in act 1 created an "atmosphere of awe, of dread." Max Beer-

The entry of Ornulf and his men on the rocky cliff of act 1 in *The Vikings*, with the dreamlike effect obtained by the gauze.

bohm, who saw the characters as inhuman monsters, described how "the strange, supernatural element" cast over every scene meant that "we shudder in unfathomable darkness, in immemorial frosts. The monsters here, as monsters, become positively real to us. We are positively afraid of them."[23]

These impressions were further reinforced by the music that Craig added to the play. As if for an opera, there was an overture, the themes from which were picked up in processional music for the entry to the banquet, in Ornulf's threnody for his dead sons, and in "storm music" for the last act – all composed by Martin Shaw in weird tones and phrases that were deliberately "unpleasing." Its discords and jarring notes were intended not only to illustrate the wild and barbaric tenth-century setting, but also to emphasize the elemental nature of the characters' emotions, emotions too powerful to find expression in tuneful or sophisticated orchestration. In addition, there was a prelude to each act, one being Wagner's thematically appropriate "Siegfried Idyll," which covered the scene changes and avoided the break in illusion that had presented such a problem in *Acis*.

Ibsen's treatment of the saga material was clearly an attempt to humanize legend, to give heroes individual faces. The characters have family ties, even occasional household concerns. However, any summary of the plot reveals a story of exaggerated violence and highly simplified motivations. The man who can slay a white bear that guards Hjordis is the man she will marry. Sigurd the Strong is in love with Hjordis, and kills the bear. But on learning of his weak half brother Gunnar's passion for Hjordis, in a spirit of Christ-like self-sacrifice, he pretends it was Gunnar who accomplished the heroic deed, and marries instead her sister Dagny. The play deals with the consequences of this act. Dagny, indignant at Hjordis, whose jealousy and discontent leads her to scorn Sigurd, reveals the truth about the bear's death. Too late, Hjordis acknowledges it is Sigurd she really loves and offers him the choice of fleeing or dying with her, so that they may live together or be united in Valhalla. When his Christian principles force him to reject both alternatives, she shoots him with her bow, then throws herself over the cliffs in despair, knowing that even in death they will be parted, he in heaven, she with her pagan gods. A subplot revolving about Käre the Peasant's feud with Gunnar leads to the death of Ornulf's seven sons and general ruin. Despite Craig's simplification of the dialogue to make it closer to colloquial speech – for instance, he substituted "you" for "thee," and "Father! She is your foster child!" for Dagny's "That meanest thou not; bethink thee, she is thy foster child!" – the whole emphasis of his production was on this *Götterdämmerung*.

In his view, the essence of Ibsen's drama was an allegorical combat, body versus soul, pagan versus Christian, rather than a human conflict, and he directed the actors to represent these qualities in their pure state: "Sigurd is little short of God. Gunnar is absolute man." Yet without involvement with the characters on a personal level, any sense of tragedy disappears. If they have no individual traits, then the ultimate loss of the lovers, parted even in death, arouses little pity. Similarly it would be hard to feel that it mattered whom Hjordis married if it doesn't affect her as an individual, but only has significance insofar as it follows or distorts patterns of fate. But Craig was clearly aiming at a more universal type of involvement on the level of archetypes. As in *Dido*, he substituted generalized, emotionally evocative scene titles for Ibsen's descriptions of specific places. "Helgeland, the seashore" and "A hall in Gunnar's house" became "Act I – The Rocks, Act II – The Feast, Act III – Light, Act IV – The Storm." To Beerbohm, "the extreme manner of fantasy" in the staging transformed "the barbarism of the North" into "something quite beyond the pale of human possibility," and another reviewer thought that Ellen Terry's positioning and gestures in the final confrontation with Sigurd made Hjordis seem "moulded on so heroic lines that she is rather a quality than a character." The masking effect of shadows, the integrating of the figures with a suggestively indistinct and mythical background, the ritualistic movement – all were designed to raise the action to this elemental but abstract plane. Every detail was intended to have symbolic resonance. One critic even described the music as "the accompanying wail of souls of those slain during the progress of the play."[24] The wood of Hjordis's bow was exaggeratedly curved into the form of a double serpent. Other weapons had twisted unsymmetrical blades or foot-long spikes that resembled gigantic fishhooks. Clubs looked like wooden dinosaur bones. Dagny's litter had a sinuous, almost organic shape, and doodled sketchnotes in Craig's promptbook clearly indicate that he was trying to create a symbolic association among the round Viking shields, the circular banqueting tables, and the truly universal image of the mythological snake eating its own tail – the Midgard serpent that encircled the world in Norse legend and the Eygptian emblem for eternity and immortality.

Perhaps no actors could be expected to play on this level, but unfortunately the conventional training of Craig's professional cast meant that their manner of characterization undermined his aims. What was needed was the style of acting that he suggested four years later in his essays entitled "On the Art of the Theatre," in which symbols drawn from the depths of the subconscious "without exhibiting the bare passions, would none the less tell us clearly about them." Instead of the "haphazard" or "incomplete" movements and gestures that imitate natural life, "a *noble* artificiality" would be created by selecting a single and clear-cut action for each moment of the play to give an effect "as solemn, as beautiful and as remote as ever" – words echoed by W. B. Yeats, who believed as strongly that the theater had to keep its distance from "a pushing world" if it were to become an art form.[25] What Craig actually got in *The Vikings* was basically naturalistic acting, which modulated into melodramatic posturing, and the customary display of the actors' personalities.

This was true even of Ellen Terry, although she was more in sympathy with his experimental approach than were the leading men. Her reading of the play as "a romantic drama" was rather different from Craig's mythic conception, and this carried through

Melodramatic acting in act 4 of *The Vikings*. (Note that the lighting created an impression of a mound so effectively that the artist has included it as a physical structure.)

into her performance. When the play was first suggested she doubted that anyone would believe her in the part of Hjordis, and several critics remarked that she was "woefully miscast" – she of all people could hardly "be imagined as a fierce virago who kept chained bears in the house." However, many others applauded her performance, claiming that "rarely of late years has Miss Terry acted with more intensity" and reporting that "when Miss Terry fights death, not many dry eyes are to be found in the house."[26] Such conflicting opinions suggest that she played the role in a traditional way that delighted her faithful public from the Lyceum days, but one that was incompatible with the dramatic context that Craig had created. Indeed, during rehearsals he had commented that "the difficulties are many and formidable – they arise one and all, from stage traditions"; and after the production had folded (by the third week the box office no longer covered the expenses) he complained:

I feel convinced that no *Vikings* can be done unless each character [*sic:* actor] will listen to the stage manager and hear what character he is to play. What the hell is the use of Act I – what's all the pother about on the rocks, the Rock and the Giants, the swords ten inches thick and blood flowing, wrestling of limb and brain, if Hjordis is not the exact opposite of all this exterior might, what is the *storm* of the play but the counterpart of the storm inside her heart, and what has exterior storminess to do with her – absolutely NOTHING. "To side with the wild sisters" and all that is the cry of her soul, not the instinct of her physique. Soul is to her what physique is to everyone else in the play.[27]

Already here one can see the seed of Craig's ideal: a spiritual theater, the expression of the soul as opposed to "the Art of the body," which led him to call for an Uebermarionette in place of the actor. His early productions can be seen not only as the source of his theories, but also as practical demonstrations, at least in embryo, of that ideal Art of the Theatre, which tends to be dismissed as unrealistic because formulating a philosophy for it took up so much of the rest of Craig's career that he effectively withdrew from the stage. At the same time the conflicts generated by *Bethlehem* and *The Vikings* help to explain his attempt "to create works of art in the theatre without the use of the written play, without the use of actors." Craig continued that sentence by reaffirming "the necessity of daily work under the conditions which are today offered us." But, in fact, after the production of *Much Ado About Nothing*, which followed directly on *The Vikings*, he was responsible for directing only two more plays – and even in his last production, *The Crown Pretenders* (staged in Copenhagen in 1926), he found that the training of a completely different generation of actors was just as inappropriate to his concepts of staging. As more than one reviewer remarked, "The actors were playing in the old realistic manner, and the better they played the more they denied their relation to the set . . . In one scene, where the actors, almost by chance, stylized their playing to meet the terms of the production, the effect was magical."[28]

Whatever its reception by the general public, *The Vikings* was recognized as the first production "to show that it is possible for a play to be produced which may be judged by the same standard and enjoyed to the same degree as poetry, painting and music." Yet this production also marks the beginning of Craig's retreat from the theater. The contrast between what he aimed at and what the actors would allow him to achieve is already clear. He had his name listed no less than five times on the program to emphasize "that a production, to be a real one, is the work of one man and a company of technicians." But even late in the rehearsals he was complaining that "all seems to me as unlike . . . what I have always strived for in [my] work as can be," and admitted privately to feeling "that I am trying to fill the position of artistic director on sufferance . . . I do not feel responsible."[29]

*Bethlehem* and *The Vikings* had made Craig begin to see that authors and the acting profession were obstacles in his march toward a new theater, and *Much Ado* brought two other conditioning factors home to him in a particularly harsh and unmistakable way: the limitations imposed on creativity by commercial pressures and by the demands of an audience with preconceived ideas. Even in his early work these influences had been present. *Acis* had closed after a single week, though the run was intended to last for two weeks or longer, because, in Craig's words, "the Public could not be brought to see it." *Dido* had barely covered expenses, not even providing any form of salary for all the hours that Craig and Martin Shaw put into it. It did not come close to producing the capital for future productions even though it had received a generous subsidy in the sense that the amateur cast devoted their time free. If Craig had had to pay the seven principals and thirty-eight chorus members (even at the rate of £2 a week for the principals, which was the minimum he had received for major roles in 1896, and £1 a week for each of the chorus), and even if the rehearsal time could have been cut to a single month, it would have required a run of six-and-a-half weeks just to cover costs. In comparison, the 1896 Lyceum production of *Richard III*, with Irving in the title role and

Craig as Edward IV, drew audiences for only four weeks and still made a profit.[30] There were no such hidden subsidies for *The Vikings*, and to keep the company solvent Craig was forced to rehearse *Much Ado* in a bare two weeks, limiting his designs to two very simple sets and using stock costumes.

This made it impossible for Craig to organize groupings in more than the broadest outline. In addition, Ellen Terry insisted on "the *old* play, and the *old* me in it" because it "would not be acceptable to the Public in a *different* style to the one they know." As Martin Shaw described it, the actors insisted on "scenery in the manner of Alma Tadema, costumes copied from Planché, conventional movements and positions – in short nothing which had not been done before." This was a fairly accurate picture of what was staged, apart from the church scene, where Craig was able to use the suggestive simplicity of draped curtains and shafts of colored light for a stained-glass effect. Here it seems likely that he saw the opportunity to give a clear definition of his stylistic reform by creating a contrast to the well-known and much-praised design for Ellen Terry's first performance in the role of Beatrice – an elaborate historical reconstruction, and one in which Godwin had a hand. Elsewhere the settings were extremely plain. A severe gray classical colonnade did duty for all, with a plain blue sky cloth behind for the garden and gray curtains drawn between the columns for indoor scenes. The only decorative props were the large circular floral wreaths for the masquerade, which Craig had used for the Harlequins of *The Masque of Love*. Even more significantly, his promptbook contains almost no directions to the actors apart from diagrams of the movements for two dances, indicating that the interpretation was left largely to the performers.

Craig's major contribution as a director seems to have been the by now characteristic insertion of almost continuous musical accompaniment – an overture, a minuet, two madrigals, a fanfare, a jig, and a Morris dance in the first two scenes of act 1, "music continually" in the third scene, and vocal pieces to cover scene changes. Two pieces for the church scene were taken straight from *Bethlehem*, and the inclusion of traditional folk songs and country dances relates directly to Craig's fascination with the masque form. This seemed to offer one possible way of unifying every aspect of a production under a single hand by making it possible for the director himself to create the "play" that he would then design and produce. But here, without sufficient time to drill the actors in the type of movement he required, the music alone was insufficient to control pacing and gesture. He may have wanted all (except Beatrice

Craig's design for the church scene of *Much Ado About Nothing* indicating the illusionistic simplicity of the setting.

and Benedick) to be "stiff and restrained," as one prompt note suggests, but when *Much Ado* went on tour the cast obviously began to discard any formalization in favor of the stock characterizations and conventional movements that had proved successful in the past and that their audiences expected.

All long-running productions tend to develop new emphases by a sort of osmosis, sometimes changing focus completely through the interplay with the audience. Yet to Craig it was "Hell – I know of nothing more tormenting." What caused him anguish was being thought responsible for something he considered a travesty of his intentions. This attitude was to be reinforced by his experiences with Otto Brahm and Reinhardt, and led him to demand nothing less than his own theater. But there was also a sense in which financial success and applause were seen as suspect in themselves, which eventually caused Craig to reject any of the more usual yardsticks of theatrical success and even to cultivate "failure" as a guarantee of aesthetic integrity:

Each time I see [*Much Ado*] a viler gaiety is added – speech is noisier and action floppier – thought infrequent, and taste unknown . . . You would get the full fervour of my feeling if you could hear Bach's Passion interpreted by the Gaiety Chorus under Raymondiana – And add to this, "contentment" on all the faces – contentment shrieking in their purses – They come off the stage and seriously take as the final verdict, the applause of a kind audience.[31]

From this point on, Craig began to think not merely of reforming the theater, but of a total revolution, one which would create an entirely new art form out of materials that owed nothing to the commercial theater. His conviction is well conveyed by the quotation he entered on the flyleaf of his promptbook for *Much Ado*: "Against stupidity the gods themselves contend in vain."

# 5  A play of ideas: Principles, theory, and an Uebermarionette

One criticism leveled at Craig is that his ideas were "a maze of suggestions . . . a mass of evasions and contradictions," a maze for which he was incapable of providing practical illustrations. Consequently, it is argued, he produced so few designs that he was forced to reprint the same ones in publication after publication.[1] In fact, repetition in his work is even more extensive than such critics have perhaps realized, though it exists for clearly different reasons than those that have been suggested. The same visual ideas can be traced from sketchbook to sketchbook, and there are constant echoes among designs for very different plays. But this is the result of a deliberate working method, rather than any inadequacy, and it indicates that Craig's theories were based on a selected number of key principles. As such, this repetition demonstrates the small value he placed on the uniqueness of a play's text. But as most of these principles derive directly from his productions between 1899 and 1903, and from the Lyceum theater, what it really brings out is his commitment to the practicable, and suggests as well that his "new theater" was not so much diametrically opposed to the old as a logical development from it.

For instance, Craig particularly admired one of Irving's scenes, the castle interior for the 1888 Lyceum *Macbeth* (see illustration on p. 19). Elements of that set reappear in Craig's designs throughout his career. A steeply rising staircase, broadened to fill the whole stage space, returned in "The Steps" (1906) and was duplicated as one of the components in the movable blocks of the Cranach *Hamlet* (1912–26). A column with steps curving up behind it recurred, progressively broadened and simplified, in a sketchbook for 1902, in a design for Lady Macbeth's sleepwalking scene in 1906, and in act 2 of the Moscow *Hamlet*, though there – as at the Lyceum – it was placed to one side of the stage instead of filling the entire center. The 1906 design was also published in *Towards a New Theatre* as well as in *Index to the Story of my Days*, and reused for one scene of Tyler's *Macbeth* in 1928. Another Lyceum scene, a rugged Scottish shoreline from *Ravenswood* in 1890, was also reflected in many different forms over the years. This image provided the inspiration for the rock structure of *The Vikings*, variations on which were used in *Macbeth*

101

designs for both Beerbohm Tree and Tyler and in one sketch for *The Crown Pretenders*. In its best-known form, Craig's 1908 "Design for a stage scene," it showed Greek warriors fighting at the foot of a steeply raked cliff.[2] In each case the illusionistic, pictorial original was transformed into simple and massive shapes, neutral in tone and with a strong tendency toward abstraction. In each case, too, three-dimensional, architectural environments were substituted for two-dimensional scenes painted on back cloths. As Craig later said, "I avoided putting any place in my picture which could *not* be travelled into actually by the actors."[3]

In the same way, not only lighting techniques and "sky" effects, but even specific visual elements from *Acis* and *The Masque of Love* reappeared consistently. Craig used the prison grille again in his design for the first scene of *Caesar and Cleopatra* for Reinhardt, and the "tent" for one of the interior scenes of *The Pretenders*. He also considered reusing the enclosed circular table from *The Vikings* for the banquet in that production, and finally settled on a variation in which the main figures were seated facing outward on the external rim with the minor characters inside the circle. The flickering light of torches behind gauze, used in *The Masque* and *The Vikings*, was repeated here too and elaborated with three superimposed gauze screens:

To show going away of torches . . . A perspective in movement. The men to stand still with torches. At X1 cover with gauze 1: lower [torches] and incline to X2: cover with 2nd gauze frame: sink and incline torches to X3: cover with gauze 3, then slowly cover torches with open hands and close fists over them.

The original design of a broad enclosed space for the Shepherds in *Bethlehem*, with a low roof and arched windows above, recurred in the conspirator's scene of *Venice Preserved*. There it became a low arcade of columns (taken from Serlio's drawing of a "pilastre d'ordre toscan" that Craig had used for the colonnade background in *Much Ado*) with lintels just over the heads of the figures and with the high walls of a piazza in the background forming a second scene above. It was also echoed in a 1904 design for *The Merchant of Venice*, and formed the basis for a generalized "scheme of a scene the height of a full sized person. Very long and low – as in low bas-reliefs on tombs" with pillars at wide intervals supporting the "roof."[4] This led directly to some of the designs for the Cranach *Hamlet*. Even details of props and costumes were reused. The dresses of floating strips of tape in *Acis* reappeared on Hjordis and Dagny (see illustrations on pp. 104–5). An elaborate handheld censer from *Bethlehem* became a focal point in the setting for the church scene of *Much Ado*,

Variations on *Acis and Galatea* and *The Vikings* in Craig's settings for the 1926 production of *The Pretenders*.

Similarities in costume design: a dancer from *Acis and Galatea* and Dagny in *The Vikings*.

and was suggested – together with a prince's costume from the *Bethlehem* procession – for the Prince of Morocco's attendant in his *Merchant of Venice* designs for Ellen Terry (1908).

In fact, what Craig was working toward was a form of universal-

ization: a multipurpose scene, which corresponded to his increasingly abstract concept of drama and which could be used for a variety of plays. One design – a high, narrow central archway in receding perspective, opening onto a platform with a cryptlike area
beneath flanked on each side by stairways leading down to the
lower stage – was titled both "Macbeth" and "Hamlet," and has
strong similarities to his later models for Bach's *St. Matthew Passion*.
Patterns of movement were treated in the same way as well. A
study of lines of soldiers marching down a ramp carrying spears and
watched by a group looking out of an immense window, originally
prepared for act 1 of *Much Ado*, became (with the window deleted
and the soldiers given more prominence) "Henry V. Enter the
Army." Finally Craig listed it, divorced from any specific play or
situation, as a generalized "Design for a Movement."

A third source for Craig's key images was art and architecture. He
created his own iconography in scrapbooks of photographs and reproductions clipped from art publications: Egyptian murals, Renaissance woodcuts, medieval palace facades, Japanese cherry blossoms.
Some provided inspiration for projects that were realized only on
paper – for example, two sky- and seascapes by Ruskin, which Craig
labeled *Peer Gynt*. Others were the sources for some of Craig's
major concepts. Beneath a picture of the stairs leading down from
the Vatican, Craig noted, "steps, a fine theme" – one that was later
realized as the studies in mood and movement that he titled *The
Steps*. Under a Gustav Doré illustration of Dante and Vergil at the
foot of a cliff he wrote, "What the theatre misses!" – and indeed, he
used it as the basis for a scene in *Hamlet*. But even more significantly, the simplified and unified shape of the background, the dra-
matically slanting light, the contrast in scale between the towering
masses and the tiny figures in this illustration, were all to become
dominant elements in the Scene that formed Craig's final vision of a
completely new art of the theater.

Still others of these pictures – such as Fra Angelico's *Dance of the
Angels* – formed the basis for patterns of movement in his productions, or provided models for specific types of scene. For instance, a
sketch of the gateway to Agamemnon's tomb in Mykenae, pasted
into an 1899 scrapbook, lies behind one of Craig's favorite scenic
shapes: the great square opening in a blank wall that rises the full
height of the stage, which was the main feature in act 3 of *The Vikings*,
in one scene for *Venice Preserved*, and in another for *Caesar and Cleopatra*, as well as in the settings of *Electra* and *Rosmersholm* designed for
Eleonora Duse. Similarly, childhood memories of "the Tall beds seen

Multipurpose setting containing the basic elements that recur in Craig's designs – flights of steps, tiered stage levels, and the use of perspective to elongate such architectural features as archways.

so often at Hampton Court," which had provided the shape of Dido's canopied throne with its four slender pillars, were repeated in exaggeratedly high four-poster beds for *Sword or Song* (1903) and in Tyler's *Macbeth* a quarter of a century later. They even provided the initial inspiration for Craig's ideal of renewing the theater and influenced his demand for the use of "precious" materials:

a room with a lofty bed haunts me . . . damask, silver, pale blue and crystal . . . the very first vision which led to an idea later on. The impossible, grand, motionless beds . . . [led to the ideal] of remaking the stage – to bring back its *apparent impossibility*. The drama was grand and perfect; great actors would come and go; but the stage itself was not fit to receive either – not like those beds. My idea was to make it fit for great plays and great acting.[5]

That 1928 New York version of *Macbeth*, Craig's last attempt to compromise with the conventional theater, did considerable damage to his reputation precisely because of this repetition, which appeared there almost as self-parody. Craig had no hand in the way his ideas were to be realized on stage. He was convinced that Tyler did not understand them, and had little respect for the American theater. He had been disappointed in his hopes (based on unrealistic visions of American wealth) of financial support from the United States, and by the failure of Bel Geddes's plans for an international theater festival associated with the Chicago World Fair (which seemed to him to have been stolen from one of his own plans, and in which he overestimated the significance of his own proposed contribution). Financial necessity alone brought him to accept Tyler's commission, and he signed all the designs "C. P. B." for "Craig pot-boiler."

In 1908 he had used *Macbeth* to demonstrate how his principles of unity, proportion, and simplicity could bring out the emotional essence of a play, creating an inner, spiritual drama:

How does it look, first of all to our mind's eye?

I see a lofty and steep rock, and I see the moist cloud which envelops the head of this rock. That is to say, a place for fierce and warlike men to inhabit, a place for phantoms to nest in. Ultimately this moisture will destroy the rock; ultimately these spirits will destroy the men . . . Set them down on your paper; *the lines and their direction*, never mind the [reality of a] cliff . . . and remember that on a sheet of paper which is but two inches square, you can make a line which seems to tower miles in the air, and you can do the same on your stage for it is all a matter of proportion and nothing to do with actuality.

What are the colours that Shakespeare has indicated for us? Do not first look at nature, but look in the play of the poet. Two; one for the rock, the man; one for the mist, the spirit . . . [use] only these two colours through your whole progress of designing your scene and your costumes, yet forget not that each colour contains many variations.[6]

But here, twenty years later, the effect was a potpourri of different elements borrowed from almost all of his previous productions. The Witches were given the grotesque bird masks and "root growth" on their legs (and Macbeth a "hedge-hog wig" for the banquet scene) from their sisters in *Dido*. The helmets and costumes came from *The Vikings*. The distorted expressionistic crosses, behind which the Witches danced beneath gaunt triangular gallows, were reminiscent of designs for Hofmannsthal's *White Fan*, which Craig had done in 1905. The pointed arch of the bridge with a stylized landscape of hills visible in the background beneath had originated as a design for *On Baile's Strand* in 1914 and was repeated from his production of *The Pretenders* two years earlier, as were the jagged windswept trees used for the heath scene. Craig's idea of lighting Macbeth's banquet with torches behind "a transparency which is kept in motion" was clearly drawn from his staging of previous banqueting scenes, though here there was one histrionic addition: Banquo's ghost appeared through the flames of the torches. When Macbeth bade his guests, "You know your own degrees; sit down," Craig's notes indicate an all-too-literal transcription of his ideas of symbolic geometry, with the "degrees" represented by four broad steps leading down from the rostrum on which Macbeth's table was placed. All these derivative elements were little more than unassimilated clichés, which Tyler's production did nothing to disguise.

Even more damaging – because it seemed to confirm the most common misinterpretation of Craig's work – was the emphasis on purely visual effects that were out of context and that detracted from the thrust of the play's action. To introduce a "Tall Bed," for example, Craig inserted a completely unnecessary scene before the sleepwalking sequence. Lady Macbeth is discovered in a canopied bed, "her body thrown about as though sleeping in disorder." Behind her the three witches appear as elongated blue fingers, moving silently. An anachronistic clock strikes midnight, "the far off sound of bagpipes is heard (marking time) and the scene fades – a pause. Curtains lowered – curtains raised . . ." Undramatic and statically pictorial, this invention demonstrates clearly (if unintentionally) that

Craig's approach could neither be reduced to a series of staging techniques nor be applied independently of his vision of a radically different kind of theater. They were of no use to a director – even, in this case, to Craig himself – who interpreted a play from the conventional focus of plot, character, or even mood, instead of subordinating every element to a unifying symbolic idea. For once Craig's interpretation here was perfunctory. His note accompanying a sketch of Macbeth's severed head, a grotesque mask on the point of a spear, sums it up: "the end of the melodrama."[7]

Craig's past experience had already sufficiently demonstrated the need for a completely unified concept of theater. If his two early productions with Ellen Terry had convinced him that working with conventionally trained actors was impossible, his subsequent attempts to collaborate with other directors were – with the questionable exceptions of Stanislavski and Poulsen – disastrous. This became clear almost at the start of his career, as soon as his growing reputation as a director brought him invitations to work outside his own company. In 1904 Otto Brahm asked him to work on Hofmannsthal's version of *Venice Preserved* for the Lessing Theater in Berlin. Quite apart from language difficulties (which led Craig to believe that he was being employed as a director rather than simply as a designer, caused an almost total failure of communication between Brahm and himself, and meant that he was unable even to read the German adaptation he was supposedly interpreting), Brahm turned out to be completely unsympathetic to Craig's principles. Craig had been hired on reputation, sight unseen as it were. Brahm's reaction to Craig's designs revealed him to be precisely the sort of realist Craig's whole approach was designed to oppose. When Craig presented a starkly plain scene that had high unbroken curtains for walls and a full-height portico on one side as the only opening, and that was bare of furnishings apart from two plain, square-shaped benches, Brahm demanded elaborate detail and doors with locks and handles. In response Craig complained that Brahm "does not know the first principles of the art [of the theater] – when lights have to imitate the hour of 5 p.m. and get down to 5.45 in an autumn evening, Brahm can absolutely wipe Tree off the face of the clock – when the Stranger enters in *The Lady from the Sea,* you can bet it is not a spirit entering but . . . an ordinary man – you can even tell what class ticket he has in his pocket." According to Craig, Brahm rejected as "impossible" anything he suggested. In reaction Craig made totally unrealistic demands: that the stage should be gutted (as the Imperial Theater had been for *The Vikings*) to create an effect of "endless sky"; that the

Asphaleia System of hydraulic lifts to raise or tilt any section of the stage floor be installed; that the auditorium be rebuilt on the model of Bayreuth (as he had wanted for *Bethlehem*), with all the seats at the same level on an inclined floor. Ultimately only three of Craig's designs were used for the play's six different scenes, and almost no reviews gave much attention to the décor. Though one reviewer praised his "sombre night scene with its dead quietness" as "more powerful than anything else that I ever saw on a European stage," the consensus was that the general level of performance fell below the Lessing Theater's usual standard. Typical comments on the design were that they "did not suit the ensemble's style" and (unsurprisingly, as half the scenes were Craig's, half Brahm's resident designer's) that there was no unity of the acting style and the setting or of one scene and another.[8]

After this, Craig insisted on total control over any production he was involved in, and his refusal to compromise meant, in fact, withdrawing from the theater. Max Reinhardt's actors were perhaps the only troupe in Europe that offered the means of realizing his theatrical vision – and indeed had some of the qualities of his ideal Ueber-marionette – because Reinhardt had trained them to take direction "almost as if they were puppets, controlling every movement and gesture, the slightest change in intonation" and subordinating their personalities "to his own conception of the play." But it was precisely this degree of training that made it impossible for Reinhardt to transfer control to anyone else. So when Reinhardt asked him to design *Caesar and Cleopatra* and *The Tempest* in 1905, and *King Lear* and *The Oresteia* in 1908, Craig's precondition that he alone "be master of the stage" was effectively a refusal. Similarly, when Jacques Rouché, the director of the Théâtre des Arts in Paris, invited Craig to produce any play he liked after seeing the Moscow *Hamlet*, Craig rejected the opportunity because "it's not a 'production' I want, but *a theatre.*"[9]

To some extent this attitude was justified. At Beerbohm Tree's request Craig designed a production of *Macbeth* despite his feeling that "even genius if it came there [Her Majesty's Theater] would never get on a step without a free hand" – and indeed Tree's traditionalist stage painter persuaded him that Craig's models and designs were impractical, so they were discarded and the models broken up. After Brahm (not unreasonably) refused to rebuild the Lessing Theater to accommodate Craig's ideas, Craig had responded "In short, change the art for the machine. Not while I'm alive!" This became his prime concern. When Scandiani offered him La Scala in

Milan, he refused because he feared his ideas would become subordinated to the stage machinery, at that time (1921) the most advanced in Europe, though once he was finally persuaded to work with such machinery in *The Pretenders* he was delighted by the technical possibilities. In Craig's view no compromise with the conventional theater was possible. Even though the Poulsens offered him "a free hand in every respect" with *The Pretenders*, he felt that "for all that I was only *assisting* in their production, not myself producing the piece." His first response to their invitation was, "Remember it is almost fifteen years since I did any work inside a theatre. The experience [with *Hamlet*] in Moscow decided me to wait until I should possess my own theatre."[10]

Already, in 1905, Craig believed he might achieve this. As he reported overconfidently to Martin Shaw, "Expect to receive wonderful news within 3 months. I may then have my own theatre and my own company. NOT ACTORS but a CREATURE of my own invention."[11] But when such hopes consistently failed to materialize, he was forced to find alternate means of defining his "Theatre of Tomorrow" – which rapidly became a new concept of drama itself – and as a result he published the first dialogue of "The Art of the Theatre." This dialogue, written in the space of a single week, recapitulated the principles that had developed out of his early productions, and pointed to the main areas that were to form his theory. There were three major points in his argument: The theater is a branch of art both equivalent to, and as unique in expression as poetry, music, and architecture. As such, it should have the same standards of aesthetic unity as the other arts. This could be achieved only if it were the work of one man; and a school should be founded to explore the principles of this art. As the London *Times* review of this booklet acknowledged, its "fundamental position" was "unassailable." But the details have led to considerable misunderstanding.

One of the most frequently quoted passages of this dialogue is usually taken as evidence that Craig was calling for the kind of synaesthesia associated with Wagner's *Gesamtkünstwerk:* "The Art of the Theatre is neither acting nor the play, it is not scene nor dance, but it consists of all the elements of which these things are composed . . . Action, words, line, colour, rhythm." Yet in his notes Craig specifically denied that combining the different arts of music, painting, and poetry, would in itself produce the kind of drama he wanted. In fact, the art that Craig was advocating is "total theater" in a rather different sense: one that singles out the different elements of drama in order to dispense with anything not specifically "theatrical." Craig draws a distinction between the "dramatic poet" and a "dramatist" who works "either in poetry or prose, but always in action: in poetic action which is dance, or in prose action which is gesture," and then dispenses with the playwright. The term "voice" replaces "words," and a "drama of silence," in which the actors express thought and emotion in movement alone, replaces the conventional "drama of speech."[12]

Revolutionary as this may have seemed, Craig's position is really an extension of Charles Lamb's well-known argument that plays such as *King Lear* should not be staged because no physical representation could ever approach their poetic vision. The implication in Lamb's argument is that the stage represents an inferior and imperfect art. For Craig, theater is the equal of literature, but a very different form of art that can reach its full potential only if it is no longer subordinated to the written word. The richer the verbal imagery of a play, and the more expressive its dialogue, the further the stage is forced into a simply illustrative function and the less it fulfills its true nature. Shakespeare and Shaw are useless to the theater, Craig claimed, because as literature their plays are complete in themselves. A third-rate script might serve as the basis for creating something close to a solely theatrical performance, like Irving's production of *The Bells*. But why incorporate a mediocre element, which can only diminish the imaginative significance of the whole? Do without the sort of dialogue created by a writer thinking in literary terms – which also means dispensing with the conventional characterization and plot contained in such dialogue – and theater might then become a "pure art" on its own terms.

To some extent, this conclusion can be traced back to the conflict between Craig and Housman. But it is also perhaps partly due to Craig's own lack of formal education: "I pick up a volume by Nietzsche. On one page alone are so many words the meaning of which I do not understand that the words are useless for me." However, this is extended into a general statement that anticipates the belief of an absurdist like Ionesco that language is a barrier to true communication, and reflects Craig's aim of reaching the broadest possible public on the most fundamental level. "Words are a bad means of communicating ideas – especially transcendent ideas – ideas which fly . . . words should not be wasted – nor used except on rare occasions – for rare things are generally simple." In place of subtle psychological thought and complex poetic language, philosophy, sermons, and epigrams, the theater should present "visions" directly through "movement which is the very symbol of life."[13]

Even in the case of plays that he admired and considered suitable for his ideal theater, like those of W. B. Yeats, Craig criticized the use of words instead of symbolic gesture or movement to express emotional states. For example, in his copy of *On Baile's Strand*, where a woman declares, "No crying out, for there'll be need of cries / And knocking at the breast when it's all finished," Craig noted, "No need for this. She should suggest by anticipation which is stronger." Where the Fool describes "a great wave going to break," he crossed the lines out and substituted mime – "He makes a movement like rising wave: hands, arms and toes" – illustrated with a sketched figure rising sinuously to curl forward with his arms stretching down over his bent head. To illustrate the simplicity and suggestiveness that he looked for in dramatic action, Craig clipped from a history book an account of how Lady Holland announced the death of Fox to his friends simply by walking through the room with her apron thrown over her head. On it he noted, "Without words. No facial expression therefore no *personal* feeling. Action."[14]

If action was the prime element in Craig's theater, dance as "the poetry of movement" – one of his favorite phrases – was action's highest form. But he was not referring to traditional ballet, which he despised as artificial, elitist, and unnatural. "Dancing is not flying – we realize that man is not a bird. Dancing belongs very certainly to the good earth. Yet . . . most trainers teach the pupils to hop, to float, to do everything to get into the air. I would teach them exactly the reverse." Equally, such modern forms as Dalcroze or Fokine's ballets for Diaghilev were rejected, despite approval of their technique and unified ensemble work, because gymnastics without what Craig considered a spiritual center seemed exotic or epileptic. For Craig, perfect movement created a mystical union with the universal rhythms of nature in such a way as to directly express the soul. By contrast, "the Russian Ballet [e.g., *Firebird* or *Scheherazade*] is essentially the Art which is created by the Body. Its perfection is physical. Its appeal is to our senses, not through them."[15]

The person who was the model for this metaphysic of movement was Isadora Duncan. In contrast to other pioneers of modern theatrical dance, like Laban and Mary Wigman, she danced alone, without conventional costume or even the barest scenery. She never performed dance dramas, took on roles or strove to evoke archetypal associations. There were no leaps or pirouettes, only floating motions and gestures in a plain white or diaphanous robe – which Craig referred to as "rags," though she thought of them more poetically as cobwebs – against a gray curtain. Her favorite music was that

Simplicity and rhythm in Isadora Duncan's dancing. The setting of a Greek amphitheater was chosen to illustrate the links between her dance and classical art.

of Chopin, lyrical rather than dramatic, but her dancing did not even require musical accompaniment. As Craig wrote to Martin Shaw, "Miss Duncan's *most* amazing dance is without music at all – and so wonderful are her rhythms that one does not miss the music . . . this dancing depends on nothing but herself." What system she had was derived from Dalcroze, whose school of movement was designed to awaken the performer to the emotional content of musical rhythms and to translate this into position and gesture. But, as she later admitted, her art was based on improvisation and her movements followed her fantasy. The keynotes were extreme simplicity and absolute naturalness, which came as a revelation to Craig in 1904 when he first saw her perform:

. . . a second prelude or étude – it was played through gently and came to an end – she had not moved at all. Then one step back or sideways, and the music began again as she went moving on before or after it. Only just moving – not pirouetting or doing any of those things which a Taglioni or a Fanny Essler would certainly have done. She was speaking her own language, not echoing any ballet master, and so she came to move as no one had ever seen anyone move before.[16]

Craig's passionate love affair with Isadora Duncan is one of the better-known parts of his life, and their letters – which span over twenty years and record a fascination with each other that borders on obsession in its extremes of ecstasy and agony, devotion and infidelity – clearly indicate her significance for Craig. The correspondence continued even after her death in 1927, in the form of his highly emotional annotations on almost every page of her posthumously published autobiography. He declared that her genius complemented his and considered her the only artist, apart from Appia, with whom he could have worked successfully.

Incongruously, because he was notoriously unable to handle even his own affairs competently, he became her business manager in 1906. He persuaded her to replace her single piano accompaniment with an orchestra, and brought in Martin Shaw as her conductor. He replaced her modest gray curtains, which were only five-and-a-half feet high and hung on rods from a row of short wooden pilasters to form an enclosed dancing area, with great blue drapes the height of the stage. She acted as his go-between with Duse and Reinhardt, and was responsible for persuading Stanislavski to employ him for the Moscow Art Theater. But, much more importantly, she was the catalyst that crystallized his artistic ideas. His early work with Martin Shaw led him to define movement and speech in terms of musical rhythm. Now Isadora Duncan's dancing brought him to see that "all written poetry and all music is based upon the laws which govern the poetry of *movement* . . . the beat of the feet upon the earth controls the musician and the poet."[17] The fact that some of her dances were performed without accompaniment convinced him that rhythm alone could form the basis of theatrical art. The arrangements of the curtains he devised for her, which derived from his designs for *Venice Preserved* and *Electra*, now struck him as appropriate for abstract movement, and when he came to work on Scene they provided one of the initial forms for its geometric shapes.

Isadora Duncan's ideas also shaped the philosophy that Craig's art eventually incorporated. What she was primarily concerned with has been called basic, even biological dance. One's first response to emotional or sensory stimuli is spontaneous movement, and her dancing was intended to reach and uncover the roots of that universal impulse. As she later described her aims when recalling her early experiments at the turn of the century, "For hours I would stand quite still, my two hands folded between my breasts, covering the solar plexus . . . I was seeking and finally discovered the central spring of all movement, the crater of motor power, the unity from which all diversities of movement are born, the mirror of vision for the creation of the dance – it was from this discovery that was born the theory on which I founded my school."[18]

Another aspect of this fundamentalist approach was the search for universal rhythms, in which form and movement would have the same unity as in nature. Isadora Duncan's earliest childhood inspiration for dancing came from the rhythm of ocean waves, and her aim in performance was to find artistic equivalents in which there was the same complete continuity among the human shape, the steps and gestures, the patterning of the dance as a whole, and the personality or emotion the dance expressed. She called this her "great and only principle . . . The waters, the winds, the plants, living creatures, the particles of matter itself obey this controlling rhythm of which the characteristic line is the wave." The result was an apparent naturalness and sincerity that struck observers as the opposite of "Art." Yet her biography shows that it took years of trial and practice to achieve this level of simplicity. As she outlined it, in terms that echoed Craig's demand for movement that would directly express the soul, her ultimate aim was to make the body "transparent . . . a medium for the mind and spirit." Her success in this reinforced his belief that a spiritual theater – as distinct from one that copied social realities – had no need of speech. "She said nothing. [Yet] she said everything that was worth hearing – and everything that everyone else but the poets had forgotten to say."[19] Soon afterward Craig was calling for "the abolition of the spoken word" because of its inevitable tendency to reduce drama to triviality; and in his copy of one of the early critical studies of his work, which quoted from "The Art of the Theatre" his decision to create the theater of the future "out of ACTION, SCENE, and VOICE," Craig noted in the margin that the word ACTION related specifically to Isadora Duncan.

These qualities of Isadora Duncan's dancing are all directly reflected in the essays and designs in which Craig defined his new art of the theater. Abstract action became its primary element, with the continuity of form and movement as its structural principle. Its aim and justification became the unmediated expression of a quasi-religious spirituality, one that rationally inclined nonbelievers might find difficult to appreciate. Its development became a process of elimination and simplification, removing even the human figure and creating a totally unified action by embodying movement in the scenery itself. By 1907 the form was set in a scenario entitled simply "Motion":

The Beginning . . . the Birth . . . we are in Darkness . . . all is still . . .

And from this Nothing shall emerge a spirit . . . Life . . . a perfect and balancing life . . . to be called Beauty . . . The Immortal Beauty of Change Eternal.

A form simple and austere ascends with prolonged patience like the awakening of thought in a dream.

Something seems to unfold, something to fold. Slowly . . . fold after fold loosens itself and clasps another till that which was void has become shapely. And now from East to West, one chain of life moves like a sea before us . . .

Without Architecture we should have no Divine Place in which to praise. Without Music no Divine Voice with which to praise. Without Motion no Divine Act to perform.[20]

Except for the fact that there is no mention of a dancer, this could well be a description of the subjective effect of Isadora Duncan in performance. The pattern of unfolding action is much the same. Even the metaphors echo hers, which may explain something of their pretentious abstraction, although Craig was always prone to this kind of inflated symbolism.

A further influence on the way in which Craig's ideas developed was Isadora Duncan's fascination with Greek art. This was shared by the avant-garde at the beginning of the century and reflected trends in philosophy and anthropology. The Cambridge School of Francis Cornford, Jane Harrison, and Gilbert Murray had documented the origins of drama in Greek religious ritual. Philosophers from Nietzsche to Ernst Cassirer were asserting that "primitive" or mythical thought, which understood experience in terms of prelogical images, was superior to the scientific rationalism of contemporary Western civilization. Yeats called his work "not drama but the ritual of a lost faith." When Reinhardt built his "Theater of the Five Thousand," his aim was to recreate the sense of community and Dionysian enthusiasm of the ancient Greek theater. Eleonora Duse claimed, in a comment that Craig liked to quote as support for his ideal of an Uebermarionette, "To save the theatre, the [contemporary] theatre must be destroyed, the actors and actresses must all die of the plague. They . . . make art impossible. It is not drama that they play but pieces for the theatre. We should return to the Greeks."[21] Similarly, Isadora Duncan traced her style of dance back to an imagined classical form, and believed the ancient open-air amphitheater provided ideal conditions for her performances.

One of the earliest inspirations for Craig's notion of theatrical reform had been a review article on the Comédie Française performance of *Oedipus* and *Antigone* in 1894, and on an opera festival in 1895 at the Roman theater in Orange.[22] This article had spoken enthusiastically about the effect of using the severely simple facade of the 120-foot-high rear wall as a permanent set, replacing the usual painted illusion of temple or palace with the reality in stone. The "majestic" architectural structure, which reduced operettas to triviality, was described as "suited only to dramas inspired by the noblest of passions and dealing with the noblest of themes." It served as a touchstone for the integrity of the dramatic vision, and in contrast to the reviewer's expectations, the heroic scale of the background "did not dwarf the human figures sustaining serious parts." In tragedy or grand opera, "play and players alike were upraised to a lofty plane of solemn stateliness by the stately reality of those noble walls." As the article commented, the physical stature of the performers would have been out of proportion even if they had worn ten-foot-high stilts, yet the grandeur of the facade acted as an emotional amplifier. In apparently instinctive reaction to their surroundings, the actors' movements took on a ceremonial slowness, and their groupings were given a natural balance and cohesion by the height of the scene. Visual simplicity, in fact, was the keynote. The lack of any wings or backstage area made it difficult to use furnishings or props, which in any case would have been incongruous against the austere backdrop. As a result, "the stage was full not of things but of people, and was wholly alive. The eye was not distracted . . . but was entirely at the service of the mind in following the dramatic action." When Craig originally read the article, it had merely opened his eyes to new spatial possibilities for the stage. Now, after 1905, his aim became a return to the values of classical theater.

At the same time he had no desire to follow Godwin in reviving the external forms of the Greek stage. Similarly, he rejected Poel and the Elizabethan Stage Society's attempts to reproduce the performance conditions of the Globe for presenting Shakespeare's plays. Poel's stripping of the stage and his removal of illusionistic settings and nineteenth-century acting conventions, together with his use of curtains, in many ways paralleled Craig's work. But Craig believed that Shakespeare's stage was meaningless without its original Elizabethan audience, and he had never been concerned with historical accuracy. As the program for *Dido* had pointed out, he took "particular care to be entirely incorrect in all matters of detail." Although he increasingly immersed himself in the study of stage history, in itself such information was of incidental interest. Almost half the essays in *The Mask* were devoted to non-European and pre-nineteenth-century forms of theater. But they were truly relevant to Craig only as evidence to support his idea of a new theater, either by providing arguments to discredit theatrical developments since the Renaissance, or proving its viability by showing that other respected traditions contained the very qualities he was advocating. In his view any imitation of the past would be an "affectation," a "sham" that simply compounded the illusionism of the old Lyceum or the new naturalistic stage. What he wished to revive was the essence of classical theater, not its archeology. On one level, the creative process of the Greek theater, in which Aeschylus had instructed the chorus in their dances as well as the protagonists in how they should deliver their lines, and in which the dramatist and director were the same person, was precisely what Craig aimed at in defining his ideal art as completely "the work of one man." But it was also the principles of an architectural, multipurpose setting (as distinct from specific or two-dimensional scenes), symbolic acting, simplicity, and perhaps above all the religious value of Greek drama that he wanted to restore. In addition, the origins of the theater provided an example for the most ambitious part of his undertaking. He was in danger of producing a stage form for which no plays had been written, and one that–given his intended "abolition of the spoken word"–would hardly attract a playwright. However, "in those days they built their theatres for their dramas, not their dramas in and for their theatres," and this encouraged him to attempt the single-handed creation of a drama that his new theater would express.[23]

After seeing *Acis and Galatea*, Yeats told Craig that he had rediscovered "an art which has lain hid under the roots of the Pyramids for ten thousand years, so solemn it is." Now, when formulating his theories, Craig repeated this almost word-for-word. The metaphor was taken literally: Instead of using "the great art which has lain buried under the fallen Temples of Greece and Asia" for the purpose of comparison, he made it a source for the qualities of what he called his "old new ideal."[24] As his phrase indicates, these essential principles were both generalized and romanticized. One of Craig's notebooks divided the whole history of European theater into six periods under three headings: "Acting or Action," "The Voice," and "Scene." The first period represented a purely notional idea of the archaic origins of drama, with marionettes only, instrumental music rather than vocalization, and no scene. Then, from the Greeks on, Craig traced what to him was a clear process of degeneration within each of the three elements. In the section on acting, Craig recounted how the chorus first appeared alone; then as set against one masked actor followed by a second (protagonist and antagonist), and after that against twelve actors and the half-masks of the *Commedia dell'Arte*. Finally the chorus was reduced to a single choral figure, or it disappeared altogether. Any form of mask vanished as well, and acting companies gradually grew from 20 to 100 people, with women added and all actors displaying individual personalities. In the section titled "Voice," Craig described a chorus of "sounds not dogma" (his term for the intellectual content in dialogue), which was followed by one or more voices distinguished from the chorus but "masked . . . and so not natural"; then, after the year 1600, by an expanding number of individual voices without any form of vocal chorus. In "Scene" he delineated the transformations of architecture from the Greeks to medieval church drama, then to imitation architecture (Palladio, Bibiena), and after that to "imitation artificial architecture" or realistic scenery.

This oversimplified and rather naive perspective reveals much more about Craig's own ideals than about stage history. His comments show that he looked on the process of renewing the theater as a progressive stripping away of accretions to return to the earliest and most fundamental forms. "I believe that the very *material* of the theatre needs simplifying . . . I do not wish to revert to an *old manner*, but I do not want to depart from a *noble tradition*. I wish to rebuild on old truths." These truths he defined as the superiority of art (which hints at a future and spiritual state) over life (which represents the physically present, and hints at nothing beyond itself). "I wish to remove *the Word* with its *Dogma* but to leave *Sound*, or the voiced beauty of the soul. I wish to remove *the Actor* with his *Personality* but to leave *the Chorus of masked figures*. I wish to remove *the Pictorial Scene* but to leave in its place *the Archetictonic* [sic] *Scene*."[25]

Although ancient Greece was his primary inspiration, Craig also found the same "universal principles" in other theatrical forms, from Indian and Cambodian dance to Javanese puppet plays and Nō drama. He had the opportunity to see a Nō performance in 1900 when a Japanese troupe visited London. Although some critics referred to Japanese qualities in Craig's work, there was no discernable Japanese influence on his early productions because the stylized acting was too alien to be immediately useful. As one reviewer complained, "The [Japanese] players . . . all have the appearance to a Western eye of grotesque mechanical toys. None of their movements resemble ours, their faces seem bizarre masks, and their voices have the peculiar metallic timbre of the gramophone. The question whether they are expressing joy or sorrow, fear or exaltation, is for the audience often the merest guesswork." Now, by 1901, the "Nō dances," as Craig called them – a description that clearly reflected his own concept of drama – provided a parallel that could help to define his ideas by offering "supreme examples of brevity and fine tradition."[26] In fact it was precisely those elements of the Nō that the public had found incomprehensible in 1900 that Craig wanted for his Uebermarionette; and the qualities he singled out were the apparent absence of violent passion in the Nō; its highly conventionalized symbolism, in which every gesture held clear significance; its distance from everyday life, or its "unnaturalness"; and its simplicity and spiritual suggestion.

One element that Greek theater shared with the Nō was the mask. Those that Craig had experimented with in his early productions were grotesque only, but now he saw the mask as the symbol of the human face. As such it came to be the symbol of his new theater itself, and gave the journal in which he published most of his theoretical essays its title. On one level, it paralleled his simplified, universalized scenery in embodying a relatively small number of archetypes that could be reused in a multiplicity of situations. On

another, masks effectively ruled out individual emotion and the egoism that made ordinary actors unsuitable material for Craig's concept of art. Simplicity and intensity replaced variety, so that "instead
of six hundred, but six expressions shall appear on the face."[27] Unlike *Commedia dell'Arte* masks, these would represent psychological
states or moral qualities such as fear and pity or justice and injustice,
rather than social types.

This corresponded to Craig's aim of creating a drama of spiritual
essences. The mask was to be restored to the stage specifically as
"the visible expression of the mind . . . the only right medium of
portraying the expressions of the soul as shown through the expressions of the face." Again, however, Craig's intention was to
design new forms that would be simultaneously universal and contemporary, not historical. Indeed, his ultimate hope was to train
actors to achieve an equivalent effect of depersonalized emotion by
muscular tension alone. In a note that prefigures one of the characteristic avant-garde acting techniques, he called Irving "a prophet
foretelling secrets of the future of the actor's art by that mask with
which he veiled the weaknesses of his face . . . to impart the secret
agonies of his soul . . . pointing with almost motionless gesture to
the path leading to the great art of gesture . . . trained to an ex-
pressionless stone nobility."[28] In using Irving as an example of the
physical control that Craig believed indispensable for capturing poetic vision as much as for its expressive qualities, the true relationship of the living actor to his notorious Uebermarionette is
summed up.

Like many innovators, Craig habitually overstated his ideas in
order to distinguish them clearly from orthodox thought and to gain
attention. Unfortunately, all too often the impact of such a tactic is at
the expense of intelligibility, and few of Craig's ideas have been
more misunderstood than the Uebermarionette. His argument was
against the "actor," but not against the human performer per se. He
rejected the conventional approach to acting, together with those
trained in it who were unable to rise above its vices. In his view, the
major of these vices was the display of personality and emotions,
which formed the main attraction of the existing theater but which
put the body at the mercy of psychological forces under imperfect
control at best. It meant that actors wanted always to be sympathetic
or central instead of subordinate to the dramatic requirements of the
piece. To produce a degree of emotional unity in which all the gestures, as a whole, would form a clear and distinct intellectual
image – one, moreover, that would not vary from performance to

Masks from *Dido and Aeneas* and *The Masque of Love:* stylization and the externalization of moral qualities.

performance – the actor had to have total physical control, which precluded personal vanity.

Instead of outlining a system of training that might achieve this, Craig chose to challenge the acting profession by calling such control an "impossible state of perfection," and went further to set up an absolute distinction between art and life. "Art arrives only by design," whereas the use of human figures as a medium for expression can only (in the present state of the theater) create accidental effects. Similarly, actors draw attention to themselves as people, whereas "the highest art is that which conceals the craft and forgets the craftsman." As general aesthetic principles such statements are unexceptional. But for the stage to be judged by the same criteria as sculpture or music demands a level of abstraction that rules out what is normally thought of as "dramatic," particularly when these

criteria are drawn from symbolist art. Craig quoted Blake and Pater to support his contention that art should not deal with physical actuality, or "flesh and blood life," but with its opposite, the world of visionary imagination that he characterized as "solemn . . . beautiful and . . . remote."[29] And as an apparently logical corollary, he proposed replacing the human being on the stage with inanimate figures or puppets.

There is, of course, a basic contradiction in using inanimate objects to express "a living spirit." But if we examine the qualities Craig attributes to puppets it becomes clear that his real aim was not quite so radical. What he specifically refers to are the puppet's "noble artificiality" in portraying abstract emotional states rather than in projecting live emotions; its symbolic character, which presents human nature in generalized or generic, rather than individual terms; and its subordination to the aesthetic requirements of the drama. Yet these qualities are not unique to puppets. Indeed the one thing that cannot be achieved with puppets is the flowing rhythms of natural movement, which Craig was simultaneously proclaiming as the basis of his new art form. It is arguable that the puppet was only pushed forward through an association of ideas from "A Note on Masks" in the very first number of *The Mask*. There Craig had quoted a comment by Anatole France that attributed precisely these qualities to M. Signoret's puppet theater: "These marionettes resemble Egyptian hieroglyphs, that is to say something mysterious and pure, and, when they perform a play by Shakespeare or Aristophanes, I seem to see the poet's vision as if unfolded by sacred figures on the high walls of a temple."

In fact Craig was really arguing for "a new form of acting, consisting for the main part of symbolical gesture. Today they *impersonate . . .* tomorrow they must *represent*." As he commented in a letter to Martin Shaw, his rejection of actors was a provisional expedient, "until a breed can be grown which are like the rest of my thought, *hard, clearcut, passionless*."[30] This remained an unrealized ideal and, in the absence of such Uebermarionettes, he experimented with eight-foot-high articulated wooden figures. He also planned productions of Maeterlinck's early plays, subtitled "Drames pour Marionettes" though written for ordinary performance. These appealed to him because the dream action required actors to model themselves on "the slow and deliberate gesture of all Puppets – each has to move as a somnambulist." But despite his claim that the puppet stage possessed "every element necessary to a *creative* and a *fine art*," with perhaps one exception his own puppet dramas were not more than parody plays, an outlet for his frustration rather than material for a new dramatic form. His real aim was to create a Western equivalent to the highly trained actors of the Nō drama, which in his view exemplified the same intrinsic qualities as the theater of ancient Greece:

The Japanese [dance drama] with its strict ritual, its noble conservatism which still preserves traditional postures without change or modification, its obedience to a fine tradition, its perfect control of its material – that is, the human body – approaches more nearly to the stately and splendid ceremonies of the past, of which, among us, some trace yet lingers in the symbolic gestures of the priests celebrating mass, and thus it partakes more nearly of the nature of an art.[31]

Craig looked on himself as a rediscoverer rather than an originator. His aim was to return the theater to its primal state, though without copying the original (and therefore alien) forms of expression, and the two elements that all the oldest traditions of theater shared were religious content and a high degree of stylization. This aim anticipates the attempts by directors like Brook and Grotowski to create a "theater of ritual" in the 1960s. But for Craig's contemporaries, a return to the religious origins of drama meant an updated mystery play or a play that incorporated direct echoes of the Mass, like Housman's *Bethlehem* and Edmond Harancourt's *La Passion* (performed on Good Friday, 1890). However, although Craig claimed to be "respectful" toward all manifestations of religion, he rejected Christianity along with conventional notions of spirituality that he characterized pungently as "white wings, upturned eyes, mutterings and mumblings devoid of humanity, and a general appearance of the sickly." Instead he proclaimed himself "a Pagan," and his "sacred theatre" was intended to express a vaguely defined pantheistic humanism. The actual forms of religious service or medieval drama were therefore of as little direct use to him as were the specific symbols and gestures of Japanese or Javanese drama. Still, at the same time the Church provided the basis for his concept of an "exquisite and precious" theater, in which the materials out of which the costumes (or in Craig's terms, vestments) and scenery were made would be as real as the devotion experienced, and in which the "noble symbols were popular without being understood."[32] Church architecture, too, became the model for one of his final scenic ideals.

In short, as Craig later emphasized, scenery in itself was of secondary importance to him. The common view that his main contribution was as a designer distorts the true focus of his art. Scenic reforms alone could be little more than decorative and superficial. To be effective they had to be accompanied by a new style of acting, and neither would have any internal coherence without a radically different concept of drama itself. As he correctly perceived, all the elements of theater – dramatic action and dialogue, the actor, scenery and lighting, audience expectations, even the architecture of the auditorium – were interdependent. Meaningful change could be achieved only by stripping away all accumulated conventions in order to redefine the whole basis of drama. By a natural association of ideas, reinforced by some of the intellectual and artistic trends of the time, this process took Craig back to the origins of drama and led him to search for equivalents in Eastern traditions. Although the direction Craig's work took is to some extent dated by its symbolist principles, his path was to be well trodden by the avant-garde after Antonin Artaud, and can be summed up by his demand that "instead of the artist of the theatre, let us in future speak of the *Ritualist.*"[33]

# 6    Toward a new theater: Masques, screens, and a *Hamlet*

Craig's view that piecemeal reforms could never change the essential nature of the theater or reverse the long-standing trend toward realism may have been correct. But the comprehensive nature of his alternative was equally self-defeating. Its scope was overambitious for one man, however gifted, and it was hardly surprising that the principles he formulated were never fully translated into practice. As a result they lacked the definition that comes only from tangible demonstration and, despite his descriptive references to parallels in other dramatic traditions, his theories seem curiously abstract. Even his stage productions and the designs that established his influence hardly provide examples, because he dismissed them as compromises with the kind of theater they were originally intended to replace. Commenting on his famous production of *Hamlet* in 1912, for example, he described it as "old work. I have passed it all, gone into places where I have really seen something – a glimpse of something wonderful." Similarly, he warned the reader of *Towards A New Theatre* that the drawings, which appeared to illustrate his vision, in fact bore little relationship to his ideal: "All that I have put in the book now lies behind me."[1] As he repeated in both his notebooks and his published work, his theater existed only in the imagination. Although he believed he was moving toward it, he never claimed actually to have reached it.

From this perspective his effective influence could be only on the level of general inspiration. He offered an ideal rather than provided a new theatrical form. Even his demand that every aspect of a performance express the vision of a single person, if theater were to qualify as an art, called for something equivalent to the Renaissance ideal of a universal man. This "Artist of the Theatre" had not only to design the scenery, costumes, and lighting, and to direct every gesture of the actors (which would require a certain degree of acting skill) but he also had to be a playwright, constructing the drama performed by the actors and writing the dialogue spoken by them; a musician, composing whatever music accompanied the performance; and even an architect, capable of redesigning a theater. A measure of Craig's achievement is how closely he came to realizing this ideal. He started his career as an actor, then taught himself to

128

draw. He studied theater architecture, collected information on every aspect of theatrical history, and built scale models of experimental stages. He also began to create his own plays.

Given Craig's rejection of the spoken word and of the kind of meaning ordinary dialogue could convey, these were scenarios rather than fully developed plays. In opposing the staging of Shakespeare, he argued that what distinguished Shakespeare's art was the poetry of ideas, which operated on a purely mental level; that acting out his words destroyed the coherence of this imagery because a spectator's mind was distracted by the appeal to his senses. Conversely, the only way such poetry could be captured in a performance was to substitute a totally visual representation, cutting all the words so that no appeal to the intellect would detract from the perception of physical images.

This was Craig's aim, a form of drama created solely from the physical elements of theatrical presentation. Figures were to be shown engaged in symbolic action and set in emotionally evocative contexts. Although he presented this as a revolutionary reversal of conventional assumptions about drama, it was really an extension of Irving's claim that "the theatre is bigger than the playwright, that its destiny is a higher one than that of the mouthpiece for an author's theses, and finally that plays are made for the theatre and not theatre for plays." The danger in dispensing with the imaginative values of the playwright is that drama becomes reduced to spectacle. As a mere show, it arouses aesthetic appreciation at the expense of the emotional involvement that can make a performance a communal act. To avoid this, Craig turned to a traditional form of drama with strong communal associations. Shakespeare had been a magnificent (yet untheatrical, in Craig's view) aberration. But Elizabethan drama provided other, very different models: "The Masques – the Pageants – these were light and beautiful examples of the Art of the Theatre."[2]

The masques of Ben Jonson and Inigo Jones had been celebrations of the Jacobean court: allegorical glorifications of the virtues attributed to the king, which were portrayed by the courtiers or by the royal family itself. As such the masques were ceremonial and their presentation was highly stylized. The figures were symbolic personifications with no individualizing traits. Plot situations were reduced to the triumph of good over evil, and the characteristic action was a dance or a tableau. Craig had already used some of these structural elements in his early productions – the masque/antimasque antiphony in *Dido and Aeneas,* and allegorical figures and dances in *The*

*Masque of Love.* However, instead of imitating the sixteenth-century form, he found what seemed to be a continuing, live tradition in which to work.

One aspect of nineteenth-century romanticism had been the rediscovery of folk art, from ballads to country festivals and Morris dancing. This was linked with the Gothic Revival, which seemed to offer moral values that might redeem Victorian materialism, and found expression as much in William Morris's artisan community and in Herkomer's art school with its theatrical performances as in Godwin's architecture. It provided much of Craig's early inspiration, and in one sense his art was an extension of this neomedievalism. The reawakened interest in mystery plays, which had brought Craig "valuable and valued instruction in theatrical craft" in the form of Theodore Child's article titled "A Christmas Mystery in the Fifteenth Century," was part of this movement. So was the founding of the Purcell Society itself. And when he defined "Ceremony" as integral to his theater of the future, among the examples he listed "The Lord Mayor's Show" as "belonging to civil rites."[3]

The kind of thing he had in mind was *Beauty's Awakening. A Masque of Winter and of Spring.* When it was performed by the Art Workers Guild at the London Guildhall in 1899, Craig found the execution inadequate – "so many designers . . . and far too few theatre craftsmen." But the imaginative qualities aimed at by the Art Workers corresponded in general terms to some of his later principles: in particular, their rejection of "realism and illusion" in favor of "an allegory of the beautiful," which led to formalized patterning – "design, then, instead of illusion" – and to an emphasis on purely "Poetic and Ethic aims, Beauty of Design and Ornament." The setting, a single central archway flanked by an arcade of columns, is echoed in many of his designs, though characteristically he elongated the arch and simplified the architectural shapes that the Art Workers had embellished with elaborate Gothic ornamentation. The pageant itself, carefully distinguished from a play by its creators, also contained thematic similarities to Craig's own masques in its mix of traditional symbols and contemporary social comment, even if its focus was rather different.

Fayremonde, representing "the Spirit of all things beautiful," is cast into an enchanted sleep by a witch with the self-explanatory name of Malebodea. Trueheart (the London County Council perhaps, in the flattering shape of a knight in shining armor with a shield bearing the city crest) searches for her, accompanied by Hope and Fortitude. He battles against "the Demons attendant upon Lon-

don . . . Bogus: who is both ancient and modern. Cupiditas: whom
we all have in our hearts tho' we fain would deny it. Jerrybuiltas or
Jerry: whom we have cherished so long and understood so well.
Ignoramus: first cousin to Philistinus"; and when these sordidly
modern demons rally, "the music tells first of their reluctance, then
of their resolution, and when at last they are of one mind they unite
in a grotesque and fantastic dance around the witch." Fayremonde's
dreaming is presented in pageants entitled "The Seven Lamps of
Architecture" and "The Fair Cities of the World." Labour, Invention, and (in a rather direct appeal to captains of industry in the
audience) Commerce awaken her, and the masque ends with a tableau of triumph. Even without dialogue, the visual symbolism, reinforced by descriptive theme music and broadly expressive acting,
was almost too accessible. Indeed, the Art Workers declared, "what
meaning there is in the Allegory that underlies our action is not far
to seek."[4] But part of the value of this model for Craig was precisely
that it demonstrated the possibility of communicating on a nonverb-
al yet popular level.

A second type of civil "ceremony," which seemed popular in a
rather more conventional sense, was the harvest festival. While
looking for material to incorporate in *Bethlehem*, Craig came across a
description of "some country people celebrating their harvest home"
near Windsor in 1598: "Their last load of corn they crown with
flowers, having besides an image richly dressed, by which they
would perhaps signify Ceres; this they keep moving about, while
men and women, men and maidservants, riding through the streets
in the cart, shout as loud as they can till they arrive at the barn."
Immediately Craig set about constructing his first original masque,
*The Harvest Home*, taking pains to emphasize its traditional and an-
tique nature by claiming that he had found the details in a scholarly
study of *Ancient Mysteries* (a book that deals solely with mystery
plays, and contains no reference whatsoever to secular festivals). In
fact, comparable festivities could still be found at that time, in a
consciously preserved, rather artificial form, on some of the larger
country estates.[5] This simple procession was elaborated into a minidrama based on a sequence of well-known folk songs. After the
harvesters, singing, "Hail to our harvest home, this day of all the
year/We reapers make good cheer" reach the barn, followed by children singing an "ABC song – Fool, Fool came to School," bells are
heard and a group of Morris dancers come on. The applause at the
end of their "capering" is counterpointed by the song of a "sad
lover" which fades away into the distance outside. The ceremonial

passing around of the garlanded straw dolly is followed by "Hobby Horses with an exact presentment of the dance which took the town and country-side by storm in the time of the Merry Monarch." Then, archetypal folk song figures are introduced. A shepherdess and a shepherd sing a kissing-duet,

and the Miller [of Dee] is called. He is slow. Business with musicians. Children with paper mills . . . 2 gunshots heard outside – they rush out and drag in Poacher – 2 dogs. 2 sons – He is made to sing [Lincolnshire] Poacher's song. Then gun dance, "can you not hit it." Final note he takes aim at audience, everyone shrieks and rushes forward to Poacher, all laugh.

This drama is punctuated by madrigals and by traditional favorites like "Go no more a' roving" and "St. George for England," and the festivities end with children dancing around a miniature maypole, and with all joining in "The King's Jig, the strains of which are heard far away in the distance as the merry makers retire to their homes."[6] Craig intended to perform this at harvest-time on country estates, and published a prospectus in 1903 advertizing it. But the potential cost of transporting thirty to forty performers, plus musicians, long distances for single performances lasting only three-quarters of an hour ("or longer, if desired") made the scheme impractical.

This was the closest Craig came to recreating an actual traditional ceremony, and there is something artificial in the idea of presenting a highly colored version of dancers and songs for the entertainment of the very people who should have been in reality performing them themselves. After this, with the exception of his plans for a festival production of *The St. Matthew Passion*, Craig restricted his concepts to the stage, where "noble artificiality" was in keeping. The intention of exactly reproducing folk dances was also an aberration for Craig. He later criticized Cecil Sharp and his troupe of Morris dancers for doing precisely that. In his view, Sharp's performers put themselves in a formal straitjacket by heeding their desire for historical authenticity instead of improvising rhythmic movement to express their inner natures. "They dress up, bells and white suits and bows. They have a look in the glass – 'Am I quite tidy?' Then with a determined air they go to their self-inflicted doom, conscious to the last."[7] But some of the *Harvest Home* material found its way into the production of *Much Ado*, which was almost transformed into a masque itself by the number of songs and dances Craig and Martin Shaw introduced. The (for Craig) unusually light and comic tone also persisted initially in association with this dramatic form, and

later that year he proposed doing an "Alhambra Masque [the Alhambra being a popular variety theater] under a *nom de ballet*" to get
away from the aesthetic preconceptions established by tragedies
such as *Dido* and *Acis* and the almost unremitting gloom of *The
Vikings.*

At the same time Craig began experimenting with more serious
themes, as evidenced by *The Masque of Hunger, The Masque of Lunatics, The Masque of London,* and *The Dance of Death.* These were developed, together with brief outlines of other scenarios jotted down in
one of his notebooks ("Theatre. Shows and Motions, 1905–1909" – a
"motion" being the traditional English term for a puppet play), as
subjects "for the best pupils of the school to attempt to improvise
on," or for Craig himself to "bring onto my stage." They therefore
have central importance, though they were little more than rough
notes; and they indicate a degree of social criticism that is usually
completely overlooked in Craig's work. For instance, London was
presented as a grimy commercial hell, akin to T. S. Eliot's "unreal
city" in *The Wasteland,* where dead souls are tormented by being
forced into degradingly materialistic trades or menial occupations.
This vision was set against an idealized world of philosophy and
poetry – a great hall flooded with light – the inhabitants of which
cannot believe that such spiritual misery could exist.

The most fully realized of these scenarios was *The Masque of
Hunger,* which went through several versions, and for which Craig
designed scenes and movements in considerable detail. He called it
a "mimo-drama," and its essence was contained in the figure of a
man in a hideous mask of grief, whose amplified breathing expresses overwhelming emotion.

From his right arm hangs a little, dead boy, which he stretches out to the
audience. He shows this figure to all, moving it from left to right and from
right to left, and all the time the sound of restrained bellowing is heard. His
movements are slow and deliberate . . . from every side, and beneath him,
come the many echoes of his solitary cry, and these echoes take new
shapes, resolving into the words "Pain – Pain – and Sorrow – "

Then a black rain begins to fall and hides the figure from sight.
Originally that single image was the whole drama, but Craig elaborated the action and distanced it by adding an on-stage audience
and turning it into a play within a play. The general statement about
human misery was transformed into a comment on social inequality
by providing a contrasting image. A brightly lit palace and Louis XV
headdresses filled the stage, so that the beggar now appeared in the

Archetypal figures and the mime-within-a-mime of *The Masque of Hunger*.

more ordinary darkness of material deprivation, rather than in the bleak night of the soul. This made the political point more specific, but at the expense of emotional immediacy. A prelude was added, which emphasized the theatricality of the performance. Figures in eighteenth-century costumes are revealed "preparing the room for a masquerade, arranging the chairs for the [on stage] spectators . . . Two others take up their positions in the centre of the stage and begin to act at acting (all of this in dumb show)." The rest seat themselves with the affected airs of aristocrats, and one "swishes back a curtain from a small circular window letting in a flood of moonlight, like a lime" that falls on the figures of the "actors." As these "spectators" applaud, "the king's waltz tune" is heard in the distance, and their sudden nervous activity makes the audience realize that what they have taken for great lords are only servants aping their masters. But when the true court enters, their mannerisms are more, not less exaggerated, and the servants' parody turns out to be more human than the grotesque reality of the rich. The king is "a kind of money king," bloated with overeating, and he is wheeled in "like a large frog" on a plushly cushioned

invalid's throne . . . those who propelled him were the chief gentlemen of the Court. Their progress was made in this manner: first four steps, and then everyone nearly fainted with fatigue – a fanning – a smelling of salts during a pause, silence, and a tiny, squeaky voice from the depths of the cushions calling for relief. Then another bold effort – four steps forward and another pause with the same play repeated.

The masked figure, holding out the shrunken body of a starved child, then provides the entertainment for these decadent courtiers, while the servants peer at them from the corners.

Such multiplying levels of theatricality and illusion are highly imaginative, and point forward to Pirandello and Genet. But their appeal is mainly intellectual, and to regain anything approaching

Rhetorical gesture and choreographed groupings in the final scene of *The Masque of Hunger*.

the emotional power of the original simple image in isolation, Craig had to use visual overkill. In the final scene he envisaged upward of sixty or seventy people on stage, massed choral groupings and swirling, rhetorically dramatic movements. Crowds of starving beggars were to invade the palace, forming a dark wall of figures along the proscenium and enclosing the brightly lit courtiers, who are huddled together in a diminishing perspective at the rear. Out of wails and sobs a somber chant arises: "Shall we show you how the peasant carries home his dead."[8] On one side a human pyramid strains upward toward a funeral pyre. On the other, ragged figures thrust out accusing arms in a gesture modeled on Fuseli's painting of the Weird Sisters from *Macbeth*. But in place of Fuseli's three pointing figures, Craig had fifteen.

Craig, like many of the socially aware but politically naive avant-garde artists of his time – Ezra Pound, the futurist Marinetti, the German expressionists Bronnen and Johst – was led by his anti-establishment feelings toward the fascist camp. His frustration with the society that declined to support his work persuaded him to offer his art to Mussolini, whom Craig admired perhaps more for his theatrical personality than for his politics. His journals became filled with anti-Jewish comments: His exaggerated ideas about the wealth of the Jewish community and his inability to persuade them to support his theatrical schemes made them the focus for his resentment. Perhaps more out of opportunism than commitment, he proposed his plans for an annual performance of Bach's *St. Matthew Passion* as a festival celebrating the principles of fascism. And even after Mussolini's patronage failed to materialize, he still felt enough sympathy for the movement to carry a message from Goebbels to Erwin Piscator, offering him a theatrical position under the Nazis, when he visited Russia in 1935.

At the same time he always realized that the essential qualities of his art were aesthetic, and came to believe that its proper function was the positive evocation of spiritual values rather than negative social criticism. But he reasoned that this was not an apolitical withdrawal, as such values in themselves were implicitly revolutionary, being antimaterialistic. As a result, his plans for "Shows and Motions" following *The Masque of Hunger* became more visionary. The political themes were transposed to a symbolic plane, as in "notes for a performance on the death of Socrates," in which an evil social establishment was to be presented as a wall of masked faces, picked out by lights from a background of darkness – a technique that anticipated the most striking visual effect in Reinhardt's expressionistic production of *A Dream Play* in 1921. In fact the scenes of this mimo-drama are explicitly labeled "visions," and the action embodies archetypal images designed to draw on the subconscious. Socrates "has only one action and his face (a glass mask) glows ever brighter and brighter . . . The jailers lay hands on him – but only seize phantoms – on each side of him has appeared [the figures of] his NAME and his DEAD BODY . . . He looks like Dionysius."[9]

Similarly, in the masque of *Psyche,* which he also called a "Project for Ballet," the swirling groups of pointing figures from *Hunger* were internalized rather than social symbols. They represented the "doubts and fears" of the heroine, who herself stood for an element of the subconscious. In his notes on seventeenth-century French theater Craig had admired the daring vision capable of conceiving *"une gloire"* on the stage, and the themes of his later notes for masques become increasingly religious, even including one titled *World Creation,* which asserted that "in the beginning . . . the Spirit of God moved upon the face of the waters – Consider – First the movement comes before all else. It was the beginning, it must be *our* beginning."[10]

When Craig looked back on his progress from the perspective of 1905, the year of his first major essay outlining the principles of his theater, he rejected even his Purcell productions on the grounds that "we may have 'interpreted' better – but we *created* not a jot," and listed his masques as the "first attempts" at creating his new art form. However, these masques were basically extensions of conventional theater and still relied on the ordinary resources of the stage. They also retained plot and motivation, however minimal, and characters, however symbolic. In essence, they simply translated the spoken word into a visual language that was its equivalent rather than an alternative. Craig's true aim was far more radical. *"If you can find in nature a new material, one which has never yet been used by man to give form to his thoughts, then you can say you are on the high road towards creating a new art."*[11]

This was a tall order. But if it meant anything, it at least meant that drama created out of conventional elements would be of as little use as the work of playwrights like Shakespeare and Shaw. The new theater had to have "pieces of its own art" to perform. Inspired by Isadora Duncan, Craig saw the artists of his future theater as "ministers to the supreme force – movement," which could act as direct revelation of the spiritual instead of obliquely representing it through the shapes of the physical world. "The Art of the Theater [by which Craig always meant his new art form, as distinct from all other types of theater] has sprung from action–movement–dance."[12] Every element had to embody this, and Craig's masques should be seen as pointers in that direction, with their affinity to ballet and their capacity for development toward such a symbolic abstraction as *World Creation*.

Working tentatively toward this, Craig had begun to make designs that he listed as "A Movement Design for Theatre" and "A Study in Scene and Movement," rather than designs for existing plays. Then he started to construct imaginary dramas around them. In these, the movement of figures and light replaced plot. There was no dramatic action in the usual sense, but rather a developing progression of emotional states. If in his view the theater had to "strive towards the condition of music," this was the spatial equivalent of a symphony or – perhaps more accurately – a tone poem. As examples he created four designs simply titled *The Steps*, each representing a "mood." Experiments with the opportunities for movement provided by steps had long occupied him, from the series of broad platforms that made up the original stage for *Dido and Aeneas* to the sharply sloping rock construct of *The Vikings*. One of the scenes for *Psyche* was little more than a complex structure of staircases, with two on each side leading up to a central platform in a pyramidal shape, and two further sets running diagonally down from their mid-point to join in a central flight of steps at the bottom. Sixteen out of thirty-eight designs in *Towards A New Theatre* included steps in one form or another, and in one the stairway was designated as a "neutral spot." Now, in 1905, this neutrality became a central dramatic focus, to be filled with subtly evocative changes in significance. "Among all dreams that the architect has laid upon the earth, I know of no more lovely things than his flights of steps . . . I have often thought how one could give life (not a voice) to these places, using them to a dramatic end . . . And so I began with a drama called *The Steps*."[13]

Each of the four "acts" or "moods" had the same setting: a long, broad flight of steps that filled the whole stage between two high walls. But different colors and angles of light, harmonizing with the expressive movement and positioning of human figures, were designed to create sharp changes in emotional effect. The brightness of morning was set against the shadows of evening, groups of children against single actors, leaping dances against solemn, flowing gestures, to create visual rhythms of counterpoint and parallels. These rhythms were intended to make such a powerful impression that the scene itself would appear to echo them. For example, in the second mood, Craig showed "many girls and boys jumping about like fire-flies" on the level above the steps, while on the flat space below "in the foreground, and furthest from them, I have made the earth respond to their movements. The earth is made to dance." By con-trast, in the fourth mood people are largely immobile or absent, and it is objects in the scene that provide the main movement. The time, night, corresponds to the emotional state represented by the only visible figure, sorrow. He moves briefly "hither and thither upon this highway of the world" from the shadowed to the moonlit wall, against which he leans, near the bottom of the steps, and remains motionless with his head sunk on his breast.

*The Steps,* fourth mood: the use of visual parallels and counterpoint to evoke mood.

Then things commence to stir; at first ever so slowly, then with increasing rapidity. Up above him you see the crest of a fountain rising like the rising moon when it is heavy in autumn. It rises and rises, now and then in a great throe, but more often regularly. Then a second fountain appears. Together they pour out their natures in silence. When these streams have risen to their full height, the last movement commences. Upon the ground is outlined in warm light the carved shapes of two large windows and in the centre of one of these is the shadow of a man and a woman. The figure on the steps raises his head. The drama is finished.[14]

The two fountains, occupying the same space where the children danced in the second mood, provide a visual equivalent to the joy the children derive from the world of nature, though the reference to autumn translates youthful innocence into stately maturity. The light cast from the windows echoes the configuration of the fountains, in the same way that the floor "danced" in response to the children's movements. An audience is clearly expected to go through the sequence of feeling presented by the stage, from world-weary sorrow and isolation to hope and the promise of fulfillment. Yet the expression of these emotional states is left abstract, so that each spectator can define them in terms of his or her personal experience. In short, the type of "revelation" contained in this art of movement relates to the audience. Each spectator is led to discover his inner nature, to accept its potential, and to perceive his existence on this level as an integral part of the cyclical patterns of nature.

The key element here, the "new material" out of which a new art form might be created, was the moving scene. Its origins were in Craig's use of plain drapes to form stark architectural shapes, suggestive rather than representational, for act 4 of *Venice Preserved*. As he commented with reference to that design, "When I began looking into the idea [of employing curtains in place of scenery], I saw almost infinite possibilities in it, and . . . developed the idea until it began to grow into a serious study." By 1907 he was creating a type of setting that would be more flexible than drapes, and that was capable of being moved invisibly to create continually changing shapes; one that could be used "to translate what we call *Movement*" independently of actors or dancers: his screens.[15] Even though these were announced as a revolutionary new principle, designed for a purely abstract form of stage presentation, they were never in fact intended to be self-sufficient. They provided a context for actors, not a replacement for them, and the way Craig pushed their adoption for poetic plays indicates that he hoped their use would revolutionize the theater from within instead of directly supersede it. Also they remained to some extent interchangeable with drapes; Craig's deployment of the screens in the first act of his Moscow *Hamlet* was modeled on a design for curtains made six years earlier (see illustration on p. 154).

The earliest sketches show screens arranged in asymmetrical geometric shapes in order to divide the stage into distinct and differently lit acting areas. As preliminary working drawings, these were indeed devoid of human figures, and it has been generally assumed that they represent the move toward pure abstraction that Craig apparently was calling for in his essays. But when he began to develop the principles for their use on a model stage, he always included actors in the form of cardboard or wooden miniatures. When photos were taken of the model without these figures, Craig inked them in. One of their functions may have been (as Edward Craig suggests) simply to give an idea of scale to those model scenes. Yet these two-dimensional cutouts were identical with his famous "Black Figures," and these show a wide variety of clearly defined characters and dramatic poses. (The folds of costumes and details of features were carved in light relief, and Craig found they could be used exactly like woodcuts to make prints). The earlier Black Figures – for "a Greek drama" – represent idealized *actors*. Later ones show actors portraying symbolic archetypes, such as "Fear" and "Lust," whereas the series for *Hamlet* is individualized. They range from heroic stylization to the grotesque, with one (the Second Grave Digger) recalling strongly the Shepherds in *Bethlehem*. These were actually used as models by the cast of the Moscow *Hamlet*. Even in the photographs recording configurations of screens that were not designed for any particular play, the clearly dramatic groupings of many of these figures and the use of sometimes ten or more in a single scene indicate the intended relationship between the screens and conventional theater.

As early as 1896, Craig's notebooks show an interest in techniques such as the use of gauzes to create scenes that could be changed during the action. Now his screens provided a medium that could create

a sense of harmony and a sense of variety at the same time. We may be said to have recovered one of the Unities of the Greek Drama . . . We pass from one scene to another without a break of any kind, and when the change has come we are not conscious of any disharmony between the new scene and that which is past.[16]

Craig saw the screens as the appropriate scenic material for his ideal religious theater because they presented the world of the poetic

Flexible architectural shapes to create the world of the poetic imagination on stage. The model with ten two-dimensional wooden figures shows a simple, architectural use of screens.

imagination, and the first arrangements that he made on his model stage were for a drama that he called "The Poetic Dreamer." There is a popular notion of fantasy as flimsy and floating. Craig's screens, with angles and mass brought out by the shadows from strong sidelighting, by contrast, seemed to give the visions of poetry a sharply-cut reality. Equally, their simplicity provided a ground for the spectators' imagination to work on, as distinct from the ornate scenery ordinarily used for fantasy settings, which presented someone else's imaginings for their admiration. Indeed, to Craig one of the selling points of his screens was their economy. Not only were their initial construction costs low, but also exactly the same screens could be reused for play after play – although Craig later limited their suitability to performances of the kind of tragedy that omits "the trivialities" of daily life and concentrates on "large happenings."[17]

These screens that allowed "1000 shapes" to be created out of a single "scene" were of canvas stretched over wooden frames and were painted in monochrome white or light yellow. (In Moscow Craig also experimented with wood and metal coverings.) They were of varying widths but of uniform height, self-supporting, double-hinged, and mounted on retractable castors to provide maximum flexibility. In themselves, they were an extension of the "flats" out of which interior scenes are ordinarily built on the stage. But although the screens' novelty lay more in the concept of how they were to be used than in the objects themselves, Craig managed to patent them as "Improvements in Stage Scenery," and his application is worth quoting as a comprehensive description of his aims:

In the representation of such plays [poetic drama] the producer has hitherto been obliged to choose between the alternatives of either employing scenery formed and painted so as to produce the illusion of the actual scene intended by the playwright, or using plain curtains as a background. Many persons have come to the conclusion that the latter method has certain aesthetic advantages and it has the material advantage of cheapness and easy transport.

The object of my invention is to produce a device which shall present the aesthetic advantages of the plain curtain but shall further be capable of a multitude of effects which although not intended to produce an illusion shall nevertheless assist the imagination of the spectator by suggestion.

My device is further intended to combine the artistic variety and mechanical advantages of painted scenery with the portable nature of the curtain . . .

The screens may be used as background and in addition . . . may be arranged as to project into the foreground at various angles of perspective so as to suggest various physical conditions, such as, for example, the corner of a street, or the interior of a building; by this means suggestion, not representation, is relied upon and nevertheless variety is obtainable.[18]

The specifications provided illustrations of how those arrangements might work in practice. Diagrams 1 and 2 show the interior of a room that could be changed in the course of a performance to suggest the walls and receding perspectives of a street or town square (in diagrams 5 and 6) by shifting only two screens.

Craig hoped originally that this invention would be picked up by other directors, who would create new arrangements and discover for themselves, through mastering its potential for mobility, that abstract movement was the essence of drama. The only principle he suggested at first was that "the aim of the Arranger is to place his screens in such a position that by moving the minimum number of leaves he may produce the desired amount of variety."[19] With this in mind he presented Yeats with a set of screens for the Irish National Theater in 1909.

Yeats experimented with them for almost a year, and was so excited by the possibilities for creating moods from expressive light and shade that he completely rewrote *Deirdre* to take advantage of them. In composing a play, once he had created an outline of the action, he worked out the context for each scene on a set of model screens, then wrote the dialogue around it. In 1911 the Abbey Theater staged three plays with Craig's ivory-colored screens. But

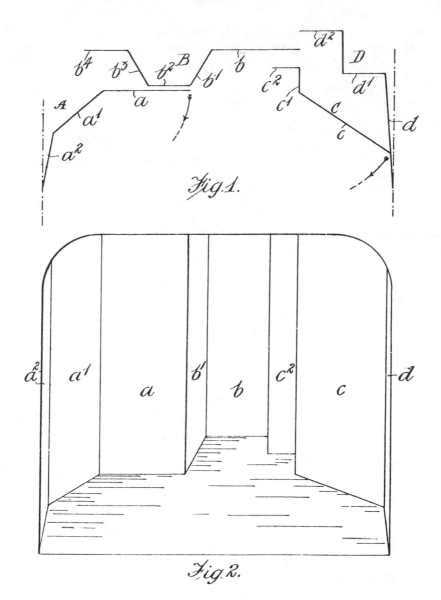

Fig. 1.

Fig. 2.

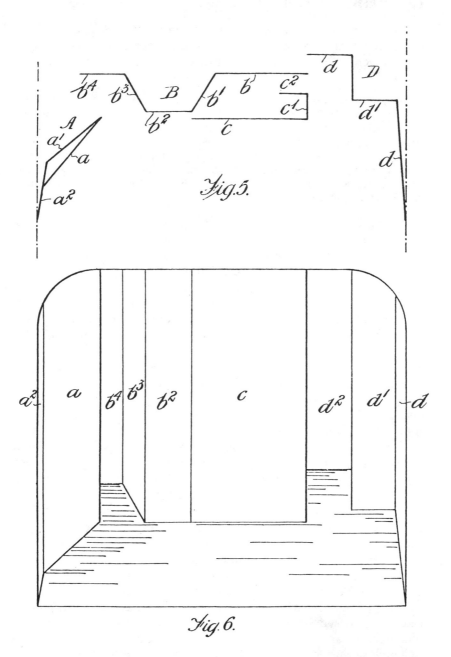

*Fig.5.*

*Fig. 6.*

The patent specifications for Craig's screens (January, 1910), illustrating the simple changes needed to transform an interior into an exterior.

for the most successful of these productions, *The Hour Glass*, Yeats turned to Craig for the screen arrangements of each scene. The results were a striking departure from Yeats's earlier practice:

Up till the present year we always played it in front of an olive green curtain, and dressed the Wise Man and his Pupils in various shades of purple (with a little green here and there) and because in all these decorative schemes, which are based on colour, one needs, I think, a third colour subordinate to the other two, we dressed the Fool in red-brown . . . Last winter, however, we revived the play with costumes taken chiefly from the designs by Mr. G. Craig, and with screens he has shown us how to make and use . . . with effects that depend but little on colour, and greatly upon delicate changes of tone.[20]

The reception was favorable, although some of the praise was hardly what Craig wanted. One review praised the "more or less *static* scene as a [harmonious] medium for the presentment of such poetic dramas," and another referred to the limelight from the auditorium as "throwing a *glaring* yellow light on the screen." Yeats was pleased with the elegant simplicity of the screens and the delicacy of natural lighting achieved with them (in contrast to having effects of highlight and shadow painted on the scenery, as had been the Abbey practice up to then). But quite apart from that, he was enthusiastic because with the screens "one enters into a world of decorative effect which gives the actor a renewed importance. There is less to compete against him, for there is less detail, though there is more beauty." After seeing these productions, Jack Yeats wrote to Craig that "all the play writers ought to have model theaters with your screens and they should fold them about until they suggest a play to them" – as he said he now did himself. He commented, however, that he had seen only interiors on the Abbey stage and could not imagine the screens suggesting any outdoor landscape, except street scenes, successfully.[21] Perhaps it was this that prompted Craig to add "extra pieces" to the screens in the form of doorways, windows, and (for *On Baile's Strand* in 1914) pictorial screens with windswept trees or rocky cliffs outlined on them.

At a public demonstration with his miniature screens in 1911, Craig created contrasting scenes for Hofmannsthal's *Electra*, a Molière comedy, a winding Italian street, and an Egyptian temple. Reports stressed how effective this simple instrument was: "One obtained vistas of colonnades and pillars, dim recesses lost in the distance or suddenly made visible by the play of electric light. The illusion was very complete." Craig received requests for his screens from two English theaters. He let Yeats, as an artist who shared his aims, experiment with them to discover new effects, but in practice Craig was not prepared to allow others the same freedom. He insisted that plans for the layout of the screens had to be obtained from him for each play, not just the first, and that "nothing be altered or added."[22]

In the same way, when he presented Ellen Terry with a set of eighteen-foot-high screens with which to perform *The Merchant of Venice,* he drew outlines of all the positions for each screen and light as well as giving her a demonstration of the intended effects on his model stage. These designs are complex, with sinuous curving shapes across the stage in one scene, necessitating a large number of thin screens, receding perspectives, and straight walls for the next. Here, as in his public demonstration, the screens were used as the

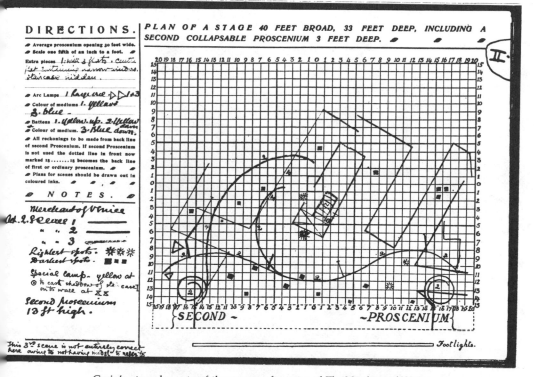

Craig's stage layouts of the screens for act 2 of *The Merchant of Venice,* 1911. In scene 3 (Shakespeare's scenes 3, 4, 5, and 6), the hidden steps lead up to an "extra piece" – a six-foot-high rostrum used for Jessica's balcony – and the false thirteen-foot-high inner proscenium is required to mask the tops of the screens.

Ellen Terry, with screens arranged for act 3 of *The Merchant of Venice*, 1911.

equivalent of conventional scenery; but the scene changes were too major for their movements to be made in view of the audience, apparently autonomously, without the stage hands appearing and without a break in the action. Perhaps for this reason Ellen Terry never used them. The only full test of their potential was Craig's own *Hamlet* production in Moscow.

Of all Shakespeare's plays, *Hamlet* was Craig's most constant preoccupation. The Prince of Denmark had been one of his first leading roles as an actor, and when he played it in London in 1896 he wore Irving's costume from the Lyceum production of ten years before. As the last piece he personally directed, with the isolated exception of *The Pretenders* sixteen years later, it therefore spans the whole of his work on the stage – as distinct from the ideal theater of his imagination – and continued to be a frequent reference point in his writing. Despite his call for "the abolition of the spoken word," and his conviction that tragedy in particular demanded the silence of naked action removed from the verbalizing that brought in everyday concerns, *Hamlet* remained in his view a play for dialogue – precisely because, to him, Hamlet's tragedy lies in the fact that he talks instead of acts. The remarkable consistency of his interpretation of the play indicates the underlying coherence of his work. Indeed, his 1912 production harked back to Irving's own reading of the character: "The eye should be wild, not vacant, and the glances piercing . . . his melancholy rises with striking and noble images, to an astounding pitch of sublimity. The tone and manner should have a correspondent weight or majesty."[23]

By 1907 Stanislavski was moving beyond the naturalistic "crickets and mosquitoes" of his Chekhov productions in search of a deeper kind of realism that would reflect "the life of the human spirit." But his experiments with symbolist drama – Knut Hamsun's *The Drama of Life,* Leonid Andreyev's *The Life of Man,* and Maeterlinck's *The Bluebird* – had been unsuccessful. The acting techniques he had developed for internalizing emotion and translating unexpressed thoughts into physical action were useless for plays that had abstract figures and no subtext. In *The Life of Man,* Stanislavski discovered some effectively illusionistic stage tricks, such as a black velvet background (allegedly taken from Beardsley's art) against which characters and props could be made to materialize or disappear like visions. But these were simply external, and Maeterlinck had complained that the mystical level of his *Bluebird* fantasy was totally missing. So, prompted by Isadora Duncan (who was as horrified by the black velvet as Craig himself was to be on seeing *The Life of Man* when he arrived at Moscow in 1908), and impressed by the first copy of *The Mask*, Stanislavski invited Craig to direct *Hamlet* for the Art Theater.

This was undoubtedly the most carefully prepared of all Craig's productions. Because of its postponement when Stanislavski fell seriously ill, Craig had three years to think it through, even though publication of *The Mask* took up much of his time. On his visits to Moscow he discussed each scene and the psychology of the characters in detail with Stanislavski, and in Italy he worked out every movement with his screens on a model stage constructed to the dimensions of the Moscow Art Theater (MAT) and fitted with eight rows of electric lights that duplicated its lighting system. He then demonstrated these to Stanislavski and to his aide Suler (Sulerzhitski), who rehearsed the actors.

Craig complained that working at such a distance forced him to create settings, to design costumes, and to dictate the *mise-en-scène* separately, instead of doing all three "things together and on the stage of the theatre, so that they should be one piece . . . so that that one piece should have one impulse behind it." Yet when he outlined an ideal method of directing, it followed his practice here, though with one significant addition: direct involvement of the actors in the creative process. After roughing in the dramatic situations in very broad terms, the scenes were to be constructed in miniature and the positions of each actor plotted with cutout figures. The "director or inventor in chief" then runs through the whole performance on the model stage for the actors, who now "elaborate the pattern" in discussion, and "such suggestions as seem to strengthen the action" are written down. At this point only is the production transferred to the full-size stage, and the actors work through the play with every improvisation carefully noted by stenographers. A second run-through on his model stage follows, incorporating the improvisations and including "each actor speaking for his special figure." Further rehearsals then "finish everything *up to a point*." Up to a point only, because (as Craig wrote, his concept of an Uebermarionette notwithstanding) even during the public performances the actors should be free to improvise, and the director's task is simply "to cut out all which is unnecessary." Indeed, after the preliminary rehearsals in Moscow, Craig reported, "I was never so clear as at present as to what I want . . . In *Hamlet* I am nearer my *Masque of Love* than *Vikings*."[24]

Although the final shape of the production fell in some ways far short of what he had imagined, Craig's interpretation was true to his concept of an interior, spiritual form of drama. His basic idea of the play as a conflict between two mutually destructive elements – Hamlet as spirit versus all that surrounds him as matter – exactly corresponded to his analysis of *Macbeth* in the first copy of *The Mask*. So did his use of a very limited range of symbolic colors to indicate the relative amounts of these two elements in each character, and to unify all the figures into a mass that would harmonize with the scene. When Stanislavski complained that the costumes were "shabby, uninteresting, quite the opposite of exquisite," he discovered that Craig indeed intended the costumes to "sink into the scene and be lost, so that for once the actors' faces and voices will tell the tale without interruption."[25] All were in shades of somber gray and beige (apart from Gertrude and Claudius, whose regal robes were gold – and Ophelia, for whom Stanislavski substituted white in deference to the romantic preconceptions of his public) with specks of scarlet or green highlighting textures, and lines of gold on folds.

Craig's design for the court scene, with Hamlet reclining downstage and the screens arranged in a flat wall across the rear.

The best example was in Craig's staging of the court scene of act 1. Gertrude and Claudius were set on a gold-backed throne high above the courtiers, whose heads appeared to protrude through slits in a single vast golden cloak that swirled down from their shoulders to hump over the seated or crouched figures massed below. (In fact the unity was illusory. An actress playing one of the courtiers has described how the effect was achieved: For this scene, all the people on stage, dressed entirely in gold, "were arranged on wooden platforms so as to represent symbolically the feudal ladder . . . The actors were distributed on various planes, their mantles flowed out and gave the impression of a monolithic golden pyramid.") Limes turned the neutral color of the straight wall of screens behind into a dull yellow, and a diagonal shaft of light fell on the throne "like molten gold." In front, alone and in a band of deep shadow, Hamlet reclined "fallen, as it were, into a dream." A light black tulle curtain, or gauze, was stretched directly behind him and cut him off sharply from these gold-draped figures, giving them a misty effect. On Claudius's line, "Come away," this gauze was slowly loosened so that, although the figures remained in place, their outlines were gradually blotted out as if they receded from Hamlet's thoughts rather than moved off the stage. As Craig explained to Stanislavski, "In this golden court, this world of show, there must not be various individualities as there would in a realistic play. No, here everything melts into a single mass." This was so impressive that the scene received an ovation (something unheard of at the MAT). One reviewer enthusiastically described the blurring of the outlines as the fog rolling in, but this effect was not simply decorative. Rather, it illustrated one of Craig's main principles: "In a poetic play the figures – faces – costumes – and all should be so much *one* that they actually resemble each other. *Unity is necessary* . . . All the parts of the play should so adhere one to the other that they make up the play."[26]

This was one of the few scenes that remained exactly as Craig envisaged it, perhaps because his concept was remarkably close to ideas that Stanislavski had already developed before Craig first arrived in Moscow.[27] It was also the kernel from which Craig's interpretation grew. It incorporated elements from some of his first ideas for *Hamlet:* The positioning of Hamlet in shadow downstage, set sharply apart from the well-lit court at the rear, had appeared in a sketch as early as 1901. The double throne and voluminous cloak came from a sketch of 1905 for the play scene, and the grouping and the gauze dividing Hamlet from the court were already set in the design of 1906, in which Craig first noted the type of curtain arrangement that developed into his screens. Here he had also envisaged a multiplying group of kings and queens ranged down each side of the scene, and on another sketch, showing a king seated on a throne with a similar zigzag arrangement of wall downstage right, Craig noted that "his thoughts [are] unfolded on the screens by his conscience, a figure who appears first." Both these ideas were discarded, although they survived in a modified form well into rehearsals for the "To be or not to be" scene. Suler recorded that "at the end of the soliloquy Hamlet stands behind the tulle with an enormous shadow in back of him. On the side screens shadows are continually moving around him and with him, flickering like black fumes"; Craig's sketch of the scene shows these shadows as elongated figures echoing and multiplying Hamlet's posture.[28] But the dreamlike symbolism carried through in more general terms, as did the single plain set that varied in shape from scene to scene, and these became the central concepts of Craig's production.

The golden court scene, representing "the note of tyranny and grandeur," was specifically Hamlet's dream, which the audience sees through his eyes. The whole play was conceived as a monodrama, and at one point Craig wanted Hamlet, in whose mind this vision was played out, on stage throughout every scene: "He can be in the distance, lying, sitting, in front of the people acting, at the side, behind, but the spectator ought never to lose sight of him." Similarly, to bring out the spiritual pole of the play, he envisaged introducing openly symbolic figures to externalize Hamlet's thoughts: Madness, Murder – and in particular, Death, a female shape who would appear at Hamlet's side during his "To be or not to be" monologue and remain there in all the following scenes, as inseparable from him as his shadow.

Death in fact became one of the keynotes of Craig's interpretation of the play. The performance opened with the Ghost. Against high gray screens, suggesting castle ramparts rising out of shadows that masked the gaps of entrances between each set of screens, the phantom appeared to emerge out of the walls. Far from the regal apparition of Shakespeare's text, this supernatural figure represented the physical horror of death in an image drawn from medieval iconography with what Stanislavski called "ultra-realism": a corpse devoured by worms and wrapped in a decaying shroud that hobbled its legs, the tatters of which suggested shreds of flesh hanging from whitened bones. By contrast, a second death figure, female instead of male, was to be associated with ecstatic music. This figure was Ham-

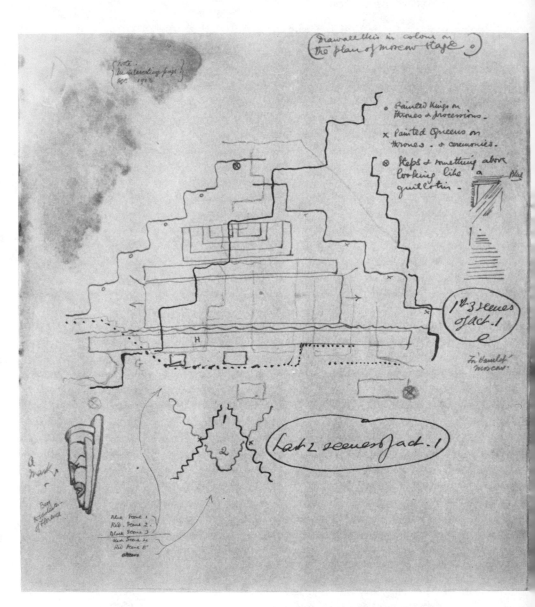

Craig's 1906 stage layout for act 1 of *Hamlet*, with the wavy lines indicating the drapes that the screens replaced. (The references to Moscow date from at least two years later.)

let's alter ego, invisible to him but enticing him onward. She embodied death in the sense that Craig referred to it in his essays: the world of the imagination, directly reflecting the life of the spirit and completely divorced from the physical world. "She must be beautiful, glowing, and during his reverie she leans towards him and lays her head on his shoulder." Stanislavski persuaded Craig to adopt a more conventional presentation of the play, for he was afraid that the Russian public would simply reject his ideas in toto if they were shown in such a radical form. Hamlet's Daemon appeared in the Cranach *Hamlet*, an edition published by Kessler in 1929 and lavishly illustrated by Craig with woodcuts – both Black Figures and compositions of movable blocks representing the screen arrangements. Craig began working on this edition immediately after the production, and considered it his definitive interpretation of the play. But even in Moscow, the psychological approach was kept. As Hamlet's vision, the court was "the grotesque caricature of a vile kind of royalty," and Claudius spoke "as if he were an automaton; his jaws snap on the words, he grunts them out ferociously."[29]

Despite Stanislavski's caution, Craig not only cut out all the stage directions (with more justice than in *the Vikings* or *Bethlehem* because, as he had pointed out in "The Art of the Theatre," these were generally later additions to Shakespeare's text, representing conventionally accepted interpretations), but also altered the emphasis of long passages considerably and introduced additional scenes. On one level, he saw the play in terms of "A Masque of Theatre," one that reflected his own artistic aims. "In *Hamlet* all that is living in the theatre is struggling with these dead customs that want to crush the theatre." He enlarged the role of the Actors, together with their dumb show of "The Murder of Gonzago." He added a scene in which they donned costumes and makeup, tuned musical instruments, and warmed up with vocal exercises and gestures. Most observers felt that this interpolated backstage activity crystallized the theatricality of the whole production, and the Actors' performance became the climax of the play. Their faces were sharply illuminated by hand-held lights stretched out immediately in front of them on the ends of long staffs. Above the sleeping king's couch was a cutout moon strung on a rope between two poles (with the grouping corresponding exactly to the print in the Cranach *Hamlet*). Their gestures were stylized and exaggerated. The emotions expressed by the Actor declaiming his set speech on Priam's death were echoed by the movements of a choral group, and the dumb show was accompanied by an on-stage orchestra who interpreted the music

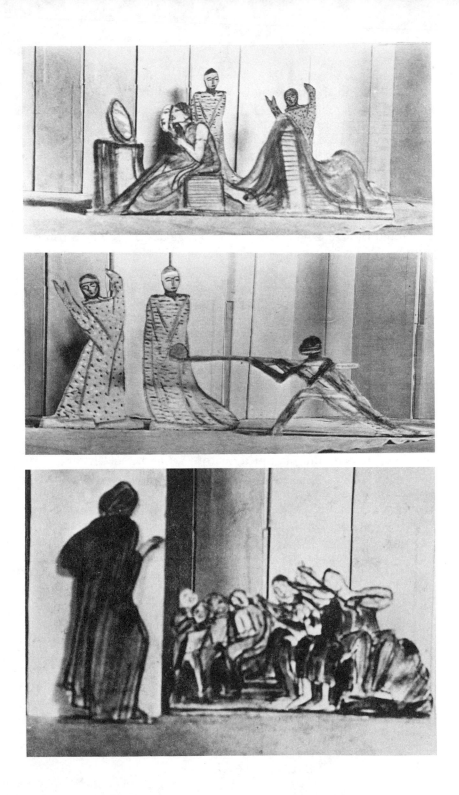

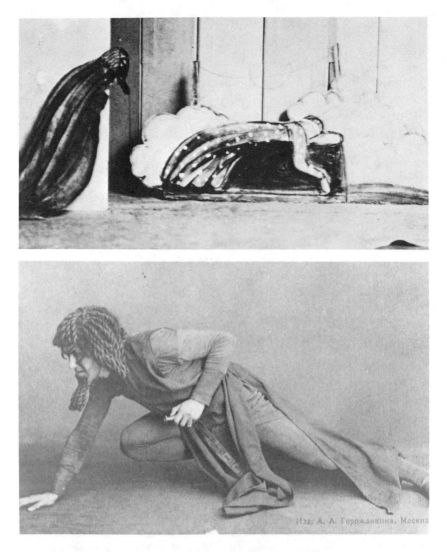

The Actors' scenes as worked out with Black Figures on Craig's model
stage, and their translation into production: Actors making-up; the use of
hand-held lamps to illuminate their performance; the orchestral accompaniment; the dumb show murder of Gonzago; B. M. Alfonin in the dumb
show.

they played with their bodies. The Actors were also intended to wear larger than life-size masks, but Stanislavski reduced these to elaborately formalized wigs and beards.

Craig had wanted this quality of overt performance to carry through the whole production, with stagehands in special costumes coming onto the stage at the beginning of each scene to set the lights and arrange the scenery. He even suggested that everything "be conveyed without words, by the movements of the actors illustrated by music," so giving the whole play the status of the dumb show. When this was rejected out of hand, he urged that there be a small orchestra on stage throughout, the music of which would key the tone for the actors' delivery and impose uniformity. True to his "system," Stanislavski opposed this on the grounds that any "music" must come from the actors' personal emotions, not from externally regulated intonation. But Craig insisted that Shakespeare, unlike Chekhov, contained no feelings to be found between the lines because everything was directly expressed in the dialogue, and he persuaded Stanislavski to try a rhetorical style of acting, "hard and cold – conventional in its movements and in its sounds." For Craig, artifice – if it were based on the play element of theatricality and not on pretentiousness – was the key to reforming drama. By reducing live human expressiveness to two-dimensional stylization it might be possible to move beyond everyday appearances to the spiritual world of the imagination. So, he claimed, "if we were to conventionalize each movement and sound we should create, as it were, an impression of something *flat* . . . To conventionalize life's movements and sounds is to create a new kind of life, and in my opinion that is the whole reason for the existence of the artist."[30]

In Craig's view, this could be achieved by the type of acting he admired in Irving, who swept on and off the stage, struck attitudes, glared, gasped, whispered with bated breath, and chanted his words. It might come perhaps more directly, from selecting only the most significant images, following the principle that a director's task was to cut out all but the essential actions. This was Craig's aim here: "No movement unless necessary. Thin out all . . . until none but the six or ten *main movements* in the scene are left." The same process of simplification was to be applied to the dialogue. For instance, Craig believed that only the first and last sentences of Hamlet's speech, "Seems, madam? nay it is; I know not 'seems,' " were needed. "These four lines express an important thought and must be spoken accordingly. All the rest of the monologue must be pronounced more as music, so that the thought becomes so much lost

in the sounds that the audience simply *does not follow* the thought."
The same kind of musical tirade, a bravura style that Craig admired
in Italian acting, was to be used for the whole of act 1, scene 3.
When Stanislavski objected that "in order to play a scene at such a
quick tempo the actors would have to move about as little as possible . . . Don't forget that the most difficult thing for an actor is to
stand still in the middle of an empty stage," Craig replied, "Yes,
yes, I know that. But can't you really see Ophelia in this scene,
crying and grimacing, but without any deep feeling, standing motionless in one place with hardly any movement?"[31]

What Craig never seemed to realize was that these stylized approaches were all too open to misinterpretation, both by the actors
and by the audience. Being derived from widely known and accepted conventions, they could hardly help but evoke the same
range of preconceptions and responses. As Bernard Shaw had already discovered, using the melodramatic form meant that a play
became limited in performance to melodrama, however different its
true content might have been. And the Irvingesque rant was just as
likely to be mistaken for the kind of artificiality that exaggerates in
order to cover the absence of real feeling. Similarly, "flat" characterization could too easily be reduced to the oversimplification that
Strindberg argued against when he rejected stock figures identified
only by a single phrase such as "Barkis is willing."

Indeed, as always, the acting in *Hamlet* failed to measure up to
what Craig had imagined. There may have been intrinsic flaws in
his theory of stylized acting, but in fact the performance could
hardly be called a fair test of it. The actors felt that he was making
impossible demands. Hamlet was to enter in one scene as if swept
in by a gale, then bend forward to touch the ground with outstretched arms, twisting his torso in movements that were simultaneously sharp, musical, and plastic, and end by stretching upward
with his spine arched backward to the audience. When Ophelia
swooned she was to hurl herself headlong down a steep flight of
stairs. Kachalov, as Hamlet, was low-key and almost scholarly –
anything but the physical actor Craig required. Alisa Koonen, who
played Ophelia, complained that Craig's directions were unrealizable and that "no actress could do it."

In the court scene – in which the actors did try to achieve the effect
Craig designed – the courtiers, whose costumes weighed as much as
thirty-five pounds, had to remain absolutely still for so long that
some of the actresses lost consciousness. But the real problem was
that the cast was never given a clear picture of Craig's concept.

From stylization to melodrama: N. O. Massalitinov as Claudius, O. L. Knipper as Gertrude, V. I. Kachalov as Hamlet.

Partly because of the language difficulties, Craig never rehearsed the actors himself, and there were complaints from the performers that he showed no interest in them. He isolated himself with his model theater, and worked entirely through intermediaries – Stanislavski and Suler – who were used to a very different style of acting.

However, Stanislavski had been well into preliminary rehearsals before any discussions with Craig about characterization or blocking, so that from the start Craig was working against preconceived ideas. Long breaks in the production process, together with cast changes, compounded the difficulties. In addition, by 1911 Stanislavski was using rehearsals to test his developing system of realistic acting. Craig wanted three quite distinct tones in the presentation: realism for the scenes of comic relief, heightened realism verging on caricature for the tragic action, and abstraction for Hamlet. Stanislavski provided Kachalov with subtexts for each of Hamlet's scenes, ignoring Craig's earlier insistence that in Shakespeare every emotion is directly expressed, and wrote asking Craig's permission to present the characters more subtly and less "naively." The result can be illustrated by the interpretation of Polonius. Craig conceived of him as a toad, and he was made to look like one. His head, with its straggling white hair and heavy-lidded eyes, was topped with a skull cap covered with wart-like diamonds and squares. But the characterization of Polonius was understated and naturalistic.

In any case it was unrealistic to hope to establish a radically unconventional acting style in a single production. Indeed, Stanislavski had originally offered Craig an ongoing contract for several productions, with at least two in the first year, as he realized that "only constant training can bring forth the results desired" from the actors. Inevitably all that could be achieved was a compromise. This was underlined in a public statement by Suler: "Our theatre, having learnt from Craig, is trying to bring to fruition everything *that it considers feasible.*" But unfortunately, as at least one reviewer noted, compromise destroyed the integrity of Craig's vision and conflicted with the effect of the screens.

A conventionalized staging requires conventionalized acting: the Art Theater did not understand this . . . life-like movements, life-like gestures should have been indicated by conventionalized gestures, like those we see in old Byzantine icons . . . monochrome denuded walls, even the very stone graveyard with square pillars would not have seemed strange and out of place if we had seen in them life as "conventionalized" in substance, with conventionalized gestures and vocal intonations.[32]

In fact it is surprising that so much of Craig's symbolic interpretation came across, and this can only be seen as evidence for the powerful imaginative effect of the screens. They clearly imposed a unity of tone and a degree of abstraction that were sufficient in themselves to color any naturalistic acting, and Jacques Rouché, the director of the Théâter des Arts in Paris, believed he had seen a work that was completely original in the stylization and simplification of both scenery and character.

Whether the conventionalized acting Craig envisaged could ever have worked remains an open question. Stanislavski reported that the actors had been forced to revert to his naturalistic method of presentation because, in attempting to speak the verse Craig's way, they "fell back upon declamation, a dead seesaw rhythm." Craig responded that they had lacked the commitment that alone could give formalization imaginative substance. "You did weakly what I would have had you do powerfully. You fell back instead of advancing . . . because you had sworn *never to be theatrical,* and that is the sole thing to be." At the same time, he was at least equally responsible, having effectively boycotted rehearsals ("For why see too often what cannot be corrected?"). There is a great deal of unintended irony in such diary entries as: "Wolkonsky also spoke of my production of *Hamlet* – he had seen 3 acts rehearsed yesterday. This is more than I have seen!! . . . it is hard to remain patient and silent while my imaginings are being messed about."[33]

As Craig spoke neither Russian nor French, and Stanislavski no English, there were problems of communication at all points in the production. It is doubtful whether either understood the other's interpretation of the play, and the transcript of their discussions gives the impression of two parallel monologues that never meet, with one of Stanislavski's constant remarks being, "that is another play." Stanislavski thought Craig believed that art could be created only out of "dead material" and that he "dreamed of a theatre without men and women, without actors. He wanted to supplant them with marionettes." This was a good example of how Craig's way of exaggerating to challenge preconceived ideas actually worked against him. All Craig later claimed to have meant was that the dead material of the existing theater and realistic acting had to be removed, and – far from wanting puppets completely subordinated to the will of a director-artist – Craig found that he disliked the cast's lack of initiative.

Although he clung to his ideal of an Uebermarionette as an actor who was totally in control of his emotions and his means of expressing them, Craig commented that "after two years of this Moscow Art Theatre I find in it a man who has an even worse opinion of the Actor than I have – Stanislavski. He uses them as one uses needle and threads – It is . . . quite inhuman." If he had in fact wanted to reduce the status of the actor, as readers of his essays popularly supposed, this was his first real opportunity. Instead he reaffirmed the necessity for improvisation, even if with the reasonable proviso that it always correspond to and reinforce the director's underlying concept.

Similarly, Stanislavski, misled by a reference in one of Craig's letters, thought Craig wanted Hamlet portrayed as a Christ figure. Actually, Craig had tried to describe a visionary like Shelley or Blake, and in fact projected himself into the play. As Craig was later to comment, "I have so much more to add about *Hamlet* under the title of 'Hamlet and my very self.' "[34] In preparing the production he

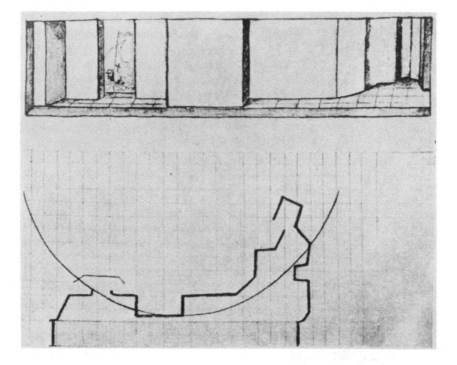

Ground plan and elevation for act 1, scene 3 (Laerte's departure), showing one of the "extra pieces" – the ship painted on a special screen.

had come to identify with Hamlet, and saw the Ghost as his own father and Ophelia as all the numerous women who had disappointed him.

It is hard to see how this suggestion could have been effectively put across on the stage. At the same time it clearly relates to Craig's concept of the play as a monodrama, and to a great extent the originality of his interpretation was due to its autobiographical nature. But even when Craig's readings were specific, Stanislavski tended to revert to conventional images. The worst example was the characterization of Ophelia. Craig had insisted that all of Polonius's family were "despicable people . . . It is only when she begins to go mad that she gradually grows into a more sympathetic figure." When asked why such an idealistic person as Hamlet would fall in love with "an insignificant little creature," the answer was that "he was in love with his own imagination, with an imaginary woman." However, by the time of the performance the accepted sentimental view of a meek Ophelia – so gentle that rejection of her love kills her, so noble that she is still able to bless the man who destroys her – had replaced this psychologically perceptive (and autobiographical) interpretation, and Ophelia was presented as "a girl with a pure soul."[35]

The same watering down of Craig's ideas affected even the screens, though this was the element of the production most directly under his control, and one that reviews singled out for praise:

Mr. Craig has the singular power of carrying the spiritual significance of words and dramatic situations beyond the actor to the scene in which he moves. By the simplest of means he is able in some mysterious way to evoke almost any sensation of time or space, the scenes even in themselves suggesting variations of human emotion . . . A completely realized success of his theories.[36]

As the evidence of Craig's models shows, there was to be a different arrangement of screens for each of the twenty scenes in the play. They could radically alter the size and shape of the acting area, changing from a flat wall across the very rear of the stage for the court scene to a claustrophobic enclosure with corners jutting forward almost to the proscenium for Polonius's study. The shape could also provide a spatial representation of a character's state of mind, as in act 3, scene 3, in which concave leading into convex curving walls echoed the indecision of Hamlet's "Now might I do it, pat . . ." Or, by moving some screens while leaving others in the same position from one scene to another, they could give a sense of progressive develop-

Model for act 2, scene 1 (Polonius's study).

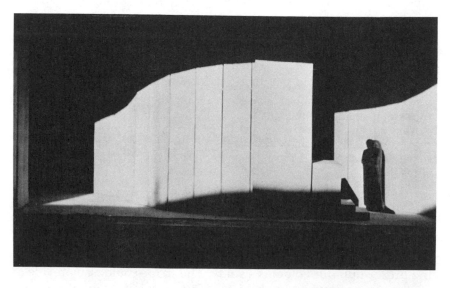

Model for act 3, scene 3 ("Now might I do it, pat"). The double Black Figure represents Hamlet with his Daemon.

ment, as in act 4. Here the continual transformations provided a
vision of subtly shifting relationships, at least in Craig's vision. (In
the actual production, the first three scenes of act 4 were all cut, as
indeed was the King's prayer scene, omitted at the final dress rehearsal to prevent the production from running overtime.)

A straight line of a wall with one large rectangle jutting forward,
set diagonally across the stage to form an exterior for the opening
scene, became an enclosed corner by swinging the further end forward onto the other diagonal, while the rectangle shrank into a
square, self-standing column. This column formed the central pillar
in a row of five placed straight across the middle of the stage for the
council hall of scene 3; a row that was then reduced to four, ranged
around a massive circular column in the center area behind as a
fortress like tent for Fortinbras. The line straightened again for scene
6 to form a battlemented wall and lower court, with the pillars being
joined by screens that linked the first with the second and the third
with the fourth at the rear corners, and extended the front edges of
the first and fourth out to the sides, while steep narrow steps filled
the center space. Finally, in the very last scene of the play, the two
center pillars were moved forward and apart, the staircase was replaced by broad low steps, and the background was filled with an
arrangement that suggested perspectives of receding columns, half
temple altar, half palace entrance – though Stanislavski reversed this,
significantly increasing its dramatic effectiveness. He filled the central archway with two rows of massed spears that moved back and
forth to suggest the approach of Fortinbras's army, so that instead of
a perspective into a distant interior, the interior with the bodies of
Hamlet and the others became the foreground.

Oddly, Craig's use of screens has come to be generally considered
an error in judgment, either because it is thought that they were
suited only to portray abstract movement (which meant that using
them as settings for specific actions reduced them to a merely illustrative function), or because it is believed that they were too much at
odds with the existing theater technology to provide the scenic fluid-
ity required for such a play as *Hamlet*.[37] It is certainly true that Craig
had to dispense with the thinly opaque roof over the acting area that
had been intended to complete the visual impression. It is also true
that the complexity of the varying shapes meant that the movement
of the screens could never have been achieved invisibly, or without
any break in the action, as Craig's patent specification suggests
should have been the case. However, most of the critics who consider the screens impractical point as evidence to the passage in

The continuing relationships created by shifting the screens in act 4, scenes 1, 2, 3, 5 and 6.

The model for the final scene of *Hamlet,* later used by Craig as a generalized example of how screens might be "employed for a large stage scene" in any play.

Stanislavski's *My Life in Art,* which describes how the screens fell over the actors like dominoes on the first night. Yet Craig himself repeatedly protested that this never happened at any performance, and demanded that Stanislavski delete the passage from future editions. Even though the description is still there, Stanislavski privately acknowledged that this did not in fact happen during a scene, nor on the first night, but in rehearsal during one of the changes. Eventually, in a letter to Craig, he enclosed a "sworn statement" from the stagehands testifying that the incident was due to their error rather than to any inherent instability in the screens themselves.[38]

The screens constructed by the MAT carpenters do not seem to have followed Craig's patent designs, and being ten feet higher than the sets presented to Yeats or Ellen Terry, may well have been less stable. But the fact that they had collapsed at all, even in rehearsal, meant that the screens were braced and weighted down for the performance, which negated a major part of their value. Any repetition of the accident would of course have been disastrous. But if the risk had been taken, and if Craig's suggestion of specially costumed

The final scene as presented on the Moscow Art Theater stage, with the central screens removed and the massed spears of Fortinbras's army visible.

stagehands had been adopted, there would have been no need for the curtain that covered each change – something on which Stanislavski indeed had always insisted – nor for the long pause that actually occurred between each scene. When there were completely different arrangements of screens in two successive scenes and the change could not be accomplished without breaking the flow, Craig had envisaged music to preserve continuity of mood, as at the end of the opening scene:

Only the glimmer of a glow remains as at the beginning of the scene, that is, in the same place where the Ghost had appeared.
    When the glow dies out, a bell is heard.
    The chime changes to a rumble – the pealing of wedding bells.
The rumble increases and the notes of a cracked bell grow prominent. They are mingled with the sounds of a funeral march, growing ever more distant.

Elsewhere the screens could have been shifted openly during exits and entrances as an integral part of the performance, and with the scenes shortened by speeding up the actors' delivery in the many extended passages that Craig considered less than essential, the effect would have been near the almost continual movement that he envisaged. "No break in the play. The scenes shall grow one out of the other and will be like the dance of the seven veils."[39]

In many ways, the screens seem to be the right instrument for creating the shapes of places "never seen before except in the mind's eye" that Craig considered the only appropriate setting for poetic drama. Even his symbolic interpretation of Hamlet, though highly idiosyncratic and limiting on one level, has fascinating potential, as his analysis of the opening shows:

A sweep of dark sky is indicated with one solitary star; it is a cold night, nothing stirs. Suddenly a bell tolls the hour. A man, hidden until now in the shadow, is seen to rise slowly, and remains listening. Then he paces restlessly to and fro, the place filling him with a certain dread. His march continues. He passes in front of us; now he is engulfed in some huge unfathomable shadow, from which he presently emerges into the grey light. He seems like some ghost; he resembles that which he fears to meet.[40]

As even Suler allowed, however one might rate Craig's instruction to the actors, the poetic quality of his concepts and their translation into an evocative composition were striking. At the same time he was undoubtedly difficult to work with. Apart from his exasperating financial demands, he quarreled with Stanislavski, abducted and seduced Stanislavski's secretary (by his own admission) when Isadora Duncan flirted with Stanislavski over dinner, and antagonized Suler by refusing to allow his name to appear on the program because Suler had questioned some of his decisions.

Such displays of temperament may have been due to Craig's own dissatisfaction with the rehearsal process. However, the production had attracted unprecedented worldwide attention and the foreign reviews were almost uniformly enthusiastic. The Moscow Art Theater's visit to Berlin in 1905 had first established its reputation outside Russia, but it was these reviews that really put the theater on the cultural map for western Europe. They were also partly responsible for Craig at last finding a patron to finance his school. The Russian reviews, however, were highly critical. The more conservative papers attacked the whole interpretation. Those who were impressed by the symbolic concept and the screens damned the acting and made Stanislavski all too aware of the "tremendous distance there is between the scenic dream of an artist . . . and its realization on the stage." Stanislavski himself attributed the gap to the unsatisfactory nature of "all the existing scenic means." But Craig put it down to working through intermediaries, who prevented him from improvising his ideas and imposed a *"pause* between the thought and the act," which "spoils all my work."[41] This immediacy, which would allow a director literally to play on the stage like a musical instrument, was one of the qualities he believed could be realized in Scene – the three-dimensional alternative to the screens that he had prefigured in 1907 with the series of etchings titled "Motion."

During the years of preparation for *Hamlet* he had also visualized other ways of extending the kind of flexibility offered by the screens. He had formulated a distinction between "Two Theatres: A. The theater of space. 1) proportion 2) relationships developing imagination – B. The theatre of speech. When the figure *fills* the space till it dominates the scene [then] its voice can be heard." This pronouncement was accompanied by three small sketches: the first with a large figure filling almost the complete frame, and a tiny tower behind it in the distance to illustrate the dominant single actor; the second with the same figure reduced to minuteness in a huge frame (represented as the same size on paper), and with the tower now a monolithic shape that fills almost the whole height of the opening, showing that when the scene dominates "the figure is not heard"; and a third of the same proportions but with a unified group of actors, in which "the tower still dominates, but the figures must now be heard – as mass."[42] As a rationale for using choral movement to balance the human figure against architectural sets in a way that would really take advantage of the visual potential of the stage, this too contains an essential element of Scene. The shape and position of the tower also strongly resemble a design for the very beginning moments of *Macbeth*, before the witches enter. This design of stony ledges rising to a single, square-sided column of rock with diagonal shafts of light striking one side provides a good example of the symbolic evocation Craig wanted from his semi-abstract scenes: "The straight pillar was to give the spectators the same feeling as Beethoven gives his hearers in the opening of his Symphony Eroica." In addition to illustrating the qualities of a "theater of space," the contrast between the relative sizes of figure and frame in the first sketch and their sizes in the other two sketches relates to the idea of a totally flexible stage that Craig outlined in describing the use of his screens: "With the scene goes a special [adjustable] proscenium, every shape being thus obtained."[43] He had intended to incorporate this into the *Hamlet* production – where, for instance, the stage opening in the grave scene would have been half-height to give the impression of a crypt – but technical limitations allowed him

Design for the opening of *Macbeth:* musical and visual correspondences.

to construct only a simple false proscenium. This gave the stage
opening proportions similar to the panoramic proscenium of *Dido
and Aeneas*, but represented no advance. Neither height nor width
could be changed during performance. However, Craig did return to
the idea in the Cranach edition of *Hamlet* (which was specifically
intended to "make good" what had been missing in the Moscow
production). For this he invented a method of creating prints with
the use of interchangeable blocks, which not only provided a continual stream of new arrangements, following each other without
pause as he had intended the screens to do, but also simultaneously
altered the shape of the frame to give a different scale to the actors.

As another variation, in one model he had constructed a circular inner proscenium, through which a scene of ramparts, towers, and steps could be seen. A note on his frequently reproduced photograph of this model reads, "Good . . . but not for *Hamlet*," and it provided one of the inspirations for his *St. Matthew Passion*.

As a result of these new interests, Craig came to feel increasingly that the *Hamlet* production diverged from his aims. It could not be altered to incorporate the next stage in the development of his ideas, and even before the performance he came to feel that it was "wasting my time. I seek to know. I do *not* seek a position or success–and this work in Moscow is old work. I have passed it all." As he admitted, he had caught only a glimpse of the final form that his concept might take. But significantly, upon rereading this passage in 1956, he related it specifically to Peter Brook. Even though Brook was still working pictorially at that time, what Craig's new position brings to mind is Brook's research into the roots of drama, which returned the stage to an "empty space." Now, as his work on *Hamlet* came to an end, Craig declared that his aim was "to study the theatre. I do not want to waste time producing plays . . . I want to leave behind me the seeds of the art–for it does not yet exist, and such seeds are not to be discovered in a moment."[44]

# 7   The theater of the future: Scene, puppets, and a religious festival

As Craig had noted in 1909, his ideal theater, which would "strive towards the condition of music," existed "only in the imagination." Its final form was never realized on the stage, and indeed – as had happened with the Moscow *Hamlet* – it effectively distracted Craig from practical work. But from 1906 on, an increasing number of jottings and scenarios in his notebooks, designs and models, and interviews and articles, culminating with the text of *Scene* in 1922, allow a fairly complete reconstruction of his visonary art form. The way these ideas are expressed is fragmentary, and their final shape evolved only gradually. So there are many contradictory elements, some of which were never fully resolved. On one hand, the thrust is away from actors to puppets and finally to abstract movement. On the other, Craig stresses the value of his concept as a context for human figures. Similarly, he claimed that his "invention" was not a mechanism, yet he realized that it would require all the resources of complex machinery; he spoke of outdoor performances lit by the sun, because the sun had become an important thematic symbol, when all his descriptions and designs presuppose artificial lighting and a roofed-in theater.

Critics have used such contradictions as arguments for dismissing Craig's vision. But these ideas have an inner consistency, and in light of this almost all of his innovations and theories – the screens, *The Steps*, the Uebermarionette – which otherwise seem eclectic, are clearly integral parts of a whole. At the same time, even though he claimed that his designs were only a poor substitute for actual performance on the stage and that he would have preferred "to work directly with the material which the theatre offers," those designs still represent a move toward abstraction and away from actual performance. In developing what he called interchangeably Scene and "A Vision," his approach was indeed visionary rather than practical, and this is the point at which anyone devoted to live theater is forced to question the validity of his ideas.

As he later noted when commenting that he could not have done another production with Stanislavski, "Had he asked me to develop some experiments with him and *not before the public* it would have been quite another matter . . . the further I went [in developing theories] the more I disliked the intrusion of the public."[1] Indeed, by the end of the First World War, Craig had developed a persecution complex. International events deprived him of funds for his work, closed the school he had finally established, made publication of *The Mask* impossible, and even caused his model theaters to be dismantled or broken up when his center in the Arena Goldoni was requisitioned by the Italian army. What made it worse was that at the same time he saw others, like Reinhardt, developing stage techniques that he looked on as his own. As a result he deliberately altered his records of the experiments he carried out on his large model stage (Model A) for fear that his ideas would be stolen, and when he published *Scene* he left his description vague, omitting any technical details.

When Craig came to analyze classical and early medieval drama, which offered very different artistic values to the modern theater he rejected, he decided that their common distinguishing factor was architecture. Whether amphitheater or church, the space in which a play was performed itself provided the setting – a permanent and "genuine" place, in contrast to a mock representation of somewhere else, "scene" rather than scenery. "A work of architecture. Unalterable except for trifling pieces here and there – except for the everlasting change which passed from morn till morn across its face as the sun and moon passed."

This architectural quality was what he wished to reproduce, but in a modern form and not as in, say, Godwin's production of *Helena in Troas*, which attempted to reconstruct an actual Greek stage, and which therefore only reintroduced illusionistic scenery in a different way. To achieve a single architectural scene that could be used to suggest many different types of location, Craig separated the strictly structural elements of buildings from the ornamental, and reduced these to "the essential parts" that were common to all, whether temple, palace, or peasant's hut, classical, Eastern, or modern European. What he was left with were "flat floor – flat walls – flat roof."[2] Variations in ground plans together with the use of light and a single detail – a certain style of door, a grilled window – would then be sufficient for an audience to visualize any particular setting from impressionistic suggestions.

All this could be, and indeed was, achieved by Craig's screens, with their "extra pieces" and the translucent ceiling he had envisaged using in conjunction with them. It was also, in fact, nothing new. As a technique of representation, this refined conventional practice rather than changed it. It was still essentially mimetic in intention. In a draft for an unpublished article Craig even referred to the nineteenth-century "eidophusikon" as a precursor of the mobile stage that he came to call "Scene." This was an almost cinemato-graphic form of spectacular realism, reproducing the sights and sounds of shipwrecks or cities in flames without the use of actors, and replacing plot with the development of an event. However, in relation to the kind of poetic drama Craig had in mind, realism was inappropriate. As he commented: "How ridiculous and how unreal!"[3] In contrast, what Craig had in mind was the representation of the heroic, which abstraction alone conjured up. The link with the eidophusikon was in the way the scenery itself had been trans-formed into an active dramatic agent. This was the true principle of Scene, although Craig continued to refer to it as an instrument that could be used for staging conventional plays with localized settings.

The quality that had made scenery dramatic in the eidophusikon was movement, and Craig put this together with his reduction of architecture to its essential elements. So when he began to work out the basis of Scene, his definition was "that it shall be of solid form, of three dimensions, and moveable." The inspiration for the actual shape that this idea eventually took came from two sources, Serlio's *Architettura* and Manfred Semper's *Handbuch der Architectur*. Craig had acquired a copy of Serlio's work in 1903 to aid him in designing settings for the hurried *Much Ado* production. Although initially he used it simply to borrow the correct shape of sixteenth-century columns and arches, he found that the geometrical diagrams "held me in 1904 or whenever it was, and today [1946] as I sit here the same book again holds me . . . I look at it and endless thoughts are born within a few moments." Then, a year later in Berlin, he came across Semper's illustration of the Asphaleia System. Together these provided him with what he referred to as his "instrument," a term coined when he exhibited the first etchings illustrating "The Art of Revelation" as "studies for fifteen separate motions or moods of movement . . . translated through an instrument."[4]

In one volume of *Architettura* Serlio deals explicitly with the theater, and Craig translated his description of the differences among tragic, comic, and pastoral scenes on the Renaissance stage for the opening number of *The Mask*. Yet the vital inspiration came from the other volume of Serlio's work, which has no theatrical reference at all. The two specific diagrams that provided Craig with the idea for Scene illustrated general principles of architectural per-spective. They showed a ground plan, divided into squares, with the elevation of walls corresponding to those squares. Craig immedi-

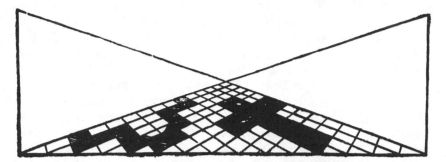

*This diagram is taken a ... in 1732 with a more complicated pattern*

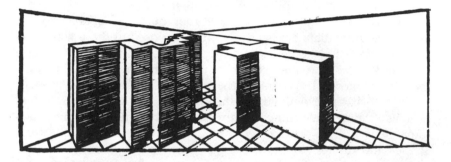

The diagrams from Serlio's *Architettura* that inspired Scene, with Craig's annotations.

ately transposed the plan into a stage floor, cut into different sections, each of which could be raised or lowered to create deep wells, open spaces, steps, platforms, or partitions. A logical extension was "a roof composed of the same shapes as the floor. Suspended cubes, each cube exactly covering (and meeting when lowered) each square on the floor."

What Craig believed he had discovered was a scene so mobile that it was capable of "scientific movement" in any direction or tempo, and uniquely responsive to the control of an Artist of the Theater: "Each section of this floor can rise and fall at will by mechanical means; each section of this roof can descend or ascend, echoing as it were the movement of the floor; each side can as it were fold and unfold at all parts and can be moved at will, and this movement of the entire stage can be so governed by time as to produce rhythm."[5] He also believed that this mechanism could be developed to the point at which a director (himself) could work it from a console at the rear of the auditorium during a performance, so responding directly to the emotional moods of the audience.

For Craig the primary advantage of this total mobility was its expressiveness. As noted on the flyleaf of the thesaurus that Ellen Terry gave him when he first began to try to formulate his ideas in writing, "Expression is the Deed of the Artist." In reviewing all the techniques of theatrical presentation from the Greeks to the nineteenth century, his primary criterion for picking out the right elements for his ideal stage was "whether or no they are capable of expression. That and little else." But there was also another motive behind this selection. The way he reduced all the varied architectural forms to universal essentials was one aspect of this. Craig's stated aim was to simplify "the possibilities of Drama." The rationale for this was that such a simplification made possible a stronger and more immediate appeal to the imagination, but there was a secondary effect that he never explicitly admitted. It was only through such reduction that the theater could become a medium a single man could control. Whatever the appropriateness to the modern spirit, which Craig defined as "the spirit of incessant *change*," there was also a practical value for a director in a theatrical form in which movement and expressiveness would be limited to architectural shapes and the play of light.

Craig's frustration with the gap between an idea and its execution was one of the main reasons for his rejection of the conventional theater. The Moscow *Hamlet* was simply an extreme example of something he had already complained about in *The Vikings* production. "I do not feel responsible, and one scene or another, one colour or another, one emotion, movement or intention or another seems to me a matter of indifference if it cannot be changed and altered . . . by a momentary idea." What he wanted was an instrument with which to translate "volcanic improvisation" directly into stage action. That meant eliminating all the accidental elements of performance, the main one being the actor, who either imposed his own interpretation or could present a director's inspiration only in a fixed form established long since in rehearsals, even when his conventional training did not distort the director's intentions. Craig believed he had found such an instrument in Scene, in which the human voice and figure could be replaced by "Light – shadow – motion through impersonal mediums – and silence."[6]

Craig's concept of a melodramatically exaggerated and emphatic form of acting, though derived from Irving and Duse, anticipated the ecstatic style of German expressionists in the 1920s, who used rhetorical gestures, glowing eyes, and facial masking to transmit emotional states directly from an actor's subconscious to the audience. The mobile scene had the same intention on a larger and more abstract scale. It would allow the director, as the artist creating a theatrical piece, to communicate a series of "moods" directly and subliminally through the symphonic movement of shapes and light. The musical analogy is one that Craig himself drew. He described the ceaselessly changing movement of three-dimensional shapes as equivalent to the orchestration of sounds in music, and his earliest jottings on the pages of Serlio compared the intended effect of Scene to that of *The St. Matthew Passion*.

Remember how imperceptibly [the Oratorio] opens – how it proceeds – advancing in its severe order – its superb rigidity without haste or delay – lawfully – how it relies on its compact and simple *form* to move us – how like a tree it rears itself upwards . . . It is so that this Oratorio catches me – and it is some such progression that I wanted to put before you in my "movement" . . .

As in Bach's music, the progression and counterpoint that created structural forms would evoke specific emotions without explanatory words or even the presence of an actor. Craig's aims had changed radically. "The desire *to impersonate* this or that character vanished, and in its place appeared the larger and far more satisfying impulse *to represent the idea* . . . to endow with soul some lifeless material."[7]

The Theater of the Soul (the title of a book by Eduard Schuré) was almost a catchphrase of the period. For Schuré and most others, it referred to conventional drama with a spiritual message, or acting techniques intended to explore and express the psyche. By contrast, Craig considered that there was no point in defining such a theater in terms of content, as it was the form that determined what the meaning would be. Therefore, *"the method of its delivery* [not the message] should be the main consideration. The soul will not speak through the body . . . Those who get nearer to the true translation of the soul's message are those who use the most divine materials." Interpreting Shakespeare, he had focused on the conflict between the spirit and the body or material world that imprisons it. Now he believed he had discovered a theatrical form that could deal with such a subject without the surface disguise of everyday life. Alongside one of his designs for *Lear*, which showed a man in a blizzard, he commented:

If we should have no snowstorm visualized, but only the man making his symbolical gestures which would suggest to us a man fighting against the elements . . . this would be better . . . Following that line of argument in its logical sequence, then, would it not be still more near to art if we had no man, but only movements of some intangible material which could suggest the movements which the soul of man makes battling against the soul of nature?[8]

However, the use of the word "intangible" is a giveaway. Craig never developed a mechanism flexible enough for the instrument he imagined.

Hydraulics were one potential solution. These had already become a regular part of stage equipment by the 1880s. At Mackaye's Madison Square Theater in New York, for example, the whole stage was a gigantic lift shaft, with two platforms, one above the other, to allow settings to be changed while a scene was being played. When the lower of the two stages was the acting area, the other was out of sight in the flies, and when it was brought down, the lower one was in the basement. Even more to the point was the Asphaleia System. This system, in use at theaters in Budapest, Prague, and Vienna around the turn of the century, made it possible to raise sections of the stage floor to form platforms of various heights, and their surfaces could even be tilted or rotated.

But the hydraulic lifts by which this was achieved were too cumbersome for the type of movement Craig had in mind. They could be installed only beneath a limited number of sections in the stage, their tempo of operation could not be varied, and they did not include the retractable walls, filling the space between a raised section and the floor, that formed the essence of Craig's visual concept. By the 1920s, the available technology was even more sophisticated, but the nearest Craig came to realizing his ideas was a simplified working model constructed in 1923 by his son, who has commented that

EGC never had a mind that could comprehend the working of even the simplest machine, so of course he had no theories as to how the mechanism for moving *Scene* would work. In early days he was sitting at the bottom of a lift shaft in which the lift moved up and down on a great shaft housed in the basement and was propelled by some hydraulic system. He took it for granted that he could mass hundreds of those shafts together and get the effect that he wanted. The little model that I made with "simple pulleys" was just to show what effects could be achieved when they were properly lighted from different angles. It was not a model to prove that it could work mechanically. I only used 25 cubes and a painted background, but it was very effective.[9]

The Asphaleia System, from Semper's *Handbuch der Architectur.*

On this miniature scale, counterweights and pulleys enabled Craig to set the wooden cubes in motion by remote control. Here he could have demonstrated the abstract play of movement that he had outlined on the flyleaf of Serlio's *Architettura.* From an initial state of nothingness, where "the floor seems to be an absence – the roof a void," one column rises in the center as "a single atom." Behind it another rises: "always a double birth, repeating and repeating." As other columns rose, the first sank again. "Now to right and left one chain of life moves like a sea . . . Slow shapes . . . continue to arise in endless numbers," folding and unfolding "until there stand before us vast columns of shapes, all single yet all united – none resting." This metamorphosis ended when an aesthetically complete form was achieved and the artist-director's vision reached its definitive expression, then "all is still."

Clearly, the subject matter of this kinetic experience was to be artistic creation itself. So the theme would always be the same, although the arrangements of light and perspective changed in each performance as each movement gave a new inspiration that was to be translated instantaneously into three-dimensional forms. The stage space was envisaged as a mindscape, a neutral ground on which the imaginations of the artist and the spectator might meet. As Craig put it, "Some spirit seems to work there in the space, as in a gentle mind," and the abstraction was designed to activate the same creative impulse, not simply passive appreciation, in a spectator. The first column rising out of the emptiness, for instance, was intended to be "like the awakening of a thought in a dream."

But without mechanical aptitude, this ideal instrument could never be developed. Instead Craig was forced to compromise. His first sketch shows screens being used in conjunction with cubes. Later notes describe them disguised as cubes, with leaves the same width as the sides of the cubes and in graduated heights, from fifteen feet to five, to give a sharply diminishing perspective. This was clearly not a viable solution. The mixture of horizontally folding screens and vertically moving columns would have been cumbersome, and the false perspective would have made it impossible to use any kind of figures. In any case, the element of fake architecture or scenic illusion inherent in it was precisely what Craig intended to abolish.

But on other levels the various compromises with which he experimented in order to find workable ways of realizing his ideas had more potential than any conceivable use of the purely abstract form he had in mind. For instance, because a scene flexible enough to provide continuously varying visual effects was beyond his reach, he was unable to dispense with human figures. Instead, he suggested ways of limiting the individuality of the actor: using masks to communicate emotion on a more precisely controllable and generalized level than facial expressions, or massing actors into large groups in which emotion would be expressed through the choreographed movement of the whole.

At first glance Craig's ideas for using this mechanized Scene seem vague and imprecise. Its actual performance qualities are described only in very general terms, and this makes them difficult to evaluate. But he also considered replacing human actors with puppets. Whatever the practical disadvantages in terms of a totally mobile stage, puppets were closely associated in Craig's mind with Scene. He wrote extensively on their use, and his ideas concerning them can be extrapolated to give concrete examples of the type of performance he intended.

Craig's earliest design for Scene, incorporating screens together with the
moving cubes.

The actor's disadvantage, in Craig's view, was that the human figure pointed inevitably toward realism on the stage, and caused audiences to confuse actuality with art. It also focused attention on personality, as opposed to vision, distracting the audience from the aesthetic pattern of the whole to particularities. The premise behind this argument is that theater should have the same characteristics and be approached with the same expectations as one of the fine arts – something that could never be achieved while human individuals themselves formed the artistic medium. At its simplest, as Craig put it in a review of a book on Marie Taglioni, "we write about an artist's *work*, but we write about the performer's person." By contrast, as "a model of man in motion," puppets represented actions in a highly stylized way that evoked a poetic vision, instead of holding "the mirror DOWN to nature." There was never any intention of disguising the artificiality of marionettes. Indeed, Craig emphasized this quality. The more a puppet's movements resembled a person's, the closer it came to giving an impression of something else – to being a surface illusion, rather than to catching "the *spirit* of the thing."[10]

In this Craig was at one with the symbolists, who had turned to marionettes as a means of abstraction and generalization. When Lugné-Poë founded his Théâtre de l'Oeuvre, he first intended it to be a puppet theater. Jarry's *Ubu* trilogy had originally been written for puppets, and Maeterlinck called his early plays "Drames pour Marionettes." For the symbolists, puppets automatically presented a hieratic image of life. They stood in the same relationship to human individuals as a national flag does to a nation. Their physical limitations reduced any dramatic action to its essentials. As artificial objects they stood for an artist's vision instead of presenting it in a fully realized form, so that the spectator had to complete the images in his own mind.

This meant that any vision gained direct imaginative relevance because each spectator filled in the details from his or her own experience. For instance, Jarry's "ABSTRACT theatre," in which puppets or puppetlike figures replaced the conventional actors' psychological and individualized self-portraits with "the effigy of the CHARACTER," was intended to confront the public "like the exaggerating mirror in the stories of Madame Leprince de Beaumont, in which the depraved saw themselves with dragons' bodies, or bulls' horns, or whatever corresponded to their particular vice." Alternatively, for Maeterlinck, this imaginative immediacy was intended to carry the spectator beyond individuality altogether onto an archetypal level of purely poetic experience.

But in both cases the value of using puppets was essentially the same. "Impersonal puppets, beings of wood and cardboard, possess a pure and mysterious life. Their aspect of truth catches us unawares, disquiets. Their elemental gestures contain the complete expression of human feelings."[11] And, even though actors, not puppets, were used for Maeterlinck's plays as well as for the first performances of *Ubu Roi* at the Théâtre de l'Oeuvre, both types of work required the actors to take on marionettelike qualities. Maeterlinck's somnambulistic action could be represented only in slow movements and deliberate gestures. Jarry's simplistic clichés and *grand guignol* slapstick ruled out psychological subtleties; his actors wore masks and (according to Yeats's description) hopped around the stage like wooden frogs.

Craig wrote puppet plays of both types. *The Drama of Fools*, a satiric and at points Jarryesque collection of minidramas, attacked society. It was an outlet for his frustration after the closing of his school and the dismantling of the model stages on which he had been working out his Art of the Theater. Others – in particular, one titled *The Scene*, written in 1914 – provide a commentary on his ideas. In *The Scene* two puppets discuss the nature of theatrical performance. One believes he has "a soul" that makes him the equal of the "God" who created him, and claims he is "absolutely self-dependent." This is demonstrably false because he has strings attached to his limbs, strings that he has to ask the other puppet to move when he wishes to change position. From his viewpoint, however, these strings connect him directly with God, and "the reason why I had to ask your help to get down just now is that God has become helpless lately." In fact he represents the human actor in the modern agnostic age, the being whose egoism has broken "the old divine unity" and whose "body refuses to be an instrument." He strikes Shakespearean poses, fills his voice with shades of personal emotion, and sees performance in terms of the stock roles of the nineteenth-century acting company. By contrast, the other puppet is fully aware of his artificial status as a man-made object and has "no 'soul' so far as I know, for I do not know what it is." But, when the first puppet typecasts him as "a Juvenile Lead," he replies, "I am a God . . . I am an Image – the Image of a God – I am therefore a God to those who believe in me." The setting of this minidrama is the movable geometrical cubes of Scene, and in a prologue the second puppet demonstrates (to a musical accompaniment that underscores their rhythmic nature) "all the movements which a marionette is capable of. These exclude all movements which are called useful or realistic."[12]

The primary quality Craig was searching for, though it is not present in the rather simplistic verbal discussion of this script, was symbolic suggestion. His jottings made in 1922 for an unpublished book referred to the Chinese theater as an example of his ideal. There everything was left to the spectator's imagination; a bare stick could become a blossoming almond tree. His aim was to create a contemporary European equivalent of this highly conventionalized Eastern theater, though he never explored the degree to which symbolic communication is dependent on fixed and widely accepted forms. Puppet drama, like classical ballet, has its own established conventions. But Craig's concepts were all designed for the ordinary theater, even if they were worked out by scaling them down to model stages. So puppets gave way to other types of figures.

One idea was to use two-dimensional human silhouettes, which would hold "a characteristic pose . . . for an entire act" (an extension perhaps of the *schemata* or fixed attitudes taken up by classical Greek actors at moments of emotional intensity). The movement was reserved for the mobile cubes of the Scene. Another idea, as inanimate figures could be of any size, was to use stature as an indicator of each silhouetted character's moral status or significance in the drama. Lesser figures – or those who existed in the world of physical action, as distinct from those who represented spiritual states – could be made one-third the size of major figures. However, in Craig's words, the essence of this art "is to be all Movement" and its chief characteristic was to be a seamless flowing of ceaselessly changing shapes, so neither puppets nor immobile silhouettes were really appropriate.

A third idea, using puppets and actors simultaneously, had been suggested by Craig for one point in the Moscow *Hamlet*. It provides a good illustration of the imaginative symbolic use of inanimate figures that he was envisaging. For Polonius's interrogation of Hamlet in act 2, Craig wanted a marionette representing the Prince to move slowly toward Polonius (waiting on a shallow forestage) down a brightly lighted central corridor designed to give a zigzag perspective of immense depth and distance. As the marionette approached, it would appear to grow larger, because scaled-up versions of the figure, book in hand, were to be substituted as it moved briefly out of sight at the end of each turn in the corridor. When it reached a gigantic size, Polonius hurries to meet it, and a strong spotlight on

An early model showing silhouetted Black Figures ("2 Roman actors and 3 others") against the background of Scene.

the now empty forestage allows the actor to take the place of his effigy and switch positions with Polonius unobserved by the audience. At the same time the flat screens on either side of the corridor move inward so that the forestage now appears to be a continuation of the passageway. The lights go up on the corridor again to show a mirror image of Polonius scurrying forward out of the depths toward Hamlet, seen in silhouette on the now darkened forestage and reading a book with his back to the audience. As they meet the dialogue begins. This staging was rejected, not without some justice, as being too complex to carry out.

In fact, despite their symbolic value, puppets were not really an appropriate means to Craig's end. If "figure and scene must both move harmoniously together – mingling their values," in practice this could be achieved effectively only by using human actors.[13] Indeed, as Edward Craig has pointed out in rebutting the notion that this ideal stage was no more than a retreat from the theater into abstraction, of the nineteen etchings published in *Scene* only two show geometric shapes without human figures.

In this series of etchings, people pursue others through passage-

Black Figures, with the difference in size standing for relative symbolic significance. The smaller figures represent Hamlet and Laertes fencing. The first of the larger figures represents Hamlet with his Daemon, and the others are general figures for a Roman drama.

ways formed by the columns, walk pensively through arcades, descend despairingly into the depths, stretch out their arms to the light that streams between high towers, or fill the stage floor in front of a single monolith. But these are not conventional actors. Their movements are dramatic, but never declamatory. There is no indication that these figures speak. They are more like dancers than actors, and in three of the designs the actions they perform are recognizable dances. In Craig's view, "all nature is silent when it acts and speech cannot take the place of action . . . let acts speak for themselves." Words appealed to reason and could communicate only limited meanings. Movement was a universal language, allowing such variety of interpretation that contact with the spectator would never be disrupted by disagreement with what was expressed. It was "simple for all to understand feelingly." Like the Japanese puppets that Craig considered particularly effective because "they use their full force of silence," a purely visual stream of images would have the strongest symbolic impact, communicating on the preverbal, subconscious level of the mind.

If dialogue were used, it would be separated from the action. The words would be recited or sung by an offstage chorus as an accompaniment to the movements of silent figures, as Craig had done with Cupid's part in *The Masque of Love* and in his experiments with silhouettes, where he had also followed the example of Japanese puppet theater. Or the actor himself might make sharp divisions among the various modes of expression, as in one of Craig's scenarios. "Harlequin enters – he moves and when he has reached the *end* of his movement he pauses – *body fixed*. Harlequin speaks – when he has finished he makes a pause – then he makes some clear and illuminating *action* [gesture] – he rests again – no sound, no movement – then the music picks up the thread of the pattern."[14]

One of the confusing aspects of the etchings published in *The Scene*, which was taken as evidence for the impracticality of Craig's ideas, is that the actors appear to change radically in size. In some designs the figures are dwarfed by columns that tower like skyscrapers. In others they fill the frame and their heads rise above their architectural background. However, these shifts in proportion make perfect sense in the context of the adjustable proscenium that Craig had intended to supply with his patent screens, though (like Scene itself) he never worked out a mechanism for putting his idea into practice.

The concept of an adjustable proscenium was not new in itself. Like the lighting techniques in Craig's early productions, it came from Herkomer, who had proposed a system of counterweights and screws to change the size of the opening from scene to scene in aid of dramatic realism (see the illustration on p. 32). But in Craig's ideal theater the proscenium was to be the most flexible part of the stage: expanding for massed crowd scenes or to put a figure into a diminishing perspective; contracting until a spread-eagled man could touch all four corners (as in Leonardo da Vinci's figure studies) to focus on the single actor alone for a soliloquy such as "To be or not to be . . ." Like the lens of a movie camera, a panorama could be changed to a close-up without breaking the action. This versatility was to be carried through to the whole structure of the stage. Craig envisaged a stage floor that could be sunk until it was five feet below the line of sight from the front row of the stalls, so that the whole audience could look down over low walls set up all over the stage floor in place of conventional background scenery and see a bird's-eye view of separate actions going on simultaneously in different rooms, as in medieval paintings. He also anticipated the concept of "environmental theater," experimented with by the American Performance Group in the sixties, suggesting that a theater be constructed in which the spectators would move around the actors to choose their own perspectives on the action.

Even if modern technology could have been used to construct such a flexible stage, the cost would have been prohibitive, and the desired effects could hardly be achieved in the conventional theater. In the last scene for his production of *The Pretenders,* Craig designed a perspective that receded to what looked like massive gates. But even if the impression of a line towering miles high could be achieved on a piece of paper only two inches square (his often-quoted example), the human figure was not responsive to such treatment. The Danish actors struggling to get through the gates looked ridiculous. Similarly, he had to content himself with a revolve in the designs he did for Tyler, though this fell far short of the flexibility he wanted:

a turntable stage is only a nuisance . . . what is needed is a stage which can move all ways – tip forward – back – sides *during the scene* – raise this X, lower that group or figure . . . For example we all need to see Macbeth exactly as placed here at moment [in the Banquet scene, stretched over the table, prostrate with shock] and, to this end, these tables – "degrees" – platforms [in the foreground] should be able to tip up gradually – Macbeth raised – the table to slant a bit – Lady Macbeth to be higher (as here), the front lines of guests lowered . . . This moving stage would be of assistance to the spectators *who cannot move around* – and to the actors – and so to the whole play.[15]

However, Craig had a more ambitious goal in mind for his Scene than providing a background for conventional dramatic plays. The most successful visual element of *The Pretenders* production was Craig's use of light – particularly his projections, which gave a free impression of tall airy columns for the cathedral scene and of a spiraling snowstorm against which the ghost of Bishop Nicholas appeared. Indeed, light had such significance for Craig, both as a symbol, as a means of evoking emotional moods, and as a technique for painting a scene, that his theater deserves to be called "The Theater of Light."

Adolph Appia is the name that springs to mind when we think of light used as a living medium to bring moving actors into emotional harmony with the stage space and to express "the inner nature of all experience." In many ways Appia shared Craig's principles. He too proposed that poetic drama be the work of a single artist – the director – who controlled the interaction of light, movement, and music, forming a synthesis of the different theatrical elements to create "a supreme union of all art." Like Craig, his aim was to find a modern equivalent for the classical Greek theater, in which drama was the event, the act itself, not spectacle. He had followed Craig, independently, in abolishing footlights, in using light and shadow instead of paint to give plastic form and color to scenery, and in replacing the realistic representation of the material world with an atmospheric suggestion of spiritual states. His concept of using light as "a means of externalizing . . . most of the colours and forms that painting freezes on the canvas and of distributing them dynamically in space" is almost an exact transcription of one of Craig's principles. So too is his vision of simplifying the stage picture while introducing sophisticated electrical equipment, which could be regulated in precise detail, so that "the actor no longer walks *in front* of painted lights and shadows; he is immersed in an atmosphere *that is destined for him* . . . We no longer seek to give the illusion of *a forest* but that of *a man* in the atmosphere of a forest."[16] Craig considered Appia to be the only theater artist with whom he could have collaborated, but believed that Appia had not gone far enough.

The human actor remained the primary means of expression in Appia's concept. Craig (perhaps overstating his position in response) insisted when they met to discuss their theatrical ideas that "the true and sole *material* for the Art of the Theatre" was "LIGHT – and through light, movement." The neutral pale gray of Scene was to be given shifting emotional tones by the changing colors of light, and the primary reason for moving the cubes was so that they could "receive the play of light."[17] But light also had a significant thematic value for Craig. God's first command in Genesis was "Let there be light." The sun had traditionally been seen as the element that fostered biological life. If on one level the subject of his theatrical art was to be artistic creation itself, on a wider level this could be seen as mirroring the creation of the universe.

In its first draft, the text of *The Scene* referred to light in quasi-religious terms. It compared the abstract movement of the cubes to the ever-changing dynamic of nature, and defined "the essential of Drama" as "Acts of God." Such phrases were omitted from the final version, perhaps because Craig felt that any touch of mysticism would only confirm the view that his ideas were impractical. However, from about 1909 on, his notebooks are filled with metaphysical scenarios that are clearly intended for performance on his mobile scene. Although these are little more than rough jottings – none were developed – their thematic consistency clearly indicates the nature of Craig's vision.

The Art of the Theater that he called for was not concerned simply with technical reforms. As he had announced in 1907, "A new religion will be found contained in it. That religion will preach no more, but it will reveal . . . it will unveil thought to our eyes, silently – by movements – in visions."[18] At the same time, these visions were to be abstract and evocative, rather than the definitive images of painting or sculpture. What they expressed was a generalized religious sense, not a theology. Craig had rejected the sentimental clichés of conventional belief when confronted with the tinsel angels and Marian pieties of Housman's *Bethlehem*. What he saw as inherent to his new forms of dramatic presentation was not a Christian message, but a pantheistic nature worship. As the sun, from Craig's perception of natural phenomena, seemed to be the source of movement as well as of light, and was one of the traditional symbols for divinity, it became the Creator, the Lawgiver, God.

The sun's rays were a rather obvious metaphor for revelation, and Craig called his scenarios *Illuminations*. They range from the representation of a single day to a *Ceremony of the 365 Days and Nights*, and were intended to have the same effect as natural manifestations of change and movement, which can appear significant and dramatic without containing any explicable message. As an art in its own right, rather than as mimetic illustration, movement would have the same quality as music, which Craig defined as "sense without meaning."

This might have been an accurate description of those *Illuminations* that represent nothing beyond the procession of hours or seasons. "The Sun is a symbolic representation of life . . . by [its] rhythm time becomes beautiful . . . A cause and effect it may have, meaning it has none. Why then do 'artists' today struggle so hard to give a meaning to everything?" But the more developed these jottings and sketches become, the further they move away from this ideal. When *The Creation* is organized into seven "days," opening "with the light, which faint at first as though travelling from afar, sets everything in motion" until "last of all a man walks into the midst," then it clearly contains conventional and extrinsic meaning. Later *Illuminations* even conflate theatrical performance and religious worship, moving toward a mythology of art in which the devotional object becomes Craig's new theater itself, as in one titled *Through Night to Light*. Here the scene becomes an imagined amphitheater in which "thousands of men and women draw together in the dark." These are Craig's followers, "waiting in *The New Theatre*" for the "consciousness of God" that the performance is to bring:

The sun has shot one ray of its immortality upon the very centre of the circle . . . It plays upon a large crystal basin in which the coldest water lies motionless . . . The force of the Ray becomes terrific. Suddenly a cry goes up – "the water is all gone" – a great conflagration . . . The Force of God is seen, is felt. A hundred men in white [enter] bearing a silver sphere upon their shoulders . . . 300 voices are chanting praise to God . . . Fountains spring up, white birds are loosed and raise themselves in air . . . voices rise higher and higher. This is the first ceremony in praise of the God of all things – the creator of life and motion – the symbol of our art.[19]

The elevated poetic prose of these *Illuminations* may be a measure of their importance to their author, but the iconography is crude and the pretentious amalgam of symbolic action and religious service is unconvincing. However, the focus of these scenarios is central to Craig's art. The intention behind his theatrical reforms is summed up in a letter from Isadora Duncan after the tragic death of her children, a letter that draws together many of the thoughts that he returns to again and again in his notebooks. "You are creating the only world that is worth living in – *the imagination* – . . . releasing poor souls from the inferno of *reality* and *matter* [you] lift them up out of 'life' into the *only life*, up where the spirit can fly – freed from this abominable bad dream of matter."[20]

Craig's rejection of naturalistic drama, his symbolist approach, his attempts to replace stage illusion with the atmospheric suggestiveness of light and the actor with a moving scene – all are aspects of this metaphysical aim. Their common factor is a move toward abstraction, which expresses an etherealization of the physical, a desire to dissolve matter into spirit and create a mystical dream of reality. In Craig's terms, it is "to get something entirely opposed to life as we see it," which he called "Death" (as being the opposite to material existence, like the female double for Hamlet).[21] But even he must have been aware that no symbolic action he could imagine would have the evocative force of Christian imagery. So he turned to *The St. Matthew Passion* as the logical extension of Scene, and dedicated the etchings illustrating *Scene* "to Old Bach."

Martin Shaw had introduced Craig to the oratorio as early as 1899, It was one of the works on his first list of planned productions in 1900, and by 1901 he was already creating designs for it with great flights of steps and shafts of light as the visual equivalents of majestic chords of music. This blending of Wagnerian concepts of synaesthesia (in which all the different arts would be united) with symbolist "correspondences," (in which visual impressions and sounds were seen as equivalents) was to become an integral part of Scene. The movement of light and three-dimensional shapes was specifically intended to elevate drama to "the condition of music" (to borrow Walter Pater's words, as Craig did), though the translation from one medium to another was more literal than this suggests. Craig in fact believed that the "laws of movement" and the "laws of music" were interchangeable, as he intended them to be in the *Macbeth* design, in which shape (the single pillar) and light (strong diagonals) were designed to reproduce in visual terms the emotions evoked by the opening chords of a symphony[22] (see the illustration on p. 174).

In fact the relationship between Scene and *The St. Mathew Passion* is explicit in one notebook, where designs for both appear on facing pages. The first sketch is inscribed, "To veil the weakness in *Human Character* and *illumine* the *Heroic*." It shows a "Hero and 6 spirits": the former standing on an upper stage with groups of figures fading on either side into the light streaming between the columns of Scene, the latter ranged on a forestage below. The second is labeled "The Hero . . . to reveal to the spectator the deity of man" and shows a similar arrangement of figures. But now the Scene is framed by the great arches that form the main feature of the later *St. Matthew Passion* model (a note gives the scale: "170 feet to top of arch from stage") and lines of steps zigzag from one edge to the other, linking the lower and upper acting areas.[23]

Already, in his polemic entitled "The Actor and the Uebermarionette," Craig had demanded acting that could represent the heroic, or reveal "the god" in man, by (again quoting Pater) "stripping away the involuntary and restless tremors of the flesh." His notebooks relate this to Scene, which is presented as the appropriate context for actors as heroes – in contrast to the "mean scene," which imitates human surroundings and drags even great actors like Irving down to its level. Scene was a space that could be dominated only by an actor "*masked* from the head to foot by sheer calculation (as in Greece before Aeschylus) . . . compelling his audience to enter into another state of being – something we call heavenly."[24] This was translated into a more conventionally religious context when Craig came across a twelfth-century church at Giornico in 1910 during one of the breaks in the *Hamlet* production. What caught his attention were the proportions of the high arches over the nave, and the unique positioning of the altar on a bridge curving over a triple archway leading down to the crypt. He immediately saw this as the natural setting for any religious drama, because it gave a perfect symbolic representation of the traditional spiritual universe. "No other church or stage," he wrote enthusiastically, "had such a bridged path from earth to heaven nor so open an inferno. The most beautiful, the most mystic – most human – theatre I have ever seen."[25]

Craig pasted two photographs of this church into his daybook for 1910. On one of them he painted white figures representing actors, and in a letter to Ellen Terry, he cited E. K. Chambers and J. A. Symonds to support the contention that the Mass was the original as well as the purest form of drama, using a thumbnail sketch of a *Quem quaeritis* performance in Giornico as an illustration. By 1914 he had constructed a twelve-foot-high model stage, specifically for *The*

A photo of the church at Giornico that inspired the model for *The St. Matthew Passion*, with Craig's annotations.

*St. Matthew Passion*, in which the main features of Giornico were reproduced. The crypt, set back from a forestage on a low platform, was now divided into acting areas of different widths and was visually cut off from the space above, which corresponded to the chancel, although narrow interior stairs united the two. The bridge now led up to vast flights of steps climbing to an upper platform with only the sky behind, a curving cyclorama to "liberate the senses" framed by the great arch.

All of Craig's major concepts were brought together in this model. It had the potential for the evocative, three-dimensional movement that he had explored in *The Steps*. It had a similar monolithic quality and allowed the same possibilities for the play of light as Scene, though the shapes were now fixed. In addition, its structure now had clear symbolic resonance, and as a universal setting for an archetypal drama the flexibility offered by the screens (the only one of Craig's concepts that was unrepresented) was unnecessary. It also had the permanent, architectural quality of the classical stage, which he had wanted to reproduce. It is worth noting that the essential elements – an upper area reached by steps over a colonnade, with a high central arch above – also appear in various combinations in the plates illustrating Roman and sixteenth-century theaters in *Scene*, as well as (together with a forestage dais labeled "pulpito") in Serlio's ground plan of the Marcellus Theater. Beside this Craig had noted: "I would develop this spot for modern theatre to new purposes."[26]

Craig never pulled his ideas for *The St. Matthew Passion* together into a formal *mise-en-scène*. Inevitably his sketches treat the different moments of the oratorio in isolation and in no particular order. But there is sufficient consistency – even though the notes, designs, and photographs of the model cover more than a decade – to give a fairly complete picture of his intentions. The figure of St. Matthew would stand on a central pillar immediately above the center of the bridge. As the Evangelist, he would start to tell the story. On the platforms on either side above the bridge would be the solo singers, attired in gray costumes that merged their figures with the architecture.[27] The scenes of spiritual crisis and "the celestial" action were to take place above the bridge: The Agony in the Garden on the topmost platform, Christ carrying his cross up the endless steps on his road to Golgotha. The other, more human scenes from Christ's Passion, such as the Last Supper, were to take place on the chancel level. "The more terrestrial parts" – Judas's betrayal and the plotting of the high priests – were to be "in the lower portion of the scene," the crypt, formed by a row of permanent openings of

The model for *The St. Matthew Passion* (twelve feet high), with Black Figures to indicate scale.

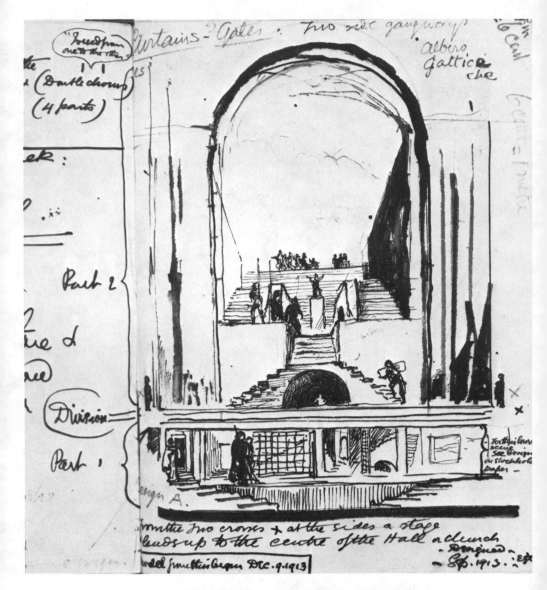

Scene design for *The St. Matthew Passion*, showing the different use of various levels and the Evangelist on the central pillar.

different sizes and designed to have the same effect as a contracting or expanding proscenium.

The principle was that the space should correspond to the number of actors, each scene "seeming crammed to overflowing." The lights would rise on the smallest cell to reveal a single disciple, enclosed by a frame that exactly fitted his standing figure. They would then dim away and rise in the largest area to show Pilate gathered with the high priests. A lurid red light might be used for Judas, pastel colors for Mary and her group. The chorus stands or reclines on the steps, moving or rising only at climactic moments, as in the aria describing the Crucifixion, in which the soprano's ecstatic vision –

See ye, see the Saviour's outstretched Hands!
He would draw us to Himself.
Come!

– catches up the chorus, which responds three times with the cry of "Where?"

Apart from these few moments, Craig wanted the complete separation of various elements of communication that he had proposed for the use of puppets or for the way figures might interact with the moving columns of Scene. The orchestra was to be invisible and, following something Craig claimed Monteverdi had once done in the seventeenth century, was distributed around the auditorium as well as behind the grilles at the rear of each opening in the crypt, so that the source of the music could not be located and sound would totally envelop the audience like an atmosphere. The singers would tell the story and give the words of the protagonists, but without gestures or facial expressions. The actions would be performed and the protagonists embodied by silent and masked figures, whose mimed gestures were precisely regulated by the tempo of the music. In outlining a proposal for the production of *The St. Matthew Passion* in Rome, Craig specified that "in addition to the *solo singers* . . . there will be: a full-sized *chorus*, the performers of a *sacred dance* . . . [and] a large number of *figuranti*," though Christ was to be "the sole Heroic figure." The sacred dance was to be a grotesque dance of death, similar perhaps to the witches' suggestively sinister antimasque in *Dido*, though very slow. It was to be performed by tap dancers in the interval between the two parts of the oratorio and "danced to the tap of drums. No music . . . the thud of the bones of the heels of the dancers – the snap of their jaws – blithe laughter in small bursts . . . the world of the grave."[28]

In contrast to this, the spiritual focus of the action was to be

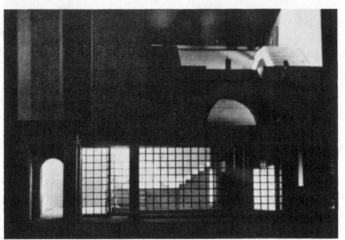

Variations of scenic effect created by lighting on the model for *The St. Matthew Passion* (Helen Craig).

translated into purely symbolic terms, with the ceremony of the Mass taking the place of the Crucifixion, and the singer's description of the elevation of Christ to the cross being represented by the elevation of the Host. Similarly, the closing moments were modeled on a benediction Craig had witnessed in Fiesole, where the candles in the church were extinguished one by one as the service progressed. One after another each area of the stage was to be darkened during the long final chorus, while the sky slowly changed from light blue to deep purple.

From the first Craig had seen *The St. Matthew Passion* as a festival drama, equivalent to the ancient Greek theater; this idea was confirmed by the first concert performance he experienced in 1906. It took place before what Craig described as an immense audience at the Kristal Palatz in Amsterdam, and convinced him that any type of chamber performance was wrong. The scope of the work demanded an audience of "several thousand people, not richer or poorer than others," and it could not be effectively produced on a small scale, for a self-selecting elite, as *Dido* and *The Masque of Love* had been. He had envisaged it initially as being performed in the ruins of some ancient amphitheater, and later tentatively proposed the open-air theatre at Marly le Roi, a semicircular raised-earth stage backed by a wall and trees, as a suitable location when he visited it in 1912. Alternatively, he considered using any large-enough building, and inspected the Panthéon and the Palace of Versailles during a stay in Paris. But because Bach's subject was the Passion, obviously it could "be best performed at Easter and in a church – some church no longer used, but large enough, which could be kept specially for this Easter performance year by year."[29] As his scenic ideas developed it became clear that they could not be realized by converting any existing building. By 1914 he was envisioning a mammoth theater, specially erected for performances of the oratorio, in which the structure of the stage would form a permanent set. His scale model deliberately preserved the architectural atmosphere of a church.

There was nothing inherently impossible in these plans. One aspect of the symbolist movement had been a religious revival. There was at least one French precedent, an updated mystery play that had been given annual performances during Holy Week in the 1890s, and the traditional passion play at Oberammergau was becoming a regular and increasingly popular festival. On the other hand there was the example of Max Reinhardt, who in 1919 built himself his Grosses Schauspielhaus, the "Theatre of the Five Thousand" which was intended to provide the same focus for the whole community as did the theater in classical Greece. One of Reinhardt's most spectacular successes had been a sacred drama, Vollmoeller's *Miracle,* and although his sentimentalized and overblown illusionistic spectacle was the reverse of what Craig had in mind – the dramatic representation of *The St. Matthew Passion* was to be "nothing like one of those Reinhardt performances, with everyone shouting and waving their arms in the air and people catching hold of a man and dragging him away and putting him on a cross" – the general effect at which Reinhardt aimed was the same as Craig's. As Reinhardt's associate Arthur Kahane described it, "Under the influence of these mighty spaces, these big, severe lines . . . the petty and unimportant – elements that are not eternal in us – cease to have effect. [Such a] theater can only express the great eternal elemental passions and the problems of humanity. In it spectators cease to be mere spectators; they become people; their emotions are simple and primitive, but great and powerful, as becomes the eternal human race."[30]

The possibility of staging *The St. Matthew Passion* continued to occupy Craig for the rest of his active life. When he received carte blanche from New York to produce any play by Shakespeare or Maeterlinck, he cabled back, "Have finished with all talk-plays – will do Bach's Passion if you wish." When Poulsen approached him in 1926, he made no attempt to disguise the fact that his interests were almost exclusively focused on musical drama, and although he agreed to design *The Pretenders,* he cautioned that "my mind likes to concern itself very little with historical tragedy." When the opportunity for meeting Mussolini arose, it was sponsorship for *The St. Matthew Passion* for which he hoped, and he drew up a "proposal for the production in Roma . . . Easter 1936 and annual thereafter." The Italian government was to construct a stage that followed his model and an auditorium that was to hold from eight thousand to over ten thousand spectators.

The artistic goals of the proposed performances were equally ambitious and summed up the symbolic, spiritual, and universal qualities that Craig had been moving toward in all his work from 1907 on. "The aim of the work will be to make an impression which will penetrate and endure . . . the dramatic will be pushed to the furthest limit possible"; what would be created in performance out of Bach's material was "the one supreme dramatic work of art which can be understood by everybody, of every land and language, of every belief."[31] However, despite the rather overly ingenuous identification of the penetrating and enduring spiritual impression with "the spirit of Fascismo," and despite references to involving "volunteer fascisti" in the performance as the silent *figuranti* who were to mime the action, this proposal came to nothing.

The St. Matthew Passion has a special place in Craig's life. It was the one work that continued to occupy him through all the different stages of his development. Yet it was the only major project that remained almost unknown until the model was reconstructed by Edward Craig for a centenary exhibition in 1972. Even details of Scene had been published, though the etchings and description gave only the most general outline of his concept. But Bach remained in his notebooks. It is significant that such a focal work was not, in a conventionally recognizable sense, dramatic. Being an oratorio, it has voices, but no action to perform; a symbolic story, but no plot; a scene – one that unites the imagined biblical context with the performance itself as part of a religious service – but no scenery; dialogue, but no conversation. As such, it could provide the model for a new form of theater, which would preserve the continuity of the dramatic tradition while making it possible to discard all the mimetic elements that were embodied in conventional plays and staging. In 1909 Craig had made a list of the theatrical elements that his Art of the Theater would discard, in descending order of importance, indicating at the side what each was to be replaced by:

> The Human face and form – Masks . . .
> The Play                          – Ceremony
> The Spoken word             – Song

Finally man himself would disappear, and what remained would be "light – shadow – motion through impersonal mediums – and silence."[32] This last step clearly related to Scene in its most abstract and extreme form, which went too far even for Craig himself, as the consistent inclusion of figures in his designs indicate. But the plans for The St. Matthew Passion give a good example of how masks and song might be used to create a drama of ceremony.

It is also characteristic, however, that Craig's production never developed beyond notes, designs, and a model. What Craig was really offering, perhaps, was an aesthetic for using the new resources of machinery and lighting now available to the stage. Many of the devices that his sketches call for are now standard equipment, but to some extent artistic creativity has fallen behind technical developments. With the exception of certain key directors, whose work may have had a leavening effect, most of the professional theater people in England and America today use equipment capable of creating highly sophisticated effects with nineteenth-century imaginations. Leaving its specifics aside, Craig's work must be seen as a challenge to find new uses for an artistic medium that has been transformed by the fallout of progress. Yet, as his reluctance to authorize others to use his screens indicates, he came to realize that imitation of his work would achieve little. This was something that the debacle of the Broadway *Macbeth* also all too graphically demonstrated. In a sense, then, his challenge was more effective without tangible examples to which to point on stage. At the same time, any artist who aims to revolutionize his medium without working in it is in a highly questionable position, and perhaps the only viable avenue for Craig to achieve general reform in the theater would have been through educating the next generation of "theater artists" in his school.

# 8    Curtain call: A school and *The Mask*

The need for a school had been clear to Craig from the start. Working with amateurs in rented halls where he could design his own stages had given him the freedom to follow his ideas, but had at the same time prevented him from realizing them fully because, as he later said, of "the limits of the money at my disposal – i.e. next to nothing – and the untrained material."[1] The apparent solution was to move into the professional theater. Yet he rapidly found that this imposed even more frustrating restrictions. When he wanted to transfer *The Masque of Love* to the Coronet Theater in 1903, its manager rejected any idea of constructing a lighting bridge immediately behind the proscenium, and refused permission to remove the footlights, to place lights on the side walls of the auditorium, or even to alter the dimensions of the stage picture by constructing a false top for the proscenium. When Craig first directed a cast of experienced actors in *The Vikings*, later the same year, he discovered that the expertise they had acquired in conventional productions worked against everything he was trying to achieve. With *Much Ado* he found that they also reverted to their old habits almost as soon as the rehearsal period was over, effectively sabotaging his conception. Not surprisingly, as soon as he came up against the inertia of established stage practices, Craig began calling for "a School for the Art of the Theatre."

In 1903 Craig announced that he was opening a school, and found suitable studios in London. Not altogether surprisingly, as his claim to attention at the time was based solely on six rather esoteric productions, two of which had received very mixed reviews, and on a prospectus that referred only to "a school of my *belief*" – a belief as yet nowhere articulated – this attracted neither financial patrons nor potential students. But this very lack of response convinced him that nothing else would serve his aims. Barely a month later he noted that "the school scheme . . . seems more necessary and inevitable every day: not because I am not producing play after play, but because it will soon be impossible for me to produce [even] a scene of a play without the school."[2]

In 1905, after the fiasco of his collaboration with Brahm, Craig again went searching for support for a school, this time in Germany,

208

and believed he had found backing from Hugo von Hofmannsthal for a small independent theater with his own company. That plan also came to nothing, but it shaped his concept of what a school should be: a workshop for developing his own theories and translating them into practice, rather than a conservatory for teaching different performance skills. Thus "students" would be apprentices instead of pupils, and he outlined the form their training would take in his "First Dialogue on the Art of the Theatre," written in the same year. Sketching in his own experience, this described a potential director as someone who had gained stage experience as an actor and who had moved on to explore how the different elements of theater might be used. Once "he had understood the right use of actors, scene, costume, lighting and dance [the level Craig himself had achieved], and by means of these had mastered the crafts of interpretation, he would then gradually acquire the mastery of action, line, color, rhythm and words."

Even in the "Second Dialogue" of 1911, which draws up what seems to be a more conventional program for a school, the true focus is still on developing Craig's Art of the Theater. This proposed five years of study, to include voice and movement training for actors and training in design for scene painters and lighting technicians. But it is this training itself, and not a trained group of artists and craftsmen, that is defined as "the results of their labours." At the top of the list of the school's aims stand "(1) A practical demonstration of the best method to be employed for building and directing a national theatre as an ideal theatre, and in a manner hitherto deemed impossible. (2) The improvement . . . of the mechanical appliances of the modern stage." The proposed school is indeed identified as "a college of experiment in which to study . . . *voice, scene* and *action*." But voice is abstracted into sound, scene translated as light, action transformed into motion. The envisaged curriculum is in fact a process of experimentation leading through "the better knowledge" of these three fundamental elements to "the invention of better instruments through which the purer beauty of both sound and light may be passed." The end product was to be written or filmed records of these experiments "of incalculable value – not only to us in our future efforts, but to those who shall resume the search when we may be forced to abandon it."[3]

This workshop concept was pathbreaking, and points directly forward fifty years to the Center for Theater Research of Peter Brook, and to the Theater Laboratories of Grotowski and others. It foreshadows them particularly in Craig's desire to discover the preverbal fundamentals of communication, to return to the roots of drama, and to refine "the material of the theatre in *words, scene, movement* to the minimum." His experiments would strip away the traditional accretions of mimetic staging, simplifying the means of theatrical expression, and then evolving a universal "vocabulary of human motion" and vowel sounds. As he outlined the program in 1911 in a proposal that Stanislavski fund a school in Florence for the Moscow Art Theater, it would build from experiments to determine first the expressive range of the human body alone, and then the potential for communication in relationships between single figures and groups, until after three years "the whole *principle* governing action" and "the *principles* of improvisation or spontaneous acting" could be demonstrated.[4]

Again, nothing came of this, though Craig claimed that Stanislavski took over this approach in developing his "method" (conveniently overlooking its basis in psychology rather than in physical movement). Meanwhile a group of Craig's supporters in England, including the critic Haldane MacFall, W. B. Yeats, and Ezra Pound, had formed a committee "to promote the Art of the Theatre as interpreted by Gordon Craig" through arranging a drama festival for him to be held at some future date in the Crystal Palace. This never got beyond initial discussions because the whole concept revolved around productions by Craig himself. Still resenting what he had come to think of as the philistinism of the British theatrical establishment, Craig refused to produce any play in London. So the committee transformed itself into "a Society for founding a School for the Art of the Theatre," with the aim of raising £25,000 through a program of lectures, exhibitions of Craig's designs, and demonstrations with Craig's model stages.[5] Meetings were held almost weekly from September 19, 1912, to June 3, 1913, when the society resolved to limit its activities to publicity for the school, as it had failed to raise sufficient money even to cover its expenses. That the school was founded at all was due to the generosity of Lord Howard de Walden, who independently provided £5,000 in 1913 and promised a further £2,500 for each of the next two years.

Four years earlier, Craig had noted that many different kinds of schools would be needed to reform the theater, ranging from the practical and technical to the theoretical and experimental. The advertisement he published in 1912 clearly opted for the second category. "It will not be an institution for 'teaching' any art, nor for learning the crafts of acting, of decorating, or of lighting." Instead, "a body of earnest workers . . . will strive by means of experiment and research to rediscover and recreate those magic and elemental principles of beauty, simplicity and grace . . . revealing the means of doing what is left undone by the modern theatre . . . and create in the course of time a solid basis upon which the workers of the future will be able to build a vital and supreme Art."[6]

Now a group of fifteen students joined Craig at the Arena Goldoni, the small neoclassical stage on the outskirts of Florence where Craig had already established the publishing offices of *The Mask*. A pamphlet was issued reaffirming Craig's artistic principles in the context of the new school. Previous theatrical reforms, it argued, had been limited to externals – changes from thrust stage to proscenium, improvements in the machinery of illusion, new methods of lighting. By contrast, here "the essence" of theater would be renewed. Freed from constraints of commercialism or public performance, ancient traditions could be revived in new forms. As a miniature copy of a Roman amphitheater, the Arena Goldoni became the architectural symbol for what Craig called the theater of the future: "a place no less sacred in its character, no less uplifting in its influence on the national life, than were the great temples of an earlier day – those temples in which were celebrated the stately and splendid exhilarating ceremonies in praise of the Creation."[7]

Although gymnastics, fencing, dancing, mimodrama, improvisation, and voice training were listed in the curriculum, the only things actually studied seem to have been the use of Craig's screens, the potential of Herkomer's lighting techniques, the effectiveness of different types of masks, the possibilities offered by marionettes, and all aspects of theater history. (One of the adjuncts to the school was to be a theatrical museum, and it was from this that Craig's own magnificent collection grew.) Unfortunately the position of the pupils was ambiguous. They were intended to be co-workers, and "at the same time students of Mr. Craig's methods."[8] In practice this meant that they functioned as unpaid technical assistants. Also, Craig printed a set of rules for the students, which showed an almost paranoid fear of his ideas being stolen – even though the very reason for the school was to spread those ideas. Students had to undertake "not to join any other School of a similar nature," and not "to send anyone outside the School any photograph or drawing of anything concerning the School or the work being done there." Even the rules themselves were "not to be shown, nor in any way made known, to any person outside the School."[9]

The result, as Craig noted parenthetically in the margin of his own copy of the rules, was that some students found themselves unable to work under such conditions. No criticism of the school was allowed, and "the first group . . . all proved unable to stick to their guns. When hard work or some self-sacrifice was needed they fled." Whether the school would ever have produced results in the form of public demonstrations or performances is an open question. In 1909 Craig had asked himself, "What then will you do in your arena?" and had answered, "I *may* give ceremonies – processions – movements . . . slight things." In 1911 he was playing with the notion that the school should "produce ONLY *Hamlet*," but in such a way that the production "will be able to be visited many times without the audience being able to say 'we have seen it before' . . . " Elsewhere, contrasting the three years and £13,000 needed for staging the Moscow *Hamlet* with his current enterprise, he envisaged that "five years after the school is founded" the simplified systems of costume, scene, movement, and vocal expression to be developed would enable his group "to produce dramas of our own souls in a material form within 48 hours and at a cost of £20."[10] However, the First World War intervened, the Arena Goldoni was requisitioned by the Italian army, and funds from Lord Howard de Walden were cut off. The school was officially disbanded and the model stages, the most tangible products of its single year of operation and the visible exposition of Craig's ideas, were dismantled – though not in fact broken up, as Craig later claimed, perhaps as a way of justifying the effective end of his career in the theater.

There was a series of abortive efforts to relaunch the school. In 1915 and 1919 Craig held exhibitions of his model stages, screens, and marionettes in Rome to raise money for the school, and published yet another prospectus. After the war Jacques Rouché, whose *L'Art théâtrale moderne* had been referred to by Craig as one of the books "which best explain the idea for which the school stands," offered him a stage in Paris. But Craig was still more interested in exploring the principles of theater than in mounting productions. In 1935 there was talk of establishing a workshop for Craig in Moscow. All came to nothing.

But throughout this period of social upheaval and thwarted personal plans, Craig continued to publish *The Mask*, which had become perhaps the most influential theater journal in all of the intense and exciting years of the first quarter of the century. From the opening issue in 1908, which set the tone with Craig's contentious polemic "The Actor and the Ueber-Marionette," it appeared first monthly and then as a quarterly until 1929. Interrupted only by war, though continually theatened by bankruptcy, which sometimes meant that several issues were compressed into one, it became Craig's mouthpiece, his soapbox, even his stage. It contained theoretical essays on movement, scene design, and the social function of drama; historical articles on all the great theatrical traditions and periods from ancient Greek tragedy to Bunraku puppets, from the Japanese Nō to the *Commedia dell' Arte;* and critical appreciations of all the main figures in the "new movement" – Diaghilev, Duse, and Isadora Duncan, Maeterlinck, Meyerhold, and Max Reinhardt. It documented what was happening in the major European theater centers; translated and reprinted source material on Renaissance theater construction, sixteenth-century masques, and eighteenth-century costume design; and reviewed theater books and exhibitions. Its range was encyclopedic, but its perspective was single and consistent. Each subject was treated in such a way as to show the superiority of stylization over realism, of aesthetic simplicity over conventional artificiality. Every argument was designed to contribute to the vision of a new theater, defining its relationship to tradition by attacking pedantic revivals of dead forms, like the Elizabethan Stage Society, and clarifying its principles by comparing classical ballet, the Ballets Russes, and the free forms of modern dance.

From the beginning, *The Mask* was conceived as an instrument for creating a radical shift in accepted ideas about theater. Its aim was to revolutionize, not simply to inform, and free copies of the first issue were sent to all the leading directors in Europe. Having come to the conclusion that any work he produced in the existing conditions would be distorted by commercialism, undermined by the star system, or compromised by the resistance to innovation he had experienced in his dealings with theater managements, and that, given the transience of performance, any stage demonstrations of his new Art of the Theater would be soon forgotten, Craig turned to a long-term program. He was the first of the twentieth-century directors to realize that publications had the potential for creating wider and more fundamental reforms than productions. Example might condition the expectations of the general public – the artistic consumer – in the one city where a reformer's theater was based. Ideas expressed in print could reach other directors, who might have little chance of seeing a production – thus influencing the artistic producer and creating a chain reaction in many different centers.

As Craig put it, "One arena does not make an Art of the Theatre . . . it needs 100 or 1000 people to make it visible to the many." His hope in issuing *The Mask* was "that through that publication I might in time come to change the whole theatre – not plays alone, but playing, sceneries, construction of theatres – the whole thing."[11] The indirect nature of this kind of influence makes it almost impossible to document, but the way so many others subsequently followed the same path indicates the effectiveness of Craig's method. The dadaists and surrealists published manifesto after manifesto. Artaud wrote extensively, even though the rejection of verbal communication was one of his major theatrical principles. The more radical the theatrical concept, the more necessary it seems to reinforce the stage with the page, to define, explain, disseminate – even to the point where writing outweighs the art form it is intended to promote. Such, for instance, was the case of Brecht, who complained that his theoretical essays had made such an impression that his plays themselves were widely misinterpreted.

In Craig's mind *The Mask* was never meant to be completely self-sufficient. It was to be complemented by his school, which was intended to "give form and substance to all that *The Mask* for six years has been saying, actualizing that for which *The Mask* has prepared the way. Thus Practice and Theory, Theory and Practice act and react, and each confirms and strengthens the other."[12] In the end, *The Mask* had to stand on its own, but it was theory in a highly dramatic (if carefully disguised) form.

Out of the twenty regular contributors, seventeen were really Craig himself, which was why the focus was so consistent. John Balance, Charles Borrow, Allen Carric, Edward Edwardovitch, Florian M. Florian, Adolf Fuerst, Franz Hoffer, Jan van Holt, Jan Klassen, Louis Madrid, George Norman, Oliver, Guilio Pirro, Schmerz, C. Ticketts, Felix Urban, and the editor, John Semar, were all pseudonyms. Each had a distinct personality, espoused a different perspective, or symbolized a particular quality in Craig's ideal theater. The name Semar came from the fat little black Javanese marionette with a white face. The significance of Balance, the most direct proponent of Craig's ideas, was spelled out in the first issue: "The king (to the artist) is . . . the delicately worked handle without which the scales could not exist, and upon which the eye of the measurer must be fixed. Therefore I have taken these scales as the device of our new art, for our art is based upon the idea of perfect balance, the result of movement." These figures corresponded, quarreled, formed alliances against each other, and resolved their disputes – always, of course, in such a way as to promote the ideals of the "new movement," particularly as those ideas were embodied in the work of Gordon Craig. They lent theory a sense of dramatic vitality, giving Craig's demands greater force by making them seem firmly rooted all over Europe, as well as allowing an apparently objective description of his concepts. As Craig wrote to Ellen Terry, "*The Mask* is an idea – a play – in it come characters, each of whom wears a mask . . . the writer becomes impersonal in assuming his mask just as an actor becomes impersonal."[13]

Whatever the direct influence of *The Mask* (and the Moscow *Hamlet* was at least one tangible effect), it certainly helped to create a climate open to new ideas and critical of conventional practices. Craig's early productions had impressed artists as different as Yeats and Granville-Barker, who invited Craig to join first the Maeterlinck Society, then the English Stage Society. Barker later commented that "as with all idealists, Mr. Craig's influence has been mainly destructive . . . *Bethlehem* destroyed for me once and for all any illusion I may have had as to the necessity of surrounding every performance of a play with the stuffy, fussy, thickly bedaubed canvas which we are accustomed to call stage scenery . . . he opened my eyes to the possibilities of real beauty and dignity in stage decoration."[14] Reinhardt sent assistants to England to report on *The Vikings*, had copies made of Craig's designs when they were exhibited in Berlin, and invited Craig to direct productions of *King Lear* and the *Oresteia*. The Moscow *Hamlet* had a lasting influence on Meyerhold and Vaktangov, and made a great impression on Rouché as well. But Craig's writings spread his ideas everywhere.

Diaghilev, Lugné-Poë, André Gide, Appia, and Copeau, who stated that he was following Craig (among others) in founding the Vieux Colombier, were all drawn by *The Mask* to visit him in Florence. Jean-Louis Barrault called *On the Art of the Theatre* his "catechism . . . the true artist's guide to the theatre" which he "was never without," and claimed that Craig was "the perfect artist of the theatre." Strindberg reportedly found "golden words" in Craig's writings.[15] But the influence of his books and journals can best be indicated by the number of invitations he received from people who had never seen his work on stage. Cochran, the impresario responsible for the famous production of *The Miracle*, approached him in 1913; Scandiani, the manager of La Scala, in 1921. In 1922 Ernest Dare invited him "to form a company on new lines" at the Bijou Theater in London, and the American Stage Company proposed an association. There were the Poulsens in Copenhagen and Tyler in New York, and in 1932 the Habima company asked him to direct for them in Jerusalem. In 1935 Amaglobeli, the director of the State Academic Little Theater in Moscow, invited him to mount a production, and Ormerod Greenwood offered the Group Theater as a nucleus for a theater company of Craig's own. Even after the Second World War there was a continuing stream of visiting playwrights, directors, and critics – among them Sean O'Casey, Julian Beck, Peter Brook, and Kenneth Tynan – all drawn by the vision preserved in his essays.

However, *The Mask* was also partly responsible for the fact that Craig never fulfilled his promise as a director. The constant need for new articles and fresh material made incessant demands on his time and diverted his energies from the stage, even during the Moscow *Hamlet*. Yet in a sense, as an ongoing collection of short essays covering the whole range of theater, it was the perfect vehicle for a man with so many diverse enthusiasms that he was seldom able to concentrate on any one thing sufficiently to complete it. Between 1906 and 1907, for instance, he was simultaneously working on designs for *Rosmersholm* and *Hamlet*; rewriting and choreographing the *Masque of Hunger*; working out the principle of his screens and making the first miniature sets for the model theater he constructed; experimenting with the concept of Scene and doing the first drawings to illustrate the kind of effects that might be achieved with such a radically new stage form; making the first of his series of Black Figures; preparing material and doing the woodcuts that were published in the first issues of *The Mask*; overseeing the construction of his costumes and sets for *Electra*; negotiating with Duse about sequels to the *Rosmersholm* production; and attempting to act as Isadora Duncan's business agent.

Hardly surprisingly, given this level of activity on so many fronts, Craig's career is a list of unfinished projects. *The St. Matthew Passion* remained a half-formed work of brilliant but disconnected insights and effects. No mechanism was ever developed for Scene, so the images of unceasing movement stayed frozen in a series of designs and etchings never to be realized in the theater. Even some of the technical problems involved in using the screens were never solved. The flexible proscenium, and the new relationships he imagined between stage and auditorium, were never translated into architectural plans, let alone bricks and mortar. None of the masques that he worked on after *The Masque of Love* reached the stage, and in his eyes not one of the productions he directed fully represented his ideas, despite critical acclaim. He later dismissed not only *Macbeth* and *Rosmersholm*, over which he had had little control, but also *The Vikings*, *Hamlet*, and *The Crown Pretenders* with the terse comment, "nothing of this to my satisfaction."[16]

Yet to some extent this was the inevitable price for such a global vision of theatrical reform. Toward the end of his career, Craig regretted having "very wantonly spent too much time throwing challenges to the old theatre" in his designs and writings, "instead of getting hold of one playhouse and steadily establishing proof upon proof of the excellence of our ideas and plans."[17] Even so, paradoxically, Craig's ideas have had a wide and lasting impact precisely because they were never given a finished, concrete expression. Some of the elements of his Art of the Theater would have dated badly. Others – in particular, the quasi-religious material around which his later theatrical forms became centered – would have seemed unacceptably pretentious or too far removed from contemporary consciousness. Those that were ahead of their time, such as Scene, could now be put into practice relatively easily with advances in technology. But even so Scene could at best provide one possibility of staging, and would be suited to only a limited range of dramatic material. At worst it might seem an idiosyncratic curiosity. Certainly that has been the fate of Terence Gray's "Dance Drama" – a direct 1930's copy of Craig's ideas, that amalgamated the concept of Scene with semitransparent screens set up in the shape of movable hollow pillars, with the rather cheaply spectacular addition of back lighting in all imaginable hues within these pillars. In either case, the elements of Craig's new theater would hardly act as the challenge to total theatrical reform that can be seen as the real value of Craig's work.

To some extent, too, projects remained incomplete and productions never measured up to his ideas because every achievement formed the basis for a fresh departure. Craig's theories were in a state of continuous development. One characteristic of modern drama seems to be that new forms supersede each theatrical reform as soon as that reform becomes established enough to react against. If Craig's ideas have survived, it is perhaps because they never became fixed in an identifiable style of production. The proposed title for one of the books that he planned, but never wrote, is characteristic: *The New Movement – and the Newer One.* It was in his notes for this book that Craig singled out the Chinese theater as an ideal, because in it everything was left to the spectator's imagination – a bare stick could become a blossoming tree. The same could be said of his own work.

# Edward Gordon Craig, 1872–1966:
## A theatrical chronology

### THE ACTOR

1878    Appears on stage in a nonspeaking part in *Olivia* at the Court Theater at the age of six.

1881    Makes a brief, nonspeaking appearance in *Charles I* at the Alexandra Theater, Liverpool.

1884    Plays nonspeaking roles with the Lyceum Company on tour in America in *Hamlet, Much Ado About Nothing, Twelfth Night,* and *Charles I.*

1885    Acts in his first speaking role in the Lyceum Company's performance of *Eugene Aram* in Chicago.

1889    Joins the Lyceum Company and makes his London debut as Arthur de Saint Valéry in *The Dead Heart.*

1890    Plays Moses in *Olivia,* Caleb Deecie in *Two Roses,* and Henry Ashton in *Ravenswood* for the Lyceum. Tours with the Haviland and Harvey Company in *Two Roses, The Day After the Wedding, The Taming of the Shrew,* and *The Lady of Lyons,* acting in roles selected by Henry Irving.

1891    Plays the Messenger and one of the Watch in *Much Ado About Nothing,* Alexander Oldworthy in *Nance Oldfield,* and Abel Quick in *A Regular Fix* at the Lyceum. Plays Charles Surface in *School for Scandal* in summer stock for Sarah Thorne's Company, then tours as Malcolm in *Macbeth* and Lorenzo in *The Merchant of Venice* with the Lyceum Company.

1892    Plays Cromwell in *Henry VIII* and Oswald in *King Lear* at the Lyceum, Ford in *The Merry Wives of Windsor* and Petruccio in *The Taming of the Shrew* at the Margate Theater, then returns to the Lyceum to play Oswald in *King Lear.*

1893    *The Merchant of Venice* is revived at the Lyceum with Craig again as Lorenzo. This is followed by Tennyson's *Becket,* in which he plays the Youngest Knight Templar. This role marks the end of his regular association with the Lyceum. Directs Alfred de Musset's *No Trifling with Love (On ne badine pas avec l'amour)* for his own company in Uxbridge, designing scenes and costumes as well as playing the lead role.

1894    Joins the W. S. Hardy Shakespeare Company to tour as Ro-

218

meo, Hamlet, Charles Surface, Cassio in *Othello*, Gratiano in *The Merchant of Venice*, and Richmond in *Richard III*.

1895 Joins the Evelyn and Leigh Company as Cavaradossi in *La Tosca*. Plays lead roles in *The New Magdalen*, *The Streets of London*, *La Dame aux Camélias*, *The Lady of Lyons*, and *Hamlet* at Paisley. Tours Aberdeen and Dundee in *François Villon*.

1896 Plays Petruccio in *The Taming of the Shrew* and the title roles in *The Corsican Brothers*, *Macbeth*, and *Hamlet* with Sarah Thorne's Company in Chatham before rejoining the Lyceum Company at Liverpool in his old parts.

### THE ACTOR-MANAGER

Directs and plays the title role in *Romeo and Juliet* with his own company at the Parkhurst Theater, then returns to the Lyceum to play Arviragus in *Cymbeline* and Edward IV in *Richard III*.

1897 Directs and plays leading roles in *François Villon* and *The New Magdalen* with his own company at the Theater Royal in Croydon, but returns to play Edward IV in the Lyceum revival of *Richard III*, then takes over the title role in *Hamlet* (wearing Irving's costume) at the Olympic Theater. Plays Young Marlow in *She Stoops To Conquer* (with Granville-Barker) at the Kingston-on-Thames Theater, and puts on an impromptu performance of *François Villon* (with James Pryde) plus a Pierrot show. Resigns from the Lyceum Company and ceases to act.

1898 Writes and publishes the first four issues of *The Page* and devises *What the Moon Saw* (a Pierrot show based on a Hans Andersen story).

1899 Publishes *The Page*, and also *The Gordon Craig Book of Penny Toys*, and *Woodcuts and Some Words* (Hackbridge, at the Sign of the Rose), as well as sketches of leading British actors for newspapers and journals, nineteen of which were reproduced in *Henry Irving, Ellen Terry: A Book of Portraits* (Chicago). Begins to design scenes for imaginary dramas.

### THE DIRECTOR

1900 Publishes *The Page* and a booklet entitled *Bookplates*. Directs and designs *Dido and Aeneas* for the Purcell Operatic Society at the Hampstead Conservatoire with Martin Shaw.

1901 Directs and designs *The Masque of Love* (adapted from Purcell's masque for *Dioclesian*) at the Coronet Theater, together with a revival of *Dido and Aeneas*. Breaks off publication of *The Page* (vol. 4, no. 2).

1902    Directs and designs Handel's *Acis and Galatea* together with a revival of *The Masque of Love*, at the Great Queen St. Theater. Directs and designs Laurence Housman's *Bethlehem* at the Imperial Institute. Starts to devise original masques with *Harvest Home*, which was advertised but never produced, and holds the first major exhibition of his drawings and woodcuts in London.

1903    Directs and designs Ibsen's *The Vikings at Helgeland* and Shakespeare's *Much Ado About Nothing* for Ellen Terry's company at the Imperial Theater. Designs costumes and three of the scenes for R. G. Legge's *For Sword or Song* at the Shaftsbury Theater. Devises an "Alhambra Masque" and begins to make designs for *The Masque of Hunger*, *The Masque of London*, and *The Masque of Lunatics*. Advertises a "London School of Theatrical Art," and holds his first exhibition of theatrical designs.

THE AUTHOR AND DESIGNER

1904    Designs scenes, which are only partially realized, for Hofmannsthal's version of Otway's *Venice Preserved* (produced by Otto Brahm at the Lessing Theater in 1905), and meets Isadora Duncan. The first exhibition of Craig's designs is mounted in Berlin.

1905    Prepares designs for *The Tempest* and Bernard Shaw's *Caesar and Cleopatra* for Max Reinhardt, though these never reach the stage because Craig demands complete control of the productions. Designs Hugo von Hofmannsthal's *Electra* for Eleonora Duse (unproduced, though the costumes and scenery were completed under Craig's direction) and illustrates *The White Fan* for Hofmannsthal. Publishes *The Art of the Theatre* in German and English (translated into Dutch and pirated in Russian in 1906, issued in Japanese in 1912 and in Hungarian and Danish in 1963). Exhibits his theatrical designs in Cologne, Dresden, Dusseldorf, Munich, Vienna, Weimar, and Zurich.

1906    Publishes *Isadora Duncan: Six Movement Designs*. Designs Duse's production of Ibsen's *Rosmersholm* (first staged at the Pergola Theater in Florence) and issues "A Note on Rosmersholm." Writes "The Actor and The Über-Marionette" (published in vol. 1 of *The Mask* and in *On the Art of the Theatre*). Develops *The Masque of Hunger*.

1907 Writes "The Artists of the Theatre of the Future," and "Motion" (later republished in vol. 1 of *The Mask* and inserted as a preface in *Scene*). Constructs his first model theater to experiment with his screens, and begins the first of his series of Black Figures.

1908 Starts to design screen scenes and costumes for *Hamlet* at Stanislavski's invitation. Publishes his first *Portfolio of Etchings* (the *Oresteia* and *King Lear*) and the first volume of *The Mask*, a monthly journal of the Art of the Theatre. Presents Ellen Terry with a set of screens and designs arrangements for their use in *The Merchant of Venice* (unproduced). Prepares designs of settings and choreography for a projected ballet of *Psyche*, and exhibits "Designs for Motion" in Florence.

1909 Publishes vol. 2 of *The Mask*. Presents W. B. Yeats with a set of screens for the Irish National Theater and designs scenes (unused) for Beerbohm Tree's production of *Macbeth*. Discusses designing a production of *King Lear* (abortive) for Reinhardt.

1910 Publishes vol. 3 of *The Mask* and a second *Portfolio of Etchings*. Travels to Moscow to work out the interpretation of *Hamlet* with Stanislavski and to begin the production process.

1911 Publishes vol. 4 of *The Mask* and the English edition of *On the Art of the Theatre* (translated into French in 1920, into Italian in 1924, and subsequently into Hungarian, Spanish, Polish, and Russian). Yeats's *The Hour Glass* and Lady Gregory's *The Deliverer* are produced at the Abbey Theater in Dublin with Craig's screen-arrangements. (The screens influence Yeats in revising *Dierdre* and are still in use for *On Baile's Strand* in 1914.)

1912 Publishes vol. 5 of *The Mask*. Craig's production of *Hamlet* (as interpreted by Stanislavski) is staged at the Moscow Art Theater using the screens. Mounts an exhibition of his stage designs, including those for *The Vikings*, *Macbeth*, and *Hamlet*, in London (transferred to Manchester, and in 1913 to Liverpool, Dublin, and Leeds).

THE THEORIST

1913 Publishes *Towards A New Theater*, and vol. 6 of *The Mask*.

Opens the School for the Art of the Theater at the Arena Goldoni in Florence, and issues "A Living Theater," which describes the school's aims and activities.

1914    Builds the large model stage for Bach's *St. Matthew Passion* and begins writing marionette plays, including *The Scene*. Publishes vol. 7 of *The Mask*.

1915    Breaks off publication of *The Mask* with the August issue, vol. 8, and closes the school.

1916–    Writes marionette plays, including *School, The Gordian Knot,*
1917    *Once Upon a Time,* and *Mr. Fish and Mrs. Bones* (published in 1918 and 1919 under the pseudonym of Tom Fool).

1918    Begins publishing *The Marionette* as a monthly journal in March; *The Mask* reappears in April.

1919    Breaks off publication of *The Mask* once more after the March issue, vol. 9. Ceases to issue *The Marionette* with the twelfth issue in August. Publishes *The Theatre Advancing* in the United States (reprinted in England in 1921 and translated into French in 1964). Advises Lovat Fraser on designs for *The Beggar's Opera* (performed at the Lyric Theater in 1920).

1921    Publishes *Puppets and Poets* (London).

1922    Shows work at the International Theater Exhibit in Amsterdam.

1923    *The Mask* reappears as a single issue. Publishes *Scene* with Oxford University Press (incorporating etchings from the portfolios of 1908 and 1910 together with the essay entitled "Motion" from 1907 and a foreword by John Masefield).

1924    Publishes vol. 10 of *The Mask* as a quarterly. Also publishes *Woodcuts and Some Words* (London).

1925    Publishes vol. 11 of *The Mask, Books and Theatres,* and *Nothing, or the Bookplate* (London).

1926    Publishes vol. 12 of *The Mask*. Designs Ibsen's *The Crown Pretenders* for Johannes and Adam Poulsen, and collaborates on the production at the Royal Theater in Copenhagen. Receives the Order of the Knights of the Danneborg for his services to the Danish theater.

1927    Publishes vol. 13 of *The Mask,* and exhibits work at the Deutsche Theater-Ausstellung at Magdeburg. (Craig was the only non-German invited.)

1928    Publishes vol. 14 of *The Mask*. Designs and outlines a production of *Macbeth* (signed C.P.B. for "Craig Pot-Boiler") for George Tyler in New York, and exhibits the designs for *Macbeth* in New York and for *The Pretenders* in London.

1929     Ceases to issue *The Mask* with vol. 15. Publication of the Cranach Press edition of *Hamlet* with seventy-five woodcuts by Craig (reprinted in England in 1930). Approached by Norman Bel Geddes to design productions for a theater festival planned as part of the Chicago World Fair, and exhibits stage designs at the International Theater Congress and Exposition in Barcelona.

1930     Publishes *A Production, 1926* (Oxford) and *Henry Irving* (London).

1931     Publishes *Ellen Terry and Her Secret Self* in a limited edition (reprinted in ordinary editions in Britain and the United States, 1932).

1932     Receives an invitation to direct the Habima Company in Jerusalem.

1934     Contributes "settings for an Ideal Theatre" to the International Exhibition of Theater Art at the Museum of Modern Art in New York, and attends the convention on theater of the Foundazione Alessandro Volta (together with Yeats, Tairov, Maeterlinck, and Pirandello).

1935     Travels to Moscow to discuss the possibility of setting up his own workshop theater, and proposes a production of Bach's *St. Matthew Passion* (as an alternative to a suggested production of *Quo Vadis*) for the Coliseum in Rome.

1946     Elected a member of the French Syndicat des metteurs en scène.

1951     Presents fourteen talks about theater on the BBC.

1956     Made a Companion of Honour by Queen Elizabeth in recognition of his services to the theater.

1957     Publishes *Index to the Story of my Days* simultaneously in London and New York.

1961     Made an honorary member of the United Scenic Artists in New York.

# Notes

To save confusion and to avoid repetition, initials have been used for those names that recur frequently: EGC for Edward Gordon Craig, ET for Ellen Terry, ID for Isadora Duncan, MFS for Martin Fallas Shaw, and WBY for William Butler Yeats. In addition, the titles of certain books are referred to in a shortened form after their first appearance: for example, *Index* for Gordon Craig's *Index to the Story of My Days*, and *Gordon Craig* for Edward Craig's *Gordon Craig: The Story of His Life*. In each case in which Craig's notebooks, daybooks, or other unpublished material is first referred to, the collection in which the work is to be found has been indicated in parentheses: BL for the British Library in London, BN for the Bibliothèque Nationale in Paris, Bledlow for the Edward Craig Collection in Bledlow, HRC for the Humanities Research Center of the University of Texas at Austin, Rood for the Arnold Rood Collection in New York, LC for the Museum of the Performing Arts at Lincoln Center in New York, UCLA for the Rare Books Collection of the University of California at Los Angeles, and V & A for the Enthoven Collection of the Victoria and Albert Museum in London.

## 1. PROLOGUE: THE ARGUMENT

1. MFS, *The Observer*, November 29, 1931; Helen Chinoy, *Directors on Directing*, ed. Toby Cole and Helen Chinoy (Indianapolis, 1976), p. 45; (First published 1953).
2. ID, *My Life* (New York, 1927), p. 185, and EGC's marginal annotation, dated 1945 (BN).
3. *The Times* (London), July 30, 1966.
4. Lee Simonson, "The Case of Gordon Craig," *Theater Guild Magazine* (February, 1931), pp. 19f. For comparison, see Chinoy, *Directors*, pp.41f., where Craig is referred to as an "evangelist . . . [and] an effective propagandist" whose "own productions were few and never completely successful," whose "sketches were basically impractical as scene designs," and whose "manifestoes were contradictory and often illogical."
5. Letter to MFS, May 20, 1905 (HRC).
6. EGC, "14 Notes on 8 pages from *The Story of the Theater* by Glenn Hughes," ed. Glenn Hughes (University of Washington Press, 1931), pp. 8 and 11; Daybook 2, 1910–11, p. 63 (HRC).
7. Theatre Designs. Notebook 1904–5–6, p. 106 (HRC); "Books on the Theatre, II," TS, n.d. (HRC).
8. Daybook 6, 1933, p. 15 (HRC).
9. For a full description of *The Pretenders* production, see Frederick and Lise-Lone Marker, *Edward Gordon Craig & The Pretenders* (Carbondale, 1982).
10. EGC, *Index to the Story of My Days* (New York, 1957), p. 213.

## 2. SCENE CHANGES: VICTORIAN THEATER, AN ACTING CAREER, AND POINTS OF DEPARTURE

1. Cf. EGC, *Henry Irving* (New York, 1930), p. 186, and EGC, "14 Notes," p. 9: "You must add that my master . . . was IRVING; my tutors, self-chosen – Walt Whitman, William Blake, Shakespeare – no realists."

224

2. EGC, *Henry Irving*, pp. 96 and 49. (Craig was not relying on memory for his descriptions of Irving's productions. Although this study was published in 1930, it is based on notes made in 1901 or earlier.)

3. Quoted in Bram Stoker, *Personal Reminiscences of Henry Irving* (London, 1906), vol. 1, p. 147.

4. EGC, *Henry Irving*, p. 74.

5. Ibid., p. 54; Henry Irving, *The Drama: Addresses* (London, 1893), pp. 55f. and 157.

6. EGC, *Henry Irving*, pp. 55 and 59; Ellen Terry and Bernard Shaw, *A Correspondence*, ed. C. St. John (London, 1931), p. 228, and Felix Emmel, *Das ecstatische Theater* (Prien, 1924), p. 37. For a full discussion of expressionist acting, see my book, *Holy Theatre* (Cambridge, 1981), pp. 46f.

7. EGC, *Henry Irving*, pp. 56–8. For a more objective description of this performance, cf. David Mayer, ed., *Henry Irving and The Bells* (Manchester, 1980), pp. 22, 45, 47, 83.

8. William Archer, *Henry Irving, Actor and Manager* (London, 1883), pp. 67–8; EGC, *Henry Irving*, p. 61.

9. EGC, *Index*, p. 154.

10. Ibid., pp. 156, 216, 159–60; Daybook 6, 1933, p. 46.

11. *The Era*, July 25, 1896; *The People*, July 26, 1896.

12. EGC, *Henry Irving*, pp. 74 and 32. For EGC's criticism of Irving's "egotistical" productions, see p. 84 of *Henry Irving*; also see EGC, *On the Art of the Theater* (London, 1962), p. 173.

13. EGC, *Henry Irving*, p. 91. Cf. also EGC, *Index*, p. 61.

14. ET, cit. George Taylor, *Henry Irving at the Lyceum* (Cambridge, 1980), p. 38.

15. EGC, *Henry Irving*, p. 113.

16. Handwritten note (d. 1948) in his program for *No Trifling with Love*, Uxbridge Town Hall, December 13/14, 1893; promptbook, pp. 148, 166, 172 (UCLA).

17. *Middlesex and Bucks Advertiser*, December 16, 1893; promptbook, p. 145 and an interleaved note.

18. EGC, *Index*, p. 149; promptbook for *A Midsummer Night's Dream* (unperformed) 1896 (UCLA).

19. Theodore Child, "A Christmas Mystery in the Fifteenth Century," *Harpers New Monthly* (1888–9), vol. 78, pp. 59f.

20. EGC, Daybook 5, 1930–3, p. 26 (HRC); Thomas A. Janvier, "The Comédie Française at Orange," *Century Magazine* (June, 1895), vol. 50, no. 2, pp. 165f.

21. Daybook 5, p. 26.

22. E. W. Godwin, *The British Architect*, May 29, 1874, p. 342.

23. Program, Prince of Wales Theater, April, 1875; *The Illustrated Sporting and Dramatic News*, April 24, 1875 and January 3, 1881.

24. Cit. J. C. Trewin, *Shakespeare on the English Stage, 1900–1964* (London, 1964), p. 14.

25. Advertisement for *Helena in Troas*, April, 1886 (Handbill, V & A); *The Illustrated Sporting and Dramatic News*, May 29, 1889, *Life*, 1886, p. 943, and *The Pall Mall Gazette*, May 18, 1886.

26. John Todhunter, *Helena in Troas* ("as adapted for the stage and produced by E. W. Godwin") (London, 1886), p. 15; *The Daily Telegraph*, May 18, 1886. The plot of Todhunter's play verges on the ludicrous. Paris alone can defend the city, and when he is wounded by a poisoned arrow only his discarded wife Oenone can save him. She will only do so if Paris will return to her, but Paris would rather die than renounce Helen, and her resulting suicide provides a melodramatic climax (p. 21):

| OENONE: | Death, Death, hail Death! |
| CHORUS: | O mighty love, self-slain in slaying her! |
| | O furious passion strangled suddenly! |

For dead she is, having with piteous shriek
O'leaped the battlements, and crushed and dead lies;
Her wild soul shrill in the shrieking air.

27. EGC, letter to MFS, September 6, 1904 (HRC); *The British Architect*, October 15, 1886. (As EGC remarked, "A *mise en scène* is childs-play when one has had an architect for a father and Irving for a master," and he wrote of Godwin that his own "vocation" could "easily seem to be his–architecture," EGC, *Index*, p. 101.)
28. "Professor Herkomer's School," *The Art Annual* (1892), n.p. Hubert v. Herkomer, *The Magazine of Art* (July, 1889), p. 316. (For a contemporary evaluation of Herkomer's influence, particularly on Irving, see Edwin Sachs, *Stage Construction* [London, 1898], cit. Herkomer, *My School and My Gospel* [London, 1908], p. 205.)
29. Cf. EGC, *Index*, pp. 100, 122, and 131.
30. *The Magazine of Art* (May, 1892), p. 261.
31. Ibid, p. 319.
32. Cf. Edward Craig, "Gordon Craig and Hubert von Herkomer," *Theatre Research*, vol. 10, no. 1 (1969), pp. 9–10.
33. Herkomer, *My School and My Gospel*, p. 203; *The Magazine of Art* (July, 1892), pp. 316, 320.
34. *The Magazine of Art* (May, 1892), pp. 261, 259, and 262; EGC, *On the Art of the Theatre*, p. 161; Herkomer, *My School and My Gospel*, pp. 151 and 140.

3. A RISING ACTION: DESIGN AND MOVEMENT

1. Notebook 1904–5–6, p. 106.
2. Daybook 6, p. 120 (d. 1949), and EGC, *Index*, p. 210.
3. Haldane Macfall, *The Studio* (1901), no. 102, p. 255, and *Review of the Week*, August 11, 1900.
4. EGC interview, *The Daily News*, April 15, 1903.
5. EGC MS. Book 13, p. 25 (BN).
6. EGC, *Towards A New Theatre* (London, 1913), p. 29.
7. Nahum Tate and Henry Purcell, *Dido and Aeneas* (London, 1887), pp. 6f., and EGC, souvenir program for *Dido and Aeneas* (May, 1900 and March, 1901), n.p.; EGC, cit. Edward Craig, *Gordon Craig: The Story of His Life* (New York, 1968), p. 121.
8. Souvenir Program, and *Dido and Aeneas* promptbook (1901, EGC's personal copy), p. 38 (BN).
9. WBY, *The Saturday Review*, March 8, 1902; *The Speaker*, May 11, 1901 (where the style of performance was also referred to as "a new and legitimate art, appealing to a taste formed by itself and copying nothing but itself"); *The Hampstead Annual* (1900), p. 138.
10. *Dido and Aeneas* promptbook, p. 38.
11. *The Hampstead Annual* (1900), p. 138; WBY, *The Saturday Review*, March 8, 1902.
12. Notebook–Dido (1900), n.p. (UCLA), and *Dido and Aeneas* promptbook, p. 24.
13. Reported by *The Musical Standard*, March 30, 1901, and by George Sampson in a letter to *The Times* (London), March 21, 1926.
14. *The Daily Chronicle*, April 1, 1901; *The Hampstead Annual* (1900), p. 138; *Review of the Week*, August 11, 1900.
15. *Dido and Aeneas* promptbook, pp. 1 and 5.
16. Edward Craig, "Gordon Craig and Hubert von Herkomer," *Theatre Research*, vol. 10, no. 1 (1969), p. 10–to which I am indebted for many of the details of this performance–and W. B. Yeats, letter to Nora Dryhurst, d. April 2 (HRC).

17. Letter to MFS, cit. Craig, *Gordon Craig*, p. 118.
18. Notebook–Dido n.p.; EGC, *On the Art of the Theatre*, p. 21 (1907); *The Musical Standard*, March 30, 1901.
19. All stage directions are taken from the *Dido and Aeneas* promptbook, pp. 16–17, 21, 26–7, 32–3, 36, and from Notebook–Dido (n.p.).
20. Notebook–Dido, n.p., and annotated copy of the souvenir program for *Dido and Aeneas* (BN).
21. Notebook–Dido, n.p., and MFS, *Up to Now* (London, 1929), p. 28.
22. Program, *Dido and Aeneas* and *The Masque of Love*, 1901.
23. EGC, *Index*, p. 235; and EGC, MS annotation to a "Biographical Note" Craig issued in 1919 (Bledlow), on which he drew a graph in 1948. The line on the graph rises from *Dido* to *The Masque*, then falls to *Acis* and *Bethlehem* (both ranked half-way between the preceding productions), and shows *Vikings* descending to the low point occupied by *Much Ado*, which leads in the direction of commercial theater and Craig's bête noir, the cinema.
24. *The Artist*, NS, vol. 1, no. 1 (May, 1902), p. 27; *Sphere*, vol. 8, no. 113, March 22, 1902, p. 291.
25. Cf. Craig, *Gordon Craig*, p. 152.
26. Graham Robertson, preface to *The Art of the Theatre*, 1905, cit. Craig, *Gordon Craig*, p. 151, and Max Beerbohm, *Saturday Review*, April 5, 1902 (reprinted in *Around Theatres* [New York, 1930], vol. 1, p. 257).
27. EGC, promptbook for *Acis and Galatea*, sketch 3 (BN), and Robertson, preface, p. 151.
28. Henry Nevinson, notebook, cit. Janet Leeper, *Edward Gordon Craig: Designs for the Theatre* (Harmondsworth, 1948), p. 7, and Craig, *Gordon Craig*, p. 136.
29. MS instructions on the costume designs (BN).
30. *The Artist*, NS, vol. 1, no. 1, p. 57.
31. MFS, *Up to Now*, p. 28, and Haldane MacFall, letter to EGC, March 13, 1902. The triple bill of *Nance Oldfield* (ET's very short curtain raiser), *Dido* and *The Masque* stretched performances from 8:00 p.m. to well after midnight with the long intervals between each scene. As a result, much of the audience had left before the work that Craig regarded as his masterpiece began.
32. Notebook–Acis and Galatea (1901–2), n.p. (HRC).
33. Program, *Dido and Aeneas* and *The Masque of Love*, 1901; Daybook 6, p. 120.
34. Christopher St. John, "The Masque of Love" (undated: BN), and note in the program for *Dido and Aeneas* and *The Masque of Love*, 1901.
35. *The Musical Standard*, March 30, 1901, p. 194.
36. Robertson, preface; Craig, *Gordon Craig*, p. 147. The advertisement was privately published by EGC in London in 1904.
37. *The Playgoer*, vol. 2 (April–September 1902), p. 31; Notebook–Acis and Galatea; promptbook for *The Masque of Love* (BN).
38. Arthur Symons, *The Monthly Review* (June, 1902) (reprinted in *Studies in the Seven Arts* [London, 1906], pp. 349–50).
39. EGC, *On the Art of the Theatre*, p. 52; Symons, *Monthly Review* (Craig's marginalia are in his scrapbook of press clippings–BN).

## 4. PROBLEM DRAMA: TEXTS AND PERFORMERS

1. Purcell, preface to *The Prophetess, or the History of Dioclesian* (London, 1691); MFS, *Up to Now*, p. 27.
2. EGC, note (dated 1943) in promptbook, *The Masque of Love*, p. 2; MFS, *Up to Now*, p. 26.

3. MFS letter to EGC, n.d. (1902: HRC).
4. *The Critic*, vol. 42 (February, 1903), p. 140; *The Times* (London), February 24, 1903. Cf. also Craig, *Gordon Craig*, p. 164.
5. Promptbook, *Bethlehem*, pp. 11 and 14 (BN).
6. *The Critic*, vol. 42 (February, 1903), p. 140.
7. Daybook 1, 1908–10 (HRC), p. 159. Cf. also EGC, *Towards A New Theatre*, p. 9.
8. Laurence Housman, letters to EGC, undated, August 24, and July 7, 1902 (UCLA).
9. Housman, letters to EGC, September 8 and 10, 1902; EGC, Sketchbook 1902, n.p. (BN); Housman to EGC, August 28 and undated; EGC, promptbook, p. 24; notes by Nora Dryhurst in her copy of *Bethlehem* (HRC).
10. For details about the reuse or rediscovery of these ideas by Artaud, Barrault, Schechner, and Piscator, see my books, *Holy Theatre*, pp. 127f. and 183f., and *Modern German Drama* (Cambridge, 1979), p. 172.
11. Promptbook, *Bethlehem*, pp. 26–7 and 29–30; notes by Nora Dryhurst; Laurence Housman, "In Spite of the Censor," *The Critic*, vol. 42 (February, 1903).
12. EGC, note on title page of the promptbook (1915); undated letter to MFS.
13. Housman, letter to EGC, June 4, 1902; *The Critic*, vol. 42 (February, 1903); letter to EGC, July 1, 1902. Paradoxically, the example Housman recommended that Craig follow here was equally out of sympathy with the theme of the play and echoed Craig's approach precisely in substituting aesthetic effects for religious content. According to William Poel, "An acted religion is all insincere . . . and the tendency of such plays is towards sentimentalism and claptrap. I did not myself produce *Everyman* as a religious play. Its theology is indefensible . . . but the whole story, Eastern not Catholic in its origin, is beautiful as a piece of art; it offers a hundred opportunities from the point of view of beauty" (*Daily Chronicle*, September 3, 1913).
14. Housman, letters to EGC, July 8, undated, and August 24, 1902.
15. Housman, letter to EGC, November 24, 1902; Charles Ashbee, journal, December, 1902 (Kings College, Cambridge); EGC, letter to ET, November, 1902 (UCLA).
16. EGC, *Towards A New Theatre*, p. 51.
17. EGC, letter to MFS, August, 1902. Cf. also *The Star*, April 16, 1903.
18. *Pall Mall Gazette*, April 16, 1903; EGC, *Towards A New Theatre*, p. 73.
19. Cf. Craig, *Gordon Craig*, p. 169, and J. G. Buckle, *Theatre Construction and Maintenance* (London, 1888); EGC, interview in *The Tatler*, no. 98, May 13, 1903, p. 260.
20. *The Saturday Review*, April 28, 1903.
21. Cf. Craig, *Gordon Craig*, p. 171; EGC notes on construction appended to sketches of props; *The Vikings* promptbook, p. 164 (BN).
22. *Lady's Pictorial*, April 25, 1903, p. 884; *The Saturday Review*, April 28, 1903; James Huneker, *Iconoclasts: A Book of Dramatists* (London, 1905), p. 31. Similarly, in Craig's production of *Much Ado* the church was suggested by a backing of gray curtains, two of which were gathered in the foreground to suggest great columns, and decorated with patterns of "dirty yellow – like old ivory – varnished all over" (EGC, promptbook: B.N.) to catch the dim light. Yet one critic gave a detailed description of "arched mosaic columns" and "Byzantine splendour." (Cf. Craig, *Gordon Craig*, pp. 175–6.) See also *Black and White*, April 25, 1903, p. 566.
23. Huneker, *Iconoclasts*, p. 32; *The Saturday Review,*, April 28, 1903.
24. EGC, letter to MFS, November 11, 1903; *The Saturday Review*, April 28, 1903, and *The Playgoer*, vol. 4, no. 19 (May, 1903), p. 397.
25. EGC, *On the Art of the Theatre*, pp. 11, 35–6, and 82. Cf. also WBY, *Essays and Introductions* (London, 1961), p. 224 (1916).

26. ET, interview in *The Daily Telegraph*, April 6, 1903; Huneker, *Iconoclasts*, p. 31, and MFS, *Up to Now*, p. 35; *The Daily Chronicle*, April 16, 1903, and *The Playgoer*, vol. 4, no. 20 (June, 1903).

27. EGC, interview in *The Daily News*, April 15, 1903, and letter to MFS, November 11, 1903.

28. EGC, *On the Art of the Theatre*, p. 53 (1907); *Theatre Arts Monthly*, vol. 11, no. 4 (April, 1927).

29. William Rothenstein, *The Saturday Review*, May 9, 1903; EGC, holograph note in the program for *The Vikings*, Imperial Theater, April 15, 1903 (BN), and letter to ET, March 8, 1903.

30. Cf. EGC, *Index*, p. 241. The costs for *Dido* were £373.10.6, of which 61 percent went to scenery, costumes, lighting and programs. For each performance the orchestra was paid £10.10.0, hairdressing and makeup cost £2.7.0, and the hire of the hall £9.10.0. If the actors and chorus had been paid 2 pounds and 1 pound respectively each week for six performances, their total salary for one performance would have been £8.12.0, and the total cost per performance £30.19.0. The sale of tickets brought in an average of £44 at each performance. (The total income for three nights was £192.15.6, out of which £60 were subscriptions to the Purcell Society; the remaining deficit was made up by donations from the cast and Ellen Terry.) The actual profit per performance would therefore have been £13.1.0, and it would have taken forty performances to clear the true cost of £513.15.6: £305.15.6, representing the actual amounts laid out on staging and advertising together with the running costs for that number of nights, plus £208 for the actors' salaries over the rehearsal period. (For a breakdown of the actual costs, see Craig, *Gordon Craig* p. 126.) In a regular theater the time needed would have been even longer, despite larger houses. EGC's correspondence with E. G. Saunders about the rental of the Coronet Theater (BN) shows that the management customarily took 50 percent of box-office receipts, though on that occasion they settled for 35 percent but only because Ellen Terry would be appearing in *Nance Oldfield*.

31. ET, letter to EGC, March 24, 1903; MFS, *Up to Now*, p. 36; EGC, letter to MFS, cit. Craig, *Gordon Craig*, pp. 176–7. (For comparison see Peter Brook's comments on the way his *King Lear* production changed during the RSC tour of Eastern Europe and the United States in *The Empty Space* [Harmondsworth, 1972], pp. 25f.)

## 5. A PLAY OF IDEAS: PRINCIPLES, THEORY, AND AN UEBERMARIONETTE

1. Lee Simonson, "The Case of Gordon Craig," p. 21.

2. Janet Leeper (*Edward Gordon Craig*, p. 9) attributes this Greek design to *The Vikings*, an error that could have come about only through Craig himself associating it with that production, as Leeper consulted with him in preparing her book and the one identifiable piece of costume is clearly not Nordic.

3. EGC, *Towards A New Theatre*, p. 18.

4. Promptbook for *The Pretenders* (Everyman ed., no. 659) pp. 54–5 (BN). "X" indicates points in the text at which these movements occur. EGC, Scenes 1, pp. 46 and 47 (BN). Cf. also a list of designs in EGC, Notebook 1904–12 (HRC).

5. EGC, *Index*, pp. 243 and 40–1.

6. "The Artists of the Theatre of the Future," *The Mask*, vol. 1, nos. 3–4 (May–June 1908).

7. EGC, holograph notes on margins of designs for *Macbeth* (BN).

8. EGC, letters to MFS, September 7 and November 25, 1904; *Vossische Zeitung*, Janu-

ary 23, 1905; *Berliner Börsen-Courier,* January 22, 1905; and *Vossische Zeitung,* January 22, 1905.

9. Morton Eustis, cit. Cole and Chinoy, *Directors* p. 51; EGC, letters to Reinhardt (cit. Craig, *Gordon Craig,* p. 199) and to ET, n.d. (UCLA).

10. EGC, letter to ET, 1909; marginal annotation on a letter from Brahm, September 30, 1904; correspondence between EGC and Johannes Poulsen, August, 1926 (published in EGC, *A Production, 1926* [Oxford, 1930], pp. 4 and 5).

11. Cit. Craig, *Gordon Craig,* p. 198.

12. EGC, *On the Art of the Theatre,* pp. 138, 140–1; Daybook 1, 1908–10, pp. 165–6 (HRC). Cf. also EGC, *Towards A New Theatre,* p. 41.

13. Daybook 1, 1908–10, p. 85; EGC letter to MFS, 1905 (cit. Craig, *Gordon Craig,* p. 199); Daybook 2, 1910–11, p. 165 (HRC).

14. WBY, *Plays for an Irish Theatre* (London, 1911), EGC's copy, pp. 80 and 85 (BN); and Daybook 1, 1908–10, p. 209.

15. EGC, "Dancing Is Not Flying." MS, n.d. (cit. Arnold Rood, *Gordon Craig on Movement and Dance* [New York, 1977] p. xxii); *The Mask,* vol. 6, no. 1 (July 1913). Cf. also *The Mask,* vol. 5, no. 1 (July, 1912), and ID, letter to EGC, February 14, 1920: "The Russian Ballet are hopping madly about in Picasso pictures . . . epileptic gymnastics with no thought or centre."

16. EGC, letter to MFS, May 20, 1905, and "Memories of Isadora Duncan," BBC radio, reprinted in *The Listener,* June 5, 1952. (The central importance of this memory for Craig is indicated by the way he repeated this passage in *Index,* pp. 261–2.) Cf. also ID, *My Life,* p. 21, and EGC, Daybook 5, 1930–3, p. 88 (HRC).

17. EGC, Daybook 2, 1910–11, p. 302 (HRC).

18. ID, *My Life,* p. 75.

19. Ibid., p. 165, and ID, *The Art of the Dance* (New York, 1928), p. 102; EGC, *Index,* pp. 263–4.

20. EGC, "Motion. Being the Preface to the Portfolio of Etchings" (originally published as a pamphlet, Nizza-Firenze, 1907), *The Mask,* vol. 1, no. 10 (December, 1908.) For further details on the relationship between Isadora Duncan's dancing and EGC's concept of Scene, see Craig, *Gordon Craig,* pp. 234–5.

21. Ursula Bridge, ed., *W. B. Yeats & T. Sturge Moore: Their Correspondence, 1910–1937* (New York, 1953), p. 156; Duse cit. Arthur Symons, *Studies in Seven Arts* (New York, 1907), p. 336.

22. Thomas A. Janvier, "The Comédie Française at Orange," pp. 169f.

23. EGC, *Towards A New Theatre,* p. 6.

24. WBY, letter to EGC, March 10, 1902; EGC note (1906), reprinted *Index,* p. 289, and *Towards A New Theatre,* p. 11.

25. EGC, Daybook 1, 1908–10, pp. 79 and 77. Cf. also EGC, *Towards A New Theatre,* p. 6, and a letter to MFS, February 18, 1906: "The people thought I was reckless–see how cautious my recklessness was. I threw overboard their old machine first– then their scenes–then their methods of moving the figures–then the playwright–then speech–now, last of all, the figures–real or pasteboard–over they go, trumpery and unworthy" (cit. Craig, *Gordon Craig,* p. 227).

26. *The Times* (London), May 24, 1900, and EGC, *The Mask,* vol. 35, nos. 4–6 (October, 1910).

27. *The Mask,* vol. 1, no. 1 (March, 1908).

28. Ibid., and Daybook 1, 1908–10, pp. 41–3. Compare Jean-Louis Barrault, who described the aim of his acting as "striving towards a purely animal state where the face becomes a natural mask" (*Cahiers Renaud-Barrault,* vol. 71, p. 22), or Peter Brook and Charles Marowitz, who discovered in their 1964 LAMDA experiment

that "facial expressions, under the pressure of extended sounds, began to resemble Japanese masks" (*The Drama Review*, vol. 11, no. 2, p. 156).

29. *The Mask*, vol. 1, no. 2 (April, 1908) (reprinted in EGC, *On the Art of the Theatre*, p. 55).

30. Ibid.; *The Mask*, vol. 1, no. 1 (March, 1908), and letter to MFS, February 15, 1906. In some ways the intellectual quality that Craig wanted in acting anticipated Brecht. It is therefore quite in line that one of the few modern dramas he should mention with complete approval should be *The Threepenny Opera*, though at first glance it might seem very far from his symbolist ideals. Cf. *The Mask*, vol. 15, no. 2 (April–June, 1929).

31. EGC, "Puppets & Poets" in *The Chapbook*, no. 20 (February, 1921), pp. 28 and 22; and *The Mask*, vol. 3, nos. 4–6 (October, 1910).

32. EGC, *Index*, pp. 34 and 24; EGC, "The Rarest Dancing in the World," *The Dancing Times* (January, 1932); Daybook 2, 1910–11, pp. 83–5 (HRC). Cf. also EGC, *On the Art of the Theatre*, p. 295.

33. "Alassio Notebook" (1911), n.p. (HRC). Cf. also EGC, *Index*, p. 293.

## 6. TOWARD A NEW THEATER: MASQUES, SCREENS, AND A *HAMLET*

1. Daybook 2, 1910–11 (HRC), and EGC, *Towards A New Theatre*, p. 2.

2. Henry Irving cit. Cole and Chinoy, *Directors on Directing*, p. 25; EGC, *On the Art of the Theatre*, p. 143 (1905).

3. EGC, *Index*, p. 99; Daybook 2, 1910–11, p. 51.

4. EGC, marginal annotation to "Beauty's Awakening," in his copy of *The Studio* (Summer, 1899), pp. 12–13 (Rood); "Beauty's Awakening," pp. 5f.

5. Paul Hentzner, *Travels in England during the Reign of Queen Elizabeth*, trans. Horace Walpole (London, 1797), p. 55, quoted by EGC in "A Masque: The Harvest Home" (prospectus), *The Green Sheaf*, no. 3 (1903), p. 3. For details of EGC's claim relating to Hone's *Ancient Mysteries* (London, 1823), see Craig, *Gordon Craig*, p. 166 – though in a letter to me (November 4, 1981) he indicates that the passage is intended only to convey "that it was there that [EGC] got the idea."

6. *The Green Sheaf*, no. 3, p. 3; EGC, Notebook 3, 1902–3, pp. 4–6 (BN); and EGC, Notebook 1, n.p. (HRC).

7. *The Mask*, vol. 5, no. 3 (January, 1913).

8. EGC, cit. Leeper, *Edward Gordon Craig*, p. 43; letter to MFS, November 11, 1903 (HRC); Notebook 1904–12, n.p. (HRC); and EGC, *Towards A New Theatre*, p. 27. (At the end of this description Craig noted that "the hunger of the poor was put down right enough, but the hunger of the rich has not been fairly treated . . . it is as tragic." "Theatre. Shows and Motions. 1905–1909" follows this up with a sketch for a drama in which "the poor men go down on their knees and begin to gild the chains of the rich men.")

9. EGC, "Theatre. Shows and Motions. 1905–1909," n.p. (HRC).

10. Ibid. Cf. also Leeper, *Edward Gordon Craig*, p. 45.

11. EGC, letter to MFS, May, 1905; EGC, *On the Art of the Theatre*, pp. 46–7.

12. EGC, *On the Art of the Theatre*, pp. 144 and 139.

13. EGC, Daybook 1, 1908–10, p. 89; cit. Leeper, *Edward Gordon Craig*, pp. 17–18. (Edward Craig dates the first notes toward *The Steps* as 1902 – *Gordon Craig*, p. 162 – but the concept only took shape in 1905.)

14. EGC, *Towards A New Theatre*, pp. 43 and 47.

15. Ibid., p. 83; EGC, *On the Art of the Theatre*, p. 50.

16. EGC, MS Book 12, p. 35 (BN). Cf. Edward Craig, *Gordon Craig*, p. 239, where Craig also suggests that the screens derived from EGC's concept of a three-dimensional, vertically moving Scene. The sketches that exist in fact show that he was formulating these ideas simultaneously. It therefore seems more logical to view Scene, with its greater complexity and abstraction, as a progression from the screens, which in turn clearly developed out of curtains; Craig's notes demonstrate that he only began to work out ways of using Scene later. To some extent he regarded both staging techniques as equal alternatives and – confusingly – he also called his screens "the Scene," with the result that the 1907 notebook (MS 12) that describes them is footnoted by Bablet and listed in the catalog of the Bibliothèque Nationale as referring to Scene.

17. EGC, note dated 1940 in MS Book 12, p. 51.

18. EGC, patent application A.D. 1910, Jan. 24, no. 1771, p. 2.

19. MS Book 12, p. 34. (This is a point he returned to in an address to the Theatre Worker's Guild on June 18, 1920; "If each artist will feel and think for himself, we can have four or five examples of mobility of scene within a year.")

20. WBY, *Plays for An Irish Theatre* (London, 1911), p. 221.

21. *The Music Review*, vol. 1, no. 2 (1912), and *The Dublin Times*, February 16, 1912 (my emphasis); WBY cit. EGC, MS Book 12, p. 40, and J. B. Yeats, letter to EGC, March 18, 1912.

22. *The Daily News*, September 19, 1911; EGC, undated letter to MFS (1911). To some extent this change of attitude was also due to Craig's realization (having taken out the patent on advice from a lawyer friend, Gilbert Cannan) that the screens could provide a source of continuing income if their use in productions was kept in his control.

23. Henry Irving, MS notes on *Hamlet* (in EGC's collection) n.p. (BN). For EGC's comments on *Hamlet* as a play in which "talk suits the whole situation so well," see *The Dancing Times* (July, 1932).

24. EGC, letter to Stanislavski, July 14, 1910; Daybook 2, 1910–11, pp. 168–9 (HRC); undated letter to MFS (1910?).

25. Stanislavski, letter to EGC, June 21, 1910, and EGC's reply, July 14, 1910.

26. Serafima Birman cit. Lawrence Senelick, "The Craig-Stanislavski 'Hamlet' at the Moscow Art Theatre," *Theatre Quarterly*, vol. 6, no. 22, p. 108; EGC, notes on sketches for *Hamlet* (Moscow, 1908); EGC, *Towards A New Theatre*, p. 81; Stenogramme des entretiens concernant la préparation de la mise en scène d'Hamlet, pp. 4–5 (BN); and Daybook 1, 1908–10, p. 225.

27. "The characters must be King, Queen and Hamlet. The rest are only a background of vileness, wealth and density . . . The problem is to show the throne, the three characters and the retinue, the courtiers, merge into one generalized background of gold. Their mantles flow together, and they cannot be perceived to have individual faces." Stanislavski, rehearsal notes, cit. Senelick, "The Craig-Stanislavski 'Hamlet,' " *Theatre Quarterly*, p. 62.

28. EGC, "Theatre. Shows and Motions. 1905–1909;" Sulerzhitski, cit. Senelick, "The Craig-Stanislavski 'Hamlet,' " *Theatre Quarterly*, p. 80. (Senelick also reproduces the sketch in question on p. 75.)

29. Stenogramme, pp. 3, 7, 18–19; and EGC, *Towards A New Theatre*, p. 81.

30. Stenogramme, pp. 22, 12, 7, 11–13. (See also EGC, *Index*, p. 290.)

31. Stenogramme, pp. 1 and 4f.

32. Stanislavski cit. Craig, *Gordon Craig*, p. 246; Sulerzhitski and Valery Bryusov, cit. Senelick, "The Craig-Stanislavski 'Hamlet,' " *Theatre Quarterly*, pp. 99 and 120 (my emphasis).

33. MS. note in EGC's copy of Constantin Stanislavski *My Life in Art*, p. 522, (London, 1924); Daybook 2, 1910–11, pp. 321, 322.
34. MS. note on typescript of "Hamlet," EGC radio talk for the BBC, 1956; Stanislavski, *My Life in Art*, pp. 509, 513, and EGC MS. notes; Daybook 2, 1910–11, p. 27.
35. David Magarshak, *Stanislavski: A Life* (Westport, Conn. 1975), pp. 328, and 299–301.
36. *The Times* (London), January 9, 1912.
37. Cf. Craig, *Gordon Craig*, pp. 250–1, and Brian Arnott, *Edward Gordon Craig & Hamlet* (Ottawa, 1975), p. 37. (Arnott, for instance, argues that the screens could not be moved because the MAT stage was raked. As Senelick has pointed out, this was not the case.)
38. EGC, "Alassio Notebook" (1907), n.p. (HRC), into which the letter from Stanislavski (1935) is pasted, and MS. note to *My Life in Art*, p. 521.
39. Production notes, reprinted by Senelick, "The Craig-Stanislavski 'Hamlet,' " *Theatre Quarterly*, p. 69; Stenogramme, p. 9.
40. EGC, draft for an article entitled "Stage Scenery," 1910 (UCLA). (Details of the quarrel with Stanislavski are given in EGC's MS. notes to Isadora Duncan, *My Life*, pp. 253f., and in Senelick, "The Craig-Stanislavski 'Hamlet,' " *Theatre Quarterly*, passim).
41. Stanislavski, *My Life in Art*, p. 519; EGC, Daybook 1, 1908–10, p. 117.
42. EGC, "Alassio Notebook" (1911).
43. EGC, *Towards A New Theatre*, p. 77; letter to MFS, 1911.
44. Daybook 1, 1908–10, pp. 150–1.

## 7. THE THEATER OF THE FUTURE: "SCENE," PUPPETS, AND A RELIGIOUS FESTIVAL

1. EGC, *Towards A New Theatre*, p. 17; Daybook 5, 1930–3, p. 88 (HRC).
2. EGC, *Scene* (Oxford, 1923), pp. 5, 22.
3. EGC, "Stage Scenery," TS, 1910 (UCLA). The "eidophusikon," little more than a curiosity in the history of the theater, was invented by de Loutherbourg, David Garrick's designer.
4. MS Book 12, 1907, p. 1; letter cit. Leeper, *Edward Gordon Craig*, p. 16; and EGC, "Catalogue of Etchings being designs for Motions by Gordon Craig, Florence 1908," pp. 1 and 6.
5. EGC, MS notes in the cover pages of Sebastiano Serlio, *Architettura*, vol. 2, p. 1545 (BN); letter to *The Times* (London), October 7, 1907.
6. EGC, *Scene*, pp. 15, 14, and 20; letter to ET, March 8, 1903 (UCLA); Daybook 1, 1908–10, p. 183.
7. EGC, cit. Maurice Magnus, unpublished TS, 1907 (HRC). For a full analysis of expressionist acting, see my *Holy Theatre*, pp. 46f.
8. Daybook 3, 1911–18, p. 25; EGC, *Towards A New Theatre*, p. 48.
9. Letter from Edward Craig to the author, September 15, 1981. (For the reason why EGC never used this model to develop his theory through experimentation, see Craig, *Gordon Craig*, p. 317.)
10. Arnold Rood, (ed.), *Craig on Movement and Dance* (New York, 1977), p. 166; EGC, "Puppets and Poets," *The Chapbook*, no. 20 (February 1921), pp. 17 and 30–1; EGC, *On the Art of the Theatre*, p. 62.
11. Alfred Jarry, *Selected Works of Alfred Jarry*, trans. Roger Shattuck and Simon Wat-

son Taylor (London, 1969), pp. 86 and 83; Paul Margueritte, *Le Petit Théâtre* (*Théâtre de Marionettes*) (Paris, 1889), pp. 7–8.

12. EGC, *The Scene*, TS, 1914 (HRC); and EGC, *The Art of the Theatre*, p. 48.
13. EGC, interview in *The Washington Post*, December 1, 1907.
14. EGC, "Puppets and Poets," p. 30; Daybook 2, 1910–11, p. 310.
15. Notes to designs for *Macbeth* (BN). See also Daybook 1, 1908–10, pp. 129 and 179, and Daybook 2, 1910–11, p. 203.
16. Adolphe Appia, "Comment reformer notre mise en scène," *La Revue*, vol. 50, no. 2, June 1, 1904, pp. 344f.
17. Daybook 3, 1911–18, p. 147 (HRC); EGC, *Scene*, pp. 20 and 23.
18. EGC, TS draft for *Scene*, pp. 3 and 19 (HRC); EGC, *On the Art of the Theatre*, p. 123.
19. Daybook 1, 1908–10, pp. 198–9; Daybook 2, 1910–11, pp. 315f; Notebook on Movement, 1907–20, n.p. (UCLA).
20. ID to EGC, June, 1913 (CD no. 231, LC).
21. EGC to ID, undated. See also EGC, *On the Art of the Theatre*, pp. 74 and 89.
22. EGC, TS draft for *Scene*, p. 19; and MS note in Craig's copy of Serlio, vol. 2. (See also EGC, *Towards A New Theatre*, p. 77.
23. Notebook 26, "Notes for Bach's *Passion*, 1912. 1913. 1914," pp. 6 and 7 (BN).
24. EGC, TS, "The Stage a Sport," 1922, p. 11 (HRC). See also EGC, *Towards A New Theatre*, p. 33, and EGC, *On the Art of the Theatre*, p. 80.
25. Daybook 2, 1910–11, p. 78.
26. It could also be pointed out that the central bridge construction at the rear of the main acting area corresponds very closely to Copeau's Vieux Columbier stage.
27. For the reconstruction of the imagined action of *The St. Matthew Passion*, I am indebted to Edward Craig, and to his article in *Theatre Notebook*, vol. 26, no. 4 (Summer, 1972), pp. 148f. I have taken the liberty of departing from his interpretation in one significant respect. He places the Evangelist "out in the auditorium, where one might perhaps expect to find a conductor on a podium," and the solo singers also outside the stage area on either side (p. 149). Quite apart from the fact that this arrangement would reduce a performance to a conventional concert piece (albeit with illustrative action in the background), several of Craig's designs specifically place a gesticulating figure on the central column at the base of the upper flight of steps. This column shows up clearly in the photograph of the lower stage area.
28. Further details of performance come from Daybook 3, 1911–18, pp. 180f., Notebook 26, pp. 12f., "Proposal for the production in Roma of Bach's *St. Matthew Passion*," TS, n.d. (HRC), Notebook 26, pp. 4 and 25, and Notebook 27, p. 5 (BN).
29. EGC, *Index*, pp. 298–9.
30. Arthur Kahane cit. Cole and Chinoy, *Directors on Directing*, p. 52. See also Daybook 3, 1911–18, pp. 39 and 55.
31. Daybook 3, 1911–18, p. 171; *A Production*, p. 5; "Proposal for the production in Roma of Bach's St. Matthew Passion."
32. Daybook 1, 1908–10, p. 183.

## 8. CURTAIN CALL: A SCHOOL AND *THE MASK*

1. Annotation in EGC's copy of the program for *Dido and Aeneas* (BN).
2. EGC, cit. Craig, *Gordon Craig*, p. 181, and letter to MFS, November 26, 1903 (HRC).
3. EGC, *On the Art of the Theatre*, pp. 163–78, 257, 239–40, 242.
4. Daybook 2, 1910–11, pp. 324, 181.
5. Cf. "Society of the Theatre," minute book, 1912–13 (UCLA).

6. EGC, "Advertisment for the School for the Art of the Theatre," London, 1912, pp. 1 and 3 (BN). See also Daybook 1, 1908–10, p. 187 (HRC).
7. EGC, "A Living Theatre," Florence, 1913, pp. 35 and 31 (BN).
8. Ibid., p. 44.
9. EGC, "Rules for the School for the Art of the Theatre," Florence, 1913 (BN).
10. EGC, holograph note on p. 53 of "A Living Theatre," d. October, 1914; Daybook 1, 1908–10, p. 54; "Alassio Notebook" (1911), n.p.; Daybook 2, 1910–11, p. 325.
11. Daybook 1, 1908–10, p. 53, and EGC, *Index*, p. 268.
12. EGC, "A Living Theatre," p. 18.
13. EGC, *On the Art of the Theatre*, pp. 45–6; EGC, undated letter to ET (1909?) (UCLA).
14. Harley Granville-Barker, *The Daily Mail*, September 26, 1912.
15. Jean-Louis Barrault, cited on the cover of the 1943 edition of EGC, *De L'Art du Théâtre*; EGC letter to MFS, 1922.
16. Undated annotation in Craig's copy of the program for *Dido and Aeneas*.
17. EGC, *Henry Irving*, p. 187.

# Select bibliography

Gordon Craig's own publications are listed in the chronology. Bibliographic details of both his major articles and the reviews of his works are to be found in the Notes.

Arnott, Brian. *Edward Gordon Craig and Hamlet*. Ottawa, 1975.
Bablet, Denis. *Edward Gordon Craig*. Paris, 1962.
Barshay, Bernard. "Gordon Craig's Theories of Acting," *Theatre Annual* (1947), pp. 55–63.
Craig, Edward. "Gordon Craig and Bach's *St. Matthew Passion*," *Theatre Notebook*, vol. 26, no. 4 (1972), pp. 147–51.
    "Gordon Craig and Hubert von Herkomer," *Theater Research*, vol. 10, no. 1 (1969), pp. 7–16.
    *Gordon Craig: The Story of His Life*. New York, 1968.
Duncan, Isadora. *My Life*. New York, 1927.
Fletcher, Ifan Kyrle, and Arnold Rood. *Edward Gordon Craig: A Bibliography*. Society for Theatre Research, 1967.
Gorelik, Mordecai. *New Theatres for Old*. New York, 1962.
Guidry, Lorelei. *Introduction and Index to The Mask*, vol. 16. New York, 1968.
Hewitt, Barnard. "Gordon Craig and Post Impressionism," *Quarterly Journal of Speech*, vol. 30, no. l (1944), pp. 75–80.
Housman, Laurence. *The Unexpected Ideas*. London, 1937.
Huneker, James. *Iconoclasts: A Book of Dramatists*. London, 1905.
Hyllestod, Morgens. "The Pretenders: Copenhagen 1926," *Theatre Research*, vol. 7, no. 3 (1966), pp. 117–22.
Ilyin, Eugene. "How Stanislavski and Gordon Craig Produced *Hamlet*," *Plays and Players* (March, 1957), pp. 6–7.
Leeper, Janet. *Edward Gordon Craig: Designs for the Theatre*. Harmondsworth, 1948.
Loeffler, Michael. *Gordon Craig's frühe Versuche zur Ueberwindung der Bühenrealismus*. Bern, 1969.
Macfall, Haldane. "Some Thoughts on the Art of Gordon Craig," *The Studio*, vol. 22, no. 2 (1901).
Marker, Frederick, and Lisa Lone. *Edward Gordon Craig and The Pretenders*. Carbondale, Ill., 1982.
Marotti, Ferrucio. *Edward Gordon Craig*. Bologna, 1961.
Newman, Lindsay. *Gordon Craig Archives: International Survey*. London, 1976.
Rood, Arnold. *Gordon Craig on Movement and Dance*. New York, 1977.
    and Donald Oenslager. *Edward Gordon Craig: Artist of the Theater*. New York, 1967.
Rose, Enid. *Gordon Craig and the Theatre*. London, 1931.
Senelick, Laurence. "The Craig-Stanislavsky *Hamlet* at the Moscow Art Theatre," *Theatre Quarterly*, vol. 6, no. 22 (1976), pp. 56–122.
Shaw, Martin Fallas. *Up to Now*. London, 1929.
Simonson, Lee. *The Stage is Set*. New York, 1932.
    "The Case of Gordon Craig," *Theatre Guild Magazine* (February 1931), pp. 18–23.
Stanislavski, Constantin. *My Life in Art*. London, 1924.
Symons, Arthur. *Studies in Seven Arts*. London, 1906.

# Index

237